Praise for
The Premier and His Grandmother

"A fascinating look into our family's Métis heritage and how it may
have impacted my father's time in public office. As a signatory to
the *Constitution Act, 1982*, my father as premier agreed to the addition of Section 35 in the Constitution of Canada, recognizing and
affirming Aboriginal and Treaty Rights and extending the definition of 'Aboriginal Peoples of Canada' to include the Métis People of
Canada. Privately proud of his heritage, he was, as the Métis Nation
of Alberta has often stated, a Métis 'hiding in plain sight.'"

JOE LOUGHEED
son of Peter Lougheed

"As Canadians continue to seek out a better understanding of our
country, we must honestly reflect on our past to understand what
has made us who we are today. To truly appreciate how people have
contributed to Canada as we know it today, we must be prepared
to understand our leaders differently today than they were at the
time. While we are beginning to honour and celebrate Indigenous
heritage in Alberta, that was not always the case. This little-known
part of Lougheed family history confronts the fact that we have not
celebrated Indigenous history and this excellent research helps us to
understand one further aspect of the true history of Alberta and the
important life of one Métis woman. It reminds us that we continue
to honour an incomplete history of Alberta to our detriment."

HONOURABLE ALISON M. REDFORD
KC, ICD.D., fourteenth premier of Alberta

"A fascinating read that tells the story of the adaptability of the Métis and our history during the fur trade and life thereafter. The Lougheeds became a powerful Métis family, and this book speaks to their strength and resilience. I would highly recommend *The Premier and His Grandmother!*"

MARILYN LIZEE
consultant for the Métis Nation of Alberta, co-editor
(with Bailey Oster) of *Stories of Métis Women:
Tales My Kookum Told Me*

"*The Premier and His Grandmother* is a unique look into the cultural and historic heritage of one of Alberta's most iconic premiers, Peter Lougheed. It is an important contribution to the canon of Métis history in Alberta and highlights the complex nature of identity and belonging, while honouring the work of our Métis matriarchs."

BAILEY OSTER
co-editor (with Marylin Lizee) of *Stories of
Métis Women: Tales My Kookum Told Me*

"A scholarly work revealing the perseverance and resilience of members of the Lougheed family, who transitioned from a traditional lifestyle and worldview and adapted to a fast-paced, chaotic, and often racist environment. Little-known details are enlightening and contribute to a foundational understanding about Indigenous Peoples that can open the door to reconciliation. A must-read for Indigenous studies."

SHARON ANNE PASULA
Urban Cultural, Educational and Spiritual Resource Person and
former Vice President Region IV, Metis Nation of Alberta.

"Doris MacKinnon has skillfully linked the story of former Alberta premier, Peter Lougheed, with that of his grandmother, Isabella Clark Hardisty Lougheed. MacKinnon's book is thoroughly researched, especially when highlighting the history of the Métis in Alberta, an area of Western Canadian history much in need of further research."

GREG N. FRASER
author of *Joseph William McKay: A Métis Business
Leader in Colonial British Columbia*

Peter Lougheed, Lady Belle,
and the Legacy of Métis Identity

THE PREMIER AND HIS GRANDMOTHER

DORIS JEANNE MACKINNON

Heritage House Publishing Company Ltd.
heritagehouse.ca

*Cataloguing information available from Library
and Archives Canada*

978-1-77203-459-2 (paperback)
978-1-77203-460-8 (e-book)

Edited by Colette Poitras
Cover design by Setareh Ashrafologhalai
Interior design by Jacqui Thomas
Cover images, from left: LHCS 2-1, courtesy Lougheed
House Archives; NA-3232-5, courtesy Libraries and Cultural
Resources Digital Collections, University of Calgary; and
GR1989.0516.1675.0001, courtesy Provincial Archives of Alberta.

The interior of this book was produced on FSC®-certified,
acid-free paper, processed chlorine free, and printed with
vegetable-based inks.

Heritage House gratefully acknowledges that the land on
which we live and work is within the traditional territories of
the Lkwungen (Esquimalt and Songhees), Malahat, Pacheed-
aht, Scia'new, T'Sou-ke, and W̱SÁNEĆ (Pauquachin, Tsartlip,
Tsawout, Tseycum) Peoples.

We acknowledge the financial support of the Government of
Canada through the Canada Book Fund (CBF) and the Canada
Council for the Arts, and the Province of British Columbia
through the British Columbia Arts Council and the Book
Publishing Tax Credit.

27 26 25 24 23   1 2 3 4 5

Printed in Canada

Friend—she understands your tears as
much as she knows your smile.

Friend—she walks alongside so that
you never walk alone.

Friend—she sees the person you seek to be.
Thank you, friends, for never doubting...

Becky Nagel
Denise Robinson
Shirley Rose Reaman
Rebecca Benedict

Introduction

Métis Connections—
The Premier and His Grandmother

ONE OF PETER LOUGHEED'S ONLY memories of his grandmother Lady Isabella Clark Hardisty Lougheed is that she once remarked "Peter. It's funny you named him Peter. That's the name of our dog."[1]

Edgar Peter Lougheed was Alberta's tenth premier, serving from 1971 to 1985. When Peter Lougheed first set his sights on becoming the premier of Alberta, he followed what some considered an unconventional path. Yet that unconventional path led to tremendous personal and political success. In 1965, Peter Lougheed was chosen as leader of the small Alberta Progressive Conservative Party, a marginal party at best, which held no seats. Regardless of the seeming impossibility of his task, some noted that Peter was "born to power," based in part on his grandfather

Sir James Lougheed's prominent role in the development of Calgary.[2] Yet James Lougheed, while amassing a grand estate and serving as the region's youngest senator, was not himself born to power. Rather, it was James Lougheed's fortuitous connection with fur trade aristocracy by way of his marriage to Peter Lougheed's Métis grandmother, Isabella Clark Hardisty, that helped establish for James a future role as a prominent community leader. Indeed, when the young lawyer James Lougheed, hailing from the poor Cabbagetown area of Toronto, arrived in the West with few connections and no material wealth, his own eventual role in the West might have seemed unbelievable to some who had known him earlier.

On the other hand, that James Lougheed's wife would be destined for a role as a community leader was not unexpected. Isabella's Hardisty family had for generations worked in the service of the Hudson's Bay Company (HBC or the Company) in fur trade country, and that family was considered to be leaders in the fur trade. Even more striking, given Peter Lougheed's eventual position among Alberta's business and political elite at a time when many viewed Indigenous Peoples as of the lowest social order in the West, is that his grandmother Isabella Clark Hardisty was of Métis ancestry. When Peter Lougheed was elected premier of Alberta, he would become the first person of Indigenous ancestry to assume that role. Yet very few people were aware of Peter Lougheed's Indigenous ancestry then, just as few remain aware of that fact today.

In reality, in 1971, when Peter Lougheed first assumed his role as premier of Alberta, most still viewed the Indigenous Peoples of North America as a simplistic people whose history and culture were static. If scholars included Indigenous people in the history of the North-West, it was primarily to present them as commodities of a fur trade that fuelled the expansion of European colonial powers.[3] It was only later in the 1970s that many began to revisit the archival material and to look to anthropology, archaeology and oral history as a way to better understand the complexity and diversity of the history and culture of the Métis People. Emerging accounts in the 1970s and 1980s of the history of the fur trade confirmed that there was a time, until approximately the early to mid-1800s, when partnerships and unions between Indigenous Peoples and European traders were considered acceptable, and even advantageous to both groups.[4] However, by the mid-1800s, when more and more European settlers began to arrive in the North-West, fear of "miscegenation"[5] grew. Thus, when Peter Lougheed's grandparents were establishing themselves as Calgary's first couple in the early 1900s, many Métis people did not realize a freedom to publicly embrace their identity. The reality was that as a pure survival strategy and as a way to avoid discrimination, some Métis people constructed a public persona as non-Indigenous people. This meant that some descendants of Métis people were often simply not fully aware of the history of their Indigenous ancestors. Even if they were aware, as was Peter Lougheed, it was often the case that Métis people did not perceive a freedom to openly express their Indigenous ancestry even into the 1970s.

Indeed, speaking to a local newspaper in 2001, in an article about Isabella Lougheed appropriately titled "A Daughter of the West Who Made a Difference," Peter remarked that his memory of his grandmother was of an "elegant woman in a rocking chair living out her last few years in the old house ... She was elderly when we knew her."[6]

During that same interview, Donald Lougheed, Peter's brother and three years his senior, recalled Isabella talking to him about those who had come to view Métis leader Louis Riel as a hero: "She told me about her brother who was killed at Batoche ... I remember her talking about Riel."[7]

The talk of Riel at that time reflected what often emerges in the dialogue of western Canadians—specifically, should Louis Riel be vilified as a traitor based on his actions in 1869–70 and 1885 when he led what some referred to as a Resistance or a Rebellion? Or should Riel be regarded as a rightful father of Confederation and a hero for standing up for the rights of the Métis as the central Canadian government encroached on Métis land? It is understandable that Peter Lougheed's grandmother Isabella would likely not regard Louis Riel as a hero, given that her own brother, a Métis, was killed as he fought for the government forces against Louis Riel's soldiers. It is also the case that Isabella, a daughter of a Hudson's Bay Company Chief Factor, William Lucas Hardisty, would be aware of the favouritism on the part of the Company for English-speaking Métis.

Whether Donald and Peter Lougheed believed that Isabella would have been upset about the idea of pardoning

Louis Riel, the reality of Métis history in Canada is that it is complicated. Indeed, the very concept of Métis identity remains complex today. It was only in 1982, just short of one century after Louis Riel's historic actions, that Métis People were recognized as Aboriginal Peoples in Canada's Constitution. Peter Lougheed, from his position as premier of Alberta until 1985, assumed a role in that process of recognition for Métis People. A 1981 article in the *Edmonton Journal* indicated that the "Lougheed, Métis compromise" was met with enthusiasm by Métis leaders. While there remained concern with the issue of "Aboriginal Rights," specifically because those rights were not being defined, Peter Lougheed proposed that Section 35 of the Constitution should define "native peoples of Canada as Indian, Inuit and Métis."[8] A *Calgary Herald* interview with Sam Sinclair, at the time Métis Association of Alberta leader, noted that "if the proposal were accepted by other governments, it will write a new page in the history of his people, affirming them as aboriginals."[9] As the talks between provinces and the federal government continued for a number of years, with some Indigenous people displeased with the provincial government's position on jurisdiction over Métis rights, Métis National Council leader Jim Sinclair once praised Peter Lougheed's work, noting that he was "instrumental" in getting the Métis into the Constitution talks.[10] Sinclair reiterated the sentiment of the Métis People in a letter to Premier Peter Lougheed in 1984, when he wrote, "You are held in high regard by the Métis people of Alberta and are generally regarded as a man who cares about our people."[11]

While the Constitution did not include a specific definition of who could legally identify as Métis, in the case of *R. v. Powley* (2003), the Supreme Court established criteria to define Métis rights and who was entitled to those rights. Today, there are Métis groups who argue that one must be able to trace their ancestry to the historic Métis Nation and community of Red River in order to rightfully identify as Métis.[12] However, there is not universal agreement with this perspective. In one example, it is the view of scholars Christopher Adams, Gregg Dahl and Ian Peach, editors of a recent collection of essays, that "Métis" is not a "signifier of a particular population situated in a specific time or place."[13] Despite what Isabella Clark Hardisty Lougheed's grandsons thought about the possibility of a Riel pardon, and despite the current arguments made about Métis identity, the fact is that Isabella was a daughter of the fur trade. It remains that her early identity and culture were inculcated by her Métis mother and her Métis father with whom she lived in the northern Mackenzie River District, where her father served the bulk of his career as Chief Factor with the Hudson's Bay Company.

While it would be difficult to find a reader in the West, and indeed in Canada, who was not familiar with Peter Lougheed and his career as premier of Alberta, many of those same readers would be surprised to learn that his paternal grandmother was Indigenous. There is some evidence that Peter Lougheed did, on some occasions, publicly acknowledge that fact while he was premier. However, there are some who believe that he more willingly embraced the Indigenous ancestry of his grandmother after he left public office. According to his son, Joe Lougheed:

> I do not believe it was widely known, but at the same time my father did not seek to hide it or deny it. In fact, he was very proud of his Métis heritage and that of his grandmother's family.[14]

Given that was the case, it is an aspect of Peter Lougheed's identity and of his history worthy of exploration from a variety of perspectives.

This book is not intended to provide an in-depth review of Peter Lougheed's political ideology, nor of his influence on the national dialogue in terms of conservative politics. Many authors have already undertaken that task. Nor does this book seek to analyze the rise of the West as an exporter of natural resources and as a contributor to the national economy, an era in which Peter Lougheed assumed a role. In the same way, this book does not reach any definitive conclusions about Peter Lougheed's personal identity as the grandson of an Indigenous woman whose family had been involved in the fur trade in the North-West for generations, and who were early pioneers and community builders of southern Alberta. Rather, this book explores the connection that Peter Lougheed had to an important Métis family, a family that included Richard Hardisty, appointed as the first Indigenous senator to serve in the Canadian Parliament. In addition to the connection to the Métis Hardisty fur trade family, this book also examines the reality for Métis people when Peter Lougheed served as premier of the only Canadian province that had earlier set aside a land base for Métis settlements.

Chapter One, *The Making of "Lady Belle,"* explores the history of Isabella Clark Hardisty Lougheed, Peter Lougheed's paternal grandmother, affectionately known as Lady Belle by many who lived in the early settlement of Calgary. Isabella was a daughter of the fur trade who spent her early formative years in the northern district of Mackenzie River. As a young girl, Isabella was sent to an eastern school and returned to live with her Métis mother and father in the North before the family retired to Lachine, Quebec, where many of the Hudson's Bay Company men lived after completing their service. After her father died, Isabella, at the age of twenty-one, was sent by her mother to Calgary to live with her uncle, Richard Hardisty, a Chief Factor of the Hudson's Bay Company, and the man who became the area's senator. Calgary became her life-long home after she married James Alexander Lougheed, a young lawyer from Ontario with few connections in the West.

Chapter Two, *It Takes a "Historical Village,"* explores Peter Lougheed's ancestry and the influences that ancestry may have had on the formation of his identity and his eventual commitment to the success of the province of Alberta. Although he was a young boy when his grandmother died, and his grandfather had passed away before Peter was born, the positions that Isabella Clark Hardisty Lougheed and James Alexander Lougheed occupied in the early province of Alberta established the Lougheed name as an important one in Alberta's history. There is no doubt that the legacy of the elder Lougheeds' roles in the boosterism[15] that established Alberta as an important contributor to the economy of early Canada would set the stage for Peter Lougheed's own passion for the success of his home province of Alberta. Exploring the history of Peter Lougheed's paternal grandparents as they followed the fur trade pattern of mixed-race marriages and survival strategies that relied on kinship connections, this chapter helps us understand Peter's history as a descendant of one of the earliest pioneer families of the West.

Chapter Three, *Métis Activism in Alberta*, explores the call to action by Alberta's Métis activists as they emerged from *Le Grand Silence*[16] in the early twentieth century to become a powerful voice for recognition as Indigenous people. It was the Social Credit government that preceded Peter Lougheed's Progressive Conservatives that set aside lands for the Métis People through the *Metis Population Betterment Act* in 1938. While the ideology that informed this legislation was one of benevolence to the Métis, many of whom lived in abject poverty at the time, the Métis viewed it as a way to begin to redress the historic wrongs of 1885 and the failed federal government scrip system. While this early success was yet again followed by periods of silence for Métis activism, the land base that was set aside in Alberta would not only impact the political realities in Alberta, but would also serve as an important building block to eventual recognition for the Métis as Indigenous People in the *Constitution Act, 1982*.

Chapter Four, *A Woman and a Man of Their Times*, explores the matter of Métis identity as historians have portrayed it and as Isabelle Hardisty Lougheed negotiated it, while beginning to explore Peter Lougheed's public engagement with Indigenous People. Lougheed led the province of Alberta during a time when the expectations for equality and justice were high amid renewed Indigenous activism. Had more people been aware of Peter Lougheed's own Indigenous ancestry when he served as premier, expectations might have been even higher. Might Peter Lougheed, as a descendant of an Indigenous grandmother who chose to establish a public role for herself in an increasingly racialized society, have been more engaged in Indigenous self-actualization? Peter Lougheed did not deny his Indigenous ancestry. This suggests that his own father (Isabella's son) also did not deny that ancestry. Without a doubt, Peter Lougheed inspired political, economic and social policy in Alberta and, indeed, in Canada in many respects. That said, it is important to explore Peter Lougheed's role in some of the policies that he influenced as they impacted Indigenous People and in the context of his times.

Chapter Five, *The Complexities of Leadership*, continues to explore the concept of identity in the context of the leadership role that Peter's grandmother Isabella assumed in the early settlement of Calgary, and how that might have impacted Peter Lougheed's own engagement with his ethnicity. There are few documented examples that speak to Isabella's personal feelings about the increasing racial boundaries in the early twentieth-century Prairie

West when she married a non-Indigenous lawyer with few personal connections and not much material wealth. Yet Isabella's determination to establish herself as a member of one of Calgary's leading social elites speaks to a quiet resistance. In reality, Isabella's role in the successful partnership that she formed with James Lougheed, and, indeed, her Indigenous ancestry, were not recognized by historians until the late twentieth to early twenty-first century, well after Peter Lougheed served as premier. Was Peter Lougheed, when he led the province of Alberta, simply a product of his time in history—a history that has, for many, progressed too slowly toward true reconciliation?

one

The Making of "Lady Belle"

It is to be regretted that she was removed so soon from the Canadian Institution where she was being educated—2 or 3 years longer would have turned out a highly accomplished and charming young lady.[1]

ALTHOUGH THERE WERE THOSE WHO knew Isabella as a young girl who doubted her future as a "lady" in the North-West, it will become clear in this discussion that she did an admirable job of establishing herself as a leading member of Calgary's society as that settlement grew into an important centre of commerce.[2]

Yet, as some of those who spent a good deal of time researching Isabella Clark Hardisty Lougheed's life have mused, it is difficult to get to know the "real Isabella." Early researchers with Lougheed House National Historic Site, Trudy Cowan and Jennifer Bobrovitz, observed that Isabella was a "private person," and that knowing her "remains a challenge."[3] It is true that there are very few of Isabella's own words that have been preserved for the historical record. To date, in addition to a few interviews given to the press, only one lone letter has been located; in it, Isabella indicated longing for her time spent away from fur trade country when she attended Wesleyan Ladies' College in Hamilton, Ontario. In the 1877 letter, Isabella wrote to her aunt, Eliza McDougall Hardisty, Senator Richard Hardisty's spouse, that she wished to spend the next winter with her. One of the reasons given by Isabella was that she found it "hard when I cannot practise my music. I will be glad when we go out, I am sure I will sit at a piano all day long if I get a chance."[4]

Although the letter to her aunt suggested that Isabella longed to leave fur trade country, she had spent her formative years as a daughter of the fur trade at Hudson's Bay Company posts in the northern Mackenzie River District. Her mother, Mary Anne Allen, was a Métis woman from the Columbia District who, as a child whose parents had died, was raised in northern fur trade country by Métis families.[5] Isabella's father, William Lucas Hardisty, was a Hudson's Bay Company man, also of Métis ancestry, whose family had served the Company for generations.

Isabella was one of nine children born to William Lucas Hardisty and Mary Anne Allen.[6] Her father, William Hardisty, son of the Company officer Richard Hardisty Sr. and his wife, Marguerite Sutherland,[7] both of Métis ancestry, always worked in the North-West with the HBC, as had three generations of Hardisty men before him. Eventually, all six of Richard and Marguerite's sons served in some capacity with the HBC. For his part, William Hardisty was an officer for thirty-six years, rising to the position of Chief Factor for the vast Mackenzie River District.

In addition to securing positions in the Company for his sons, Isabella's grandfather, Richard Hardisty Sr., ensured that all of his children received Euro–North American educations. It was in 1842, after completing his education at Red River Academy, that Isabella's father began his own career with the HBC, accepting the position of apprentice at Fort Halkett, in the Mackenzie River District. At the time of his employment, William Hardisty's parish was listed as "Native."[8]

As a Hudson's Bay Company officer with some European-style education, Isabella's father often bemoaned the lack of education that his wife, Mary Anne Allen, had received. In a letter to Sir George Simpson, governor of the HBC, dated November 10, 1857, Hardisty described not only his recent marriage to the seventeen-year-old Mary Anne Allen but also the emphasis he placed upon formal education:

> I was up at Fort Simpson in August and got married there in a very offhand way to a Miss Allen—she is an orphan, her parents having died when she was an infant—her education has been very neglected, and it is my intention to send her to school for a year or two. It is a very unusual thing to send a Wife to school and no doubt will cause a laugh at my expense, but I don't care a fig and won't mind the expense, so long as she is enabled thereby to act her part with credit in the society among which she is

15

placed—as for the rest, the woman who I consider good enough to live with, is good enough for my friends to look at.[9]

Researchers Judith Hudson Beattie and Helen Buss concluded that William Hardisty did follow through on his plans to educate his wife, and they wrote that she became an "educated elite of fur trade society."[10] However, there appears to be no formal written record of Isabella's mother attending any educational institution, and no letters have been found that were written by her, suggesting that she received little or no formal education. In fact, William and Mary Hardisty were married in 1857, and their first surviving child was born in 1858, followed by another in 1861 and yet another in 1862. There is no way to know if any children were lost in between these births, which was often the case in early fur trade marriages. Further, in 1869, William still held his wife and her lack of education responsible for problems with his children. In a letter to Miss Davis, the mistress of the school at Red River, William apologized for his children's behaviour, writing,

> I have to thank you for the trouble you must have had with him (Richard). It is very difficult in this District to keep the children away from the Indians who are always about the house & my children labour under this further disadvantage that their mother has no education. I am generally absent from them all summer, and at intervals during winter, so that they are to be pitied more than blamed for their mischievous

habits. I hope therefore that you will excuse them if they are not so good or so well behaved as those who have educated mothers to instil virtuous habits into them from their infancy & to teach them the rudiments of their education ... I am willing to recompense you for the extra trouble.[11]

William Hardisty was always concerned with formal education for his family and there is some evidence that he was anxious to have a convent school built in the Mackenzie River District. In a letter to Hardisty from Roman Catholic Bishop Henri Faraud in 1863, the bishop "assured the chief trader he would try to bring the Grey Nuns north not later than the summer of 1865, provided Hardisty helped build them a suitable house." William may have assisted in the building, since nuns were brought to Fort Providence in 1867.[12] Possibly Mary Allen Hardisty attended there for some education, but all indications are that she never left fur trade country for an extended period of time in order to attend school, as her husband had initially hoped. In addition, as William confirms in this letter, "Indians" were always close at hand, and he was away a good deal of the time, including most of the summers and intervals in winter. Further, he noted that his wife had no education and no ability to instill "virtuous habits" in her children. Thus, with her father away so much of the time, and her mother likely having no Euro–North American education, it is reasonable to assume that much of Isabella's early role modelling was from her Métis mother, and that she had ample exposure to Indigenous culture as a child.

Despite Mary taking on the primary parenting role due to his own extended absences, in an 1870 letter William was still complaining about his wife, this time to the woman who had married his brother Richard, Eliza McDougall Hardisty, writing that

> I wish my Mary had your kind and gentle way, for I am sure there is the making of a good respectable father of a family in me, if managed in the proper way. It is true I am getting rather crabbed as I increase in years, which makes it all the more necessary to receive a few [sic] to make me a good boy.[13]

It appears from his letters that, in regard to raising his children, William felt he was at a disadvantage in part because he had chosen to marry an Indigenous woman, unlike his brother Richard.[14] It is important to note, though, that William's letters, in which he despaired over his wife's shortcomings, were written during the latter part of the fur trade era. This coincided with the later nineteenth century, when attitudes toward miscegenation were hardening.

Despite the shifting perceptions of mixed marriages (which was not the case for William and Mary Hardisty, as both were Indigenous), William Hardisty's desires to correct his wife's shortcomings by way of a Euro–North American education were hampered by the same reality that early fur traders came to understand. Indigenous women possessed a wide range of skills, in effect the "education" that was critical for survival in fur trade country. With the privations of the North and his extended periods away, William likely soon realized that he could not spare his wife for a "year or two" as he had intended so that she might receive a formal education, even as near at hand as Fort Providence.

In addition to the changed attitudes generally, William's desire to educate his new wife may have been influenced by the feelings that his own father expressed in a letter to his son Richard. In it, the senior Hardisty wrote,

> When I received your letter, I received one also from William, and in it he tells me of his marriage with a Miss Allen from the Columbia. It is a pity she has no education, but I hope William will set to work and educate her himself, as he is well able to do it.[15]

In another letter to William's younger brother Richard, Richard Sr. again implored his son to be cautious about a marriage partner himself, and perhaps revealed that he was not so pleased with William's choice: "I hope you will not think of marrying any girl who is not the Daughter of a respectable family. I do not wish to interfere with you in your choice, but hope you will make a good choice."[16]

Despite his own expressed dismay with his wife's lack of education, and while Isabella's time in the eastern school is discussed later, it speaks to her father's appreciation

The Making of "Lady Belle"

for fur trade culture that he wrote in a letter to Miss Davis, the head of the Red River school that Isabella had briefly attended, that

> I can never thank you or pay you enough for your kindness and attention to my little girl—whom I fully intended from the first should have finished her education under your direction—had her health permitted.[17]

When Isabella eventually returned to the North after her time at school in Ontario, it was only a few years before her father retired from his post with the HBC. In 1878, Isabella's father moved his family to the home of his brother-in-law Donald A. Smith, later Lord Strathcona, in Winnipeg and then on to Lachine, Quebec, where many fur trade employees retired.

The early attempts to groom Isabella to "gracious womanhood" at European-styled schools would have faced some challenges, given the realities of survival strategies in the North. While Isabella's mother tended to her traplines, in effect serving as the head of household and provider of sustenance for the family while her father tended to Company business, what were the young ones doing? This was a concern for William, who surely worried about the freedom his children had in "running wild."[18] No doubt many HBC men had similar misgivings about their children adopting an Indigenous way of life that was increasingly viewed as "primitive, heathen, and dangerous."[19]

The fact that Isabella was able to become "Lady Lougheed" of Beaulieu House in Calgary's pioneer community is due, in part, to the fact that her mother and father did send her away from northern fur trade country to be educated in Euro–North American schools. It was perhaps even more important for William to ensure that his daughter was educated, given he was not able to provide his wife with a formal education and that she was considered to be of a "lower position." The fact that her husband considered her to be of a lower position may have induced Mary Allen to desire that Isabella receive a Euro-Canadian education and thus lend her support to her young daughter undertaking such an arduous journey out of fur trade country.

As an adult, speaking of her journey out of the North to attend the school operated by Miss Davis near present-day Winnipeg, Isabella recalled for her interviewer that she first set out by York boat,

> walking portages of ten and twelve miles through mos-
> quito-infested areas, voyaging down the Saskatchewan
> River via Fort Carleton and Prince Albert, and over-
> land by prairie Schooner. On this trip she caught
> scarlet fever and for a year and a half afterward lay
> ill in bed. Then her grandmother, who was living at
> Lachine, Quebec, sent for her.[20]

Although she was speaking by this time as Belle, the First Lady of Beaulieu House, Isabella still seemed intent on reminding her contemporaries that she was, at the very least, a pioneer capable of walking portages and of surviving privations.

Today, there sits a plaque outside Isabella's first school in Red River identifying it as Twin Oaks. To Miss Davis (of Indigenous ancestry) and her students, it was known as Oakfield. As the plaque explains, the house was built in the mid-1850s to serve as a residence for a private girls' school operated by Matilda Davis until 1873.[21] The girls at Miss Davis's school were primarily daughters of HBC men, sent there to be educated as English ladies by a woman who had become one herself when she left fur trade country to attend school in Europe. To that end, the girls were taught such skills as French, music, drawing, dancing, needlework and deportment.[22]

It is not clear exactly how long Isabella attended Miss Davis's school, since there is only record of her tuition for the year 1867.[23] While Isabella's father expressed a preference for her to be educated in Red River, shortly after arriving there to attend school, Isabella became ill and was sent to Lachine to be cared for by her grandmother. Isabella would have been around six years old at that time. It was in the same year that tuition was paid for her at the Red River school, 1867, that Isabella's grandmother Marguerite Sutherland Hardisty reported in a letter to her son Richard that Isabella was in Lachine, and that she had "improved wonderfully since she arrived, the cough she was so much troubled with has almost entirely left her."[24] Isabella remembered that the man who escorted her to Lachine from Red River was the son of the man who had built Whitby Ladies' College in Ontario.[25] Whoever that man was, he likely had a role in Isabella later being sent to Wesleyan Ladies' College in Ontario.

There were surely some concerns with a young child being so far removed from her family, and this is likely why Isabella's father, William Hardisty, expressed a clear preference for a school in Red River rather than the Ontario school Isabella eventually attended. Regarding the culture with which Isabella was familiar, it is true she was born at Fort Resolution, an isolated post on the south shore of Great Slave Lake,[26] so she cannot be considered a "Red River Métis." Yet the majority of residents at this northern post with which Isabella would have had contact were Dené or Métis, and both of her parents were Indigenous. Clearly, some of the culture she encountered at Red River would have been familiar to Isabella, given that

> in such centres as Fort Smith, Fort Chipewyan, Fort Simpson, and Fort Liard, the Métis formed an integral part of the community ... These people carried the culture, values and personal identifications of the southern Métis; they ... deemed themselves a distinct social group.[27]

In addition to the lack of educational facilities, perhaps it was this socialization and the recreational pursuits in the North that convinced Isabella's father that it was best for his daughter to attend school elsewhere, but in a culture with which she was familiar in the Red River Settlement. There is no way to know what occupied Isabella while at the northern posts, but she undoubtedly joined in some traditional activities alongside her mother (particularly when she returned to the North as a teenager), such as dressing skins, gumming canoes and making moccasins, clothing, fishnets and snowshoes.[28] So it is clear that, while Isabella had the benefit of a Euro-Canadian education, she was well schooled in the ways of the northern Métis.

While Isabella was at the school in Ontario, her father wrote a letter to Miss Davis, explaining the reason for her departure. Following the lengthy quotation included earlier, William went on to express regret that Isabella had "gone back in everything, and what is still more to be regretted, she has lost a good deal of that religious feeling and firm reliance on her Creator that she learnt [sic] from you."[29] There is further indication that William and his family did not feel the quality of the education, or at least the cultural experience, at Wesleyan Ladies' College measured up to that offered at Miss Davis's school. Isabella's brother Thomas wrote to Miss Davis, complaining that he did not think Isabella was improving much. Rather, he said,

> if I may judge from her writing … it is not so good as when she came down here [Montreal] last fall. Anyway I know if she were my daughter I would never send her to a school such as she is at just now—for the reason that there are too many scholars and the teachers can never look after all of them properly.[30]

One might think that the Hardistys, with their adherence to the Protestant faith and the value of work and

education for both sons and daughters, would appreciate a more liberal education like that offered at Wesleyan.
Perhaps a primary concern for William in particular in
regard to Isabella was that she was so far removed from
other children of the fur trade, most of whom remained in
Red River.[31] At the time of William's letter to Miss Davis
in 1870, "Bella" was in Lachine for a visit during a school
break, and her father again expressed his concern for his
daughter, particularly that she may become a "woman of
the world." As he wrote,

> Bella was quite well—her cough had entirely left
> her—but they were spoiling her by allowing her to
> pass her holidays with too many different families.
> She will form no real or lasting friendship and settle
> down at last into a mere woman of the world.[32]

Perhaps some of William's concerns were born of
the fact that Isabella had left her immediate family at
a relatively young age and that she was so far removed
from northern fur trade country. There is some indication that Isabella may have had a brief visit from either
her father or mother in 1868, when both were in Lachine
to bury their young son, Edward Stewart Hardisty,[33] but
she would not have enjoyed many visits from them. On
one occasion, when Isabella was approximately twelve
years old, Donald A. Smith referred to "little Isabelle"
in his letter to Richard Hardisty in December of 1872,
noting that "all at Lachine are well as are also those
of my own household."[34] Although Isabella was not

always in the North with her parents, when she was not at school she was being cared for by her grandmother Marguerite Sutherland Hardisty, another woman of Métis ethnicity familiar with Hudson's Bay Company fur trade culture.

Although she was in close contact with her grandparents while she was at school, being separated from her family must have been difficult for Isabella. While there do not appear to be any letters remaining that she might have written home while she was away at school, there is one from her cousin, a young Richard Hardisty, written while he was at school in Europe. In a letter addressed to "my dear father," postmarked Merchiston Castle, Edinburgh, October 28, 1885, and signed "your loving son," Richard not only expressed his desire to please his father but implored him to write.

> I wish you would write to me I have not had a letter from across the ocean for nearly seven weaks [sic] and so now if I was to get a letter I would feel so much better because it seams [sic] so dul [sic] to see the other boys getting their letter and I standing and looking at them reading and I have nothing to do so I wish you would write as often as you can … I would feal [sic] a great deal better so pleas [sic] write … Perhaps you are to [sic] busy to write but if you are surly [sic] Ma or Clara are not too busy … I wish you would write to Mr. Rogerson and tell him all you would like me to do.[35]

We might assume that Isabella shared some of the same sentiments of loneliness expressed by her cousin Richard when she found herself so isolated from her parents and the familiarity of the North-West. This is particularly so, given that school calendars confirm that Isabella was one of only a few students at Wesleyan from northern Hudson's Bay country, while most others came from Ontario, Quebec or the United States.[36]

Perhaps William was aware of some of Isabella's challenges in her new school. In a letter to Eliza McDougall Hardisty, William again expressed his concern that Isabella would become too worldly, and continued:

> You did not say much about my little girl. It is a theme I never hear of poor child [*sic*] they are knocking her about very much and I fear will become worldly minded and superficial, a kind of cosmopolitan lady of the world, with hosts of acquaintances, but few real friends in the proper sense of the term. She was very attentive to her religious duties when she left Miss Davis school but I was sorry to observe that she became less so after she went to Canada. I have not had a line from Dr. Rice or even Mr. and Mrs. Wright about Bella since I left Canada and she herself is so nervous and frustrate [*sic*] that she cannot write an intelligible letter. She is always in such a hurry to get to the end of it in fact it is altogether illegible and unintelligible. I have told her now that she must try to write a good plain hand before she attempts

The Making of "Lady Belle"

a running hand. Her ideas go faster than her pen and the poor girl makes a sad mess of it but she may improve as she grows older.[37]

Again, William bemoaned the shortcomings he saw in his own wife when compared to Eliza, writing, "I wish my Mary had your kind, gentle way."[38]

In 1872, while still at Wesleyan, Isabella was again mentioned in a letter from Marguerite Sutherland Hardisty to her son Richard. In the letter, Marguerite referred to Isabella's mother as Mrs. William, for whom Bella was sending a "small parcel." The letter, which suggested that Marguerite was aware of her grand-daughter's unhappiness at Wesleyan, went on to say that William had written to her, advising that he "thought of removing his daughter Bella from Hamilton, but as he did not intend staying much longer in the service, he thought it hardly any use to do so."[39]

There is some correspondence from others who were not family that suggests Isabella stood out as "different" while at Wesleyan, and this likely contributed to her unhappiness and the nervousness her father noted. Reports about Isabella surfaced later when a few of the alumnae also returned to the West after they left Wesleyan.[40] It is from one alumna in particular that we learn about some of the students' perspectives on Isabella. In the annual report of 1962–63, Louise Purchase noted that she

read an interesting paper on the life of her mother who was Nettie (Janet) Coatsworth, daughter of

Emerson Coatsworth, [and who] attended the Hamilton Ladies College from 1875–1879. She emphasized the influence of her years in the college on her life as a pioneer mother and community leader on the prairie in Saskatchewan.[41]

Purchase went on to explain that her mother, Nettie Coatsworth, received her Mistress of English Literature Degree from Wesleyan. According to Purchase, her mother recalled that fellow classmate Isabella Hardisty, now "Lady Lougheed, wife of Senator Lougheed, [was the] daughter of an Indian Chief. Her name was Bella Hardisty. She attended in Mother's time."[42] Where the girls at Wesleyan got the idea that Isabella was the daughter of an "Indian Chief" is not clear, but they were clearly aware that she was Indigenous and "different."

In 1927, the *Hamilton Herald* alluded to the different classes of girls who had attended Wesleyan, when it referred to tuitions that ranged from "$143 per annum to $275." The newspaper concluded that "one could imagine the arrogant misses of that time boasting that they were on the $275 course to some poor lass who was paying $175 or less."[43] Many of Wesleyan's records were destroyed by fire, so there is no way to know the tuition her father paid for Isabella's attendance. Yet the fact she seemed to have achieved some notoriety as the daughter of an "Indian Chief" suggests she was regarded as belonging to a different class than other girls, regardless of the tuition paid. It is not totally clear what effect her "special" status had on Isabella, but she did not graduate like many of the other

The Making of "Lady Belle"

girls did. Rather, she returned to her family in the North while still in her teens.

After having been away at school in Ontario, life was no doubt different for Isabella at the northern posts. Yet, later in life, Isabella continued to refer to a "genteel" life-style when she spoke of some aspects of her youth, such as the time she had spent with her grandmother in Lachine prior to her arrival at Wesleyan. She commented that, although there had been many "privations" in her early life, she had never had to do "much hard work, having been in school, and my grandmother had had twelve servants."[44] Surely Isabella's early years at Forts Resolution, Liard and Simpson, along with the three years spent at Fort Rae and again at Fort Simpson after her time at Wesleyan, were key periods in her life. In reality, life in these northern posts necessitated that *all* family members contribute to some amount of the physical labour required to ensure survival. This is particularly so given that Isabella once noted the shortage of food and having been sent to another post with her mother and siblings in order to survive one particularly difficult winter. In fact, it appears that, after 1821, there was often limited capacity on the part of the Hudson's Bay Company's transportation system, mean-ing that the quantities of supplies sent to the Mackenzie River area were inadequate to meet the demands of both Indigenous people and fur trade families.[45] After hav-ing been away at school in the East, the privations of the North were no doubt difficult to re-accustom to. When speaking to the media later in life, Isabella may not have wanted to recall those difficulties as she focused on maintaining the higher status that she enjoyed in her southern Alberta community.

Despite her higher status in Calgary, her own personal history would have remained with Lady Belle as the Métis clashed with the new central Canadian government over their land rights. It is not clear if Isabella fully understood her uncle Donald Smith's role in the political happenings of the North-West. Donald Smith, later Lord Strathcona, who was married to Isabella's aunt, was sent to the Red River by the central Canadian government in an attempt to quell any possibility of conflict. For her part, Isabella was at the eastern school when fighting erupted in the first Métis resistance in 1869. Thus, she would have been exposed to the sentiments of Euro-Canadians with regard to the Métis.[46] Also, not long after her marriage to James Lougheed, when fighting erupted again between the Métis and government troops, Isabella may very likely have attended and then read the account of the military funeral held for her brother, Private Richard Hardisty, whose body was being sent from Moose Jaw to Winnipeg in May of 1885.[47] She may have been there on May 24, 1885, as all heard the "Toll for the Brave" when her brother was laid to rest during a funeral service that resulted in a gathering the size of which was never "before seen in Winnipeg or in the North West." During the funeral service, Isabella would have heard that the community, although mourning the dead, recognized the necessity of the losses so that the "stability of our institutions and security under good government" would continue.[48] If in Winnipeg for the funeral, Isabella, fully understanding that there were Métis

The Making of "Lady Belle"

who fought on both sides of this conflict, would likely have read the story of the battle that led to her brother's death. Soldiers' accounts in the local newspaper reported that, while Riel assured his followers of their reward in heaven should they die, Isabella's brother was "shot through the head" at 8:00 PM on May 16, 1885, and died the following morning at 5:00 AM.[49]

No doubt Isabella read the tribute to Private Hardisty, published on May 28, 1885, which indicated that Richard Hardisty had lived with the Inkster family in Seven Oaks from the time he was ten until he was seventeen years of age, while he attended St. John's College. Given that he was at the school in the Red River area for so long, those who spoke of him at his funeral likely knew Richard better than did his sister Isabella. "Liberal, bright, chatty, cheerful and interesting . . . he was the life of his friends" are words used to describe Richard.[50] Despite her physical distance from her brother, the words used to describe him could also be used to describe Isabella, given that she made such a lasting impression as a "gracious woman" when she became first lady and primary hostess of the new North-West.

The persona of the gracious woman that she was cultivating likely prevented Lady Belle from commenting publicly about the fighting in Batoche, even though her family had been very personally involved in the politics of the day. For the most part, gracious womanhood necessitated the appearance of publicly embracing the emerging Anglo-dominated society of the new North-West and refraining from political commentary. Yet Isabella's appearance always thwarted a completely successful subsuming of her ethnicity.

Her facial features confirmed her Métis ancestry. Indeed, a man who was himself familiar with attempted assimilation, Sylvester Clark Long, confirmed Isabella's ancestry for the public. Long was better known to his contemporaries and in history as Chief Buffalo Child Long Lance, a man believed at the time to be the son of a Blackfoot Chief. As Chief Buffalo Child, Sylvester Long, who was actually descended from enslaved Black people, achieved some notoriety and many residents of the West read his words. Long confirmed what many already knew about Isabella but perhaps did not speak of, noting in an article for the *Mentor* that "some of western Canada's best citizens are of Scotch and Indian descent. Lady Lougheed, wife of Sir James Lougheed, minister of the interior, is a half-breed."[51]

This was public confirmation, along with her physical appearance, and a brief but rather telling assessment of Isabella's character, that belies the simplistic conclusion that the agenda of "gracious womanhood" and the abandonment of her Métis culture were a *fait accompli*. According to a letter written on December 11, 1876, to her uncle Richard Hardisty from Fort Chipewyan, the unnamed author expressed regret that Isabella had left Wesleyan so soon. The author shared his doubts about Isabella's ability to assimilate to European-inspired gracious womanhood, saying,

> Miss Bella Hardisty is passing the winter at this place—it is to be regretted that she was removed so soon from the Canadian Institution where she was being educated—2 or 3 years longer would have

The Making of "Lady Belle"

turned out a highly accomplished and charming young lady.[52]

Given the isolation in which Isabella lived during a good part of her childhood, it is understandable that some who knew her as a youngster might doubt her eventual ability to succeed as Lady Belle. There is some indication that even Isabella might have felt she was not fitting in with the other "young ladies" at Wesleyan, which was so far removed from her family and the northern fur trade posts where she spent her early childhood and her later teens.

However, those who doubted Isabella's abilities to become "highly accomplished" and "charming" not only underestimated Isabella, but also underestimated the resilience of her Métis family network. Like many HBC men, William Hardisty had sent his daughter to school so that she might be adept at presenting herself as English rather than Métis, and for the most part Isabella did not disappoint. She became the gracious "English" wife of a man who would become one of the new economy's most successful businesspeople and community leaders. Yet, as an adult, Isabella continued to rely on the extended family network of the Métis Hardistys and on the culture that she had learned in her formative years—a culture and family that helped her to transition from a child of the northern fur trade to a respected pioneer who was known to many as Lady Belle.

two

It Takes a "Historical" Village

My wife was a Hardisty, of Lady Strathcona's family,
so that, in a way, I'm a Hudson's Bay man, my father-
in-law having been chief factor of the company. In
early western days people spoke of "The Company"
pretty much as a man from Prince Edward Island
spoke in New York of "The Island," and asked "What
other Island is there?"[1]

ON ONE OCCASION WHEN PETER Lougheed
spoke to the Calgary Chamber of Commerce
about the top six events in Alberta history,
three of those were directly related to his grandparents,
Senator Sir James Lougheed and Lady Isabella Hardisty
Lougheed. Firstly, both James Lougheed and Isabella's uncle
Donald A. Smith, Lord Strathcona, were linked with the
Canadian Pacific Railway when it arrived in the North-
West.[2] Secondly, James advocated for the creation of the
province in 1905, and thirdly, he strongly advocated for
the Natural Resources Transfer Agreement, which came
to fruition in 1930, only five years after the senator's death

in 1925.[3] Indeed, in Peter Lougheed's personal papers held by the Provincial Archives of Alberta, among other papers that supported his 1974–75 political campaign, is an excerpt from his grandfather James Lougheed's observation in July 1905 (just as Alberta and Saskatchewan were to gain official status as provinces) that

> I have no hesitation in saying, that the time will come when these provinces will occupy a more important position. Their natural resources are calculated to make them more important than ... any of the older provinces.[4]

In 1980, when Peter Lougheed was embroiled in an epic battle with Ottawa over control of resources on behalf of the West once again, Peter's emotions were evident as he referenced the historic events that were intertwined with his own personal history.

> For 25 years we were not really a full province— we were still, in part, a colony or territory of Ottawa. We did not have, like most other provinces, the control of our own natural resources ... My roots go very deep in this Alberta—my grandfather played a part in preserving those resources for Alberta. Our predecessors, 50 years ago this year— in a basic agricultural area—considered the Natural Resources Transfer Bill as, and I quote them, "the most important legislation ever before the Alberta House." I think it still is! ... It is difficult to explain—

let me try. I have very deep feelings about this province, its people, its history, its pioneers.[5]

Peter's grandparents, James and Isabella, were indeed important pioneers in what would become Alberta. Yet James Lougheed's western story begins in a manner similar to the stories of many pioneers to the West. Although as a lawyer he may have been a valuable addition to Calgary society, Peter's paternal grandfather was one of those pioneers who had a fairly humble background when he arrived in the West with few assets and no influential connections.

James Alexander Lougheed was born in Brampton, Ontario, on September 1, 1854, to a Methodist family of Scottish and Irish descent. His father was a carpenter, a trade he had hoped to pass along to James. The family resided in Cabbagetown, the poor eastern section of Toronto, which was English-speaking, Protestant and highly British and Orange in sentiment and tradition. The Cabbagetown of James Lougheed's youth was comprised of

lines of utilitarian frame houses, largely covered over in roughcast plaster ... thinly built, lacking central heating, and boasting privies out back ... a drab industrial environment with dirt, debris and fumes of factories close at hand.[6]

It was his mother who believed that James should aspire to more than carpentry,[7] and she encouraged him to accept a position as assistant librarian at Trinity

Church in Toronto. Trinity was sometimes referred to as "the Poor Man's Church," where parishioners were likely to be bricklayers, mariners, servants and tavern keepers, with only a few listed as "gentlemen."[8] It was at this church, however, that James was encouraged by the Anglican layman, Samuel Blake (who went on to become a member of Parliament),[9] to further his education at Weston High School.

According to the *Newsletter of the Lougheed Families of North America*, James spent his spare time as a young man attending church meetings, listening to the speeches at the Houses of Parliament or fulfilling his duties as chaplain in the Orange Order, duties that included donning a white gown and carrying a Bible in parades.[10] There is no evidence of James continuing his involvement with the Orangemen when he later lived in Calgary, perhaps in part because it was no longer convenient to do so, perhaps because this group fell out of favour in the West and perhaps in part because he married an Indigenous woman with an influential kinship network.

While still in Ontario in 1877, James had studied law with the Toronto firm of Beatty, Hamilton, and Cassels. In 1881, James opened his own law office in Toronto but only practised a short time before heading west in 1882 with his brother Sam, who would eventually work at the Indian industrial schools.[11] The 1880s were times of expansion in the North-West, and James quickly gained an appointment to practise law in the Manitoba Court of Queen's Bench and County Courts.[12] James kept a diary for most of his adult life, and while the entries for the years when he was married to Peter's grandmother Isabella are not very detailed, those entries for his days in Winnipeg are more revealing of his personality. As a young man intent on making his fortune in the West, James was quite pleased to include information on everything from who preached the Sunday services he attended to the amount he spent on his first suit, even noting in his diary the first time he wore that new suit.[13] Although he was beginning to make some good connections in Winnipeg, James was not there long. When the Canadian Pacific rail line was completed to Medicine Hat in 1883, he soon travelled to the end of that line, where he set up a general store in a tent with business partner Thomas Tweed.[14] There is no official record of this, but Lougheed family history holds that, during this time, James reportedly met William Van Horne and secured a position as legal counsel for the Canadian Pacific Railway (CPR).[15]

Whether he made this early connection to a business elite such as Van Horne or not, in the late summer, James and his brother Sam moved to Fort Calgary,[16] where James rented the back half of a log cabin for his legal practice. If James was not the first lawyer in Calgary, he quickly became the busiest.[17] It did not take much time for this enterprising young man to make even more important personal connections. In December of 1883, James was elected as one of the first stewards of Central Methodist (later United) Church "at the first meeting of the quarterly official board," held at the home of Richard Hardisty.[18] Soon after forging the connection with Richard Hardisty, James and Isabella Hardisty (niece of Richard) became a couple. Richard Hardisty was at one time reported to be one of the wealthiest men in the North-West, holding both the position of Chief Factor of the Hudson's Bay Company and senator for the region. But it was not only her important family connections that convinced James of Isabella's suitability as a wife, but also her Euro–North American education.

There is no doubt that James's marriage into the Hardisty family was a fortuitous one for him, having demonstrated himself to be an ambitious young man. Yet, according to some newspaper articles, James often attributed his success to his mother, Mary Ann Alexander, a "beautiful Christian woman … It is said that from her he inherited his Scotch shrewdness and cleverness that characterized him in later years."[19] Mary Ann Alexander, who had given her son the middle name of Alexander, died before James went west. Thus, she unfortunately never did witness the tremendous success her son achieved after he had forged ties with the Hardisty family.

Indeed, it was not long after James Lougheed arrived in the North-West that he became what some referred to as a "pedigreed Westerner through marriage" to Isabella.[20] The social significance of the marriage on September 16, 1884, was clear when the *Calgary Herald* reported that

last evening, the youth and beauty of our town might be seen wending their way to the Methodist Church, where a scene of no common interest was being enacted … Before the hour the building was packed, a number having to satisfy themselves with a peep through the windows. The principals were James Alexander Lougheed, Esq., Barrister, and Miss Isabella Hardisty.[21]

The invitations for James and Isabella's wedding indicated that Richard Hardisty organized the event, with no mention made of Isabella's Métis mother. After the death of Isabella's father, William Hardisty, Isabella's mother, Mary Anne Allen Hardisty, had sent Isabella to live with her uncle Richard Hardisty in the new hamlet of Calgary. Isabella's mother had subsequently married another Métis man and settled in Manitoba. Whether Mary Hardisty was even at her daughter's wedding is not clear, but the invitations requested the presence of guests at the Methodist Church and then at the home of Richard and Eliza Hardisty to celebrate the marriage of their niece.[22] Newspaper reports were focused on the "youth and beauty" in attendance, and no mention is made of Isabella's mother or siblings, if they were present.

Regarding Isabella's marriage to James, at least one author believes the union was sanctioned by the elders of the Hardisty family. Popular historian J.G. MacGregor wrote:

Evidently Dick Hardisty, keeping an eye on the budding romance (between Isabella and James) had made up his mind that his brother's eldest daughter was making a good match. There is nothing to show how one of her other uncles, Donald

A. Smith, regarded the union, but undoubtedly his interest in the affair would have boded well for the young couple.[23]

Regarding the wealth and stature of Isabella's uncle Richard Hardisty, MacGregor continued,

Whatever it cost Dick Hardisty to send his children away to school it made little dent in his wealth. Undoubtedly he was the richest man in the western prairies and besides his mill had his hand in several other ventures.[24]

Although MacGregor's sources are sparse, Hardisty was well connected enough for it to be plausible that he was one of the wealthiest men in the North-West during the transitional period that followed the end of the fur trade economy. In addition to his own stature as a Chief Factor of the Hudson's Bay Company, which at that time controlled the development of the western lands, and as a member of the McDougall family because of his marriage to Eliza, Isabella's uncle Richard Hardisty often employed and formed partnerships with other McDougall men, also a fairly wealthy group. The McDougall family were well known in the area. Eliza McDougall was the descendant of George Millward McDougall, missionary, pioneer and treaty negotiator, who established several missions in the North-West, including in Edmonton and Morley. In fact, recognizing the changing times, Eliza's husband Richard Hardisty worked "hand in hand with … David

[McDougall] who competed with the Hudson's Bay Company for trade."[25] After his marriage to Isabella, the new family member James Lougheed soon also became Richard Hardisty's close business associate.[26]

Despite the excitement generated by the marriage of the future senator to the daughter of what might be considered fur trade "aristocracy," James and Isabella still began married life in a small log hut next to James's law office. The only renovation was a bay window, imported from central Canada, a renovation that no doubt served as notice to the townspeople that this couple already viewed themselves to be "distinct."[27] The Lougheeds physically moved the house twice to new locations, suggesting that it was somewhat more substantial than a traditional "log hut," until they finally left it to move into their grand home, Beaulieu, in 1891.[28]

Confirming that Peter's grandmother Isabella had not married out, but rather that his grandfather James had married *into* an established Hudson's Bay Company family, and as though he was now a Company man himself, James had chosen the HBC man Charlie Parlow to stand for him as best man. In fact, when James was interviewed in 1921, he indicated that he had sensed a new beginning for himself as a "Company man" upon his marriage. In the excerpt referenced at the start of this chapter, James Lougheed said:

My wife was a Hardisty, of Lady Strathcona's family, so that, in a way, I'm a Hudson's Bay man, my father-in-law having been chief factor of the company. In

It Takes a "Historical" Village

early western days people spoke of "The Company" pretty much as a man from Prince Edward Island spoke in New York of "The Island," and asked "What other Island is there?"[29]

Indeed, James's contemporaries noted that when he ventured west, "like most men who came to Calgary in those days he was not over burdened with surplus wealth."[30] Yet by 1889, just six years after his arrival in Calgary and his marriage into the Hardisty family, the local paper could refer to James as "one of our heaviest real estate owners, having accumulated property to the extent of nearly $70,000 worth."[31] Given that the 1881 census does not even list Calgary, but rather a region identified as the Bow River, which contained "five shanties, seventy-five houses, and four hundred people, of whom fifty were women,"[32] James and Isabella's accumulation of property by 1889 was impressive.

While researching members of Isabella's kinship network, historian Donald B. Smith located what he believed to be the earliest surviving letter written by James, dated November 25, 1885. Speaking about this letter, Smith wrote,

One can also see from this letter how the young lawyer has worked himself into the network of his wife's influential family connections, who included not only Richard Hardisty, the richest man in the Northwest Territories, but also Donald A. Smith, soon to be the richest man in Canada.[33]

In this letter to Isabella's uncle Richard Hardisty, James did give some indication of the close connection he quickly developed with Richard. After some personal details about his first-born son "growing like a weed in a potato field," James went on to speak of other family members, referring to an upcoming visit by Lord Strathcona, the "worthy driver of the last C.P.R. Spike." James also confirmed some of the investments he held with Richard Hardisty—in this case, cattle. In the same letter, James noted that his brother Sam was looking after the herd for Richard and James.[34]

Like James after him, Richard Hardisty was never elected as a representative of the North-West in the Canadian government (although Richard had run unsuccessfully in the 1887 election before receiving his senate appointment). Rather, both men took advantage of political connections and were successful in part due to the long fur trade history of the Hardisty family. In fact, when Richard was appointed to the senate in 1888 as the first senator for the District of Alberta, he continued to hold the position he had been appointed to in 1872, that of Chief Factor for the Upper Saskatchewan District of the HBC with headquarters at Fort Edmonton, and comprising all of Manitoba, Saskatchewan, Alberta and the Territories.[35] The fact that Richard could retain his post as an HBC man and at the same time serve in the senate demonstrates not only the continuing importance of the fur trade company, its employees and their family networks, but also the close connections that government officials retained with the fur trade company during the transitional period.

As both Chief Factor and the area's senator, Richard Hardisty was well placed to monitor changing times and to identify political and financial opportunities. According to the man who would eventually become a business partner to James, Edmund Taylor (another HBC man), it was Richard who had encouraged the HBC to expand its operations to include "Flour Mills, Lumber Mills, and caused the company to become the pioneer cattle ranchers in the North after the buffalo made their last trek southward about 1870."[36] As the senior HBC officer when settlers began arriving on the western prairies, Richard was ideally situated, not only to assess material needs, but also to personally profit from land speculation.

As a partner to the Hardisty men in business, Peter's grandfather James Lougheed served as an example of one individual who embraced the ideologies of expansion, diversification and challenging Ottawa for provincial control of its resources. Despite James's involvement in the lobbying for control of resources for his adopted province, and the wealth they had amassed, James and Isabella Lougheed's vast estate, like so many others, fell victim to the economic crisis of the late 1920s and ensuing Great Depression, so that Peter's father, Edgar Lougheed, never achieved political and business success to the degree that his father had. Rather, it was James's grandson Peter Lougheed who, by championing many of the same things, was able to restore the family name and economic fortunes to the "glory days" of the past, when Isabella and James were members of prairie aristocracy. There were clearly unique challenges for James and Isabella's children

46

that served as obstacles to their success during the severe downturn in Alberta's economy. When Peter Lougheed's father, Edgar, was the only son left to manage his parents' estate, one report suggests that he turned to alcohol and that his wife suffered a nervous breakdown and was hospitalized.[37] Researchers Pratt and Richards attribute Edgar's problems to those "typical ... of the offspring of the privileged and powerful."[38] However, many people from varied backgrounds suffered similar problems during the 1930s. Nonetheless, it is true that the

> age of prairie elegance did not long outlive Sir James Lougheed. Like many other members of the old mansion set of Winnipeg, Edmonton, and Calgary, the Lougheed family did not fare well during the Depression. Indeed, it very nearly wiped them out ... The Depression severely trimmed the values of the family properties ... Following the death of the senator's widow, the Royal Trust Company, which held the mortgages on the Lougheed properties, ordered the family mansion auctioned off.[39]

After James died, Peter's father, Edgar Lougheed, like his brother Clarence before him, was expected to defer his law career to manage his father's estate. Despite the challenges Edgar faced, Allan Hustak mused that temperament and circumstances beyond his control denied Edgar the "opportunity of coming out of the Senator's shadow and equaling his accomplishments."[40] Edgar did assume a difficult task in a situation over which he had little control. The Depression was followed by the war, and, according to Hustak, based on a conversation with Peter Lougheed, his father's drinking caused "sporadic difficulties."[41] Peter went on to say that the family went through the Depression and the war in much the same way that everyone else did. That may be a slight exaggeration, given the Lougheeds continued to enjoy the services of a housekeeper throughout the period.

Although they were somewhat better off than many people during the Depression, Isabella's other sons also experienced tragedy. After his father's death in 1925, and until his own death, Clarence, as well as his brothers Edgar, Norman and Douglas Lougheed, had become executors of their parents' vast estate, which was full-time work. The youngest Lougheed son, Douglas, was the first to die, in 1931, at the age of thirty, prior to the real downturn in family financial fortunes. Yet the bulk of the estate Douglas left was an amount of eighteen thousand dollars in life insurance.[42]

The economic depression that created severe financial problems for Isabella's family may have contributed to Clarence's sudden death in 1933 at the age of forty-eight of a heart attack.[43] With Clarence's early death, Peter's grandmother lost the son who had most often accompanied her as she continued her public duties after she was widowed in 1925. Despite the loss of Clarence, Isabella was financially able to carry on with her duties until the 1930s.[44] However, by 1933, a lawsuit brought by the executors of the Lougheed estate against the province gives some indication of the struggles the family now faced. Following Clarence's death, the Lougheed family sought to receive fifteen thousand dollars in life insurance being withheld for payment of succession duties on Clarence's share of his father's estate. At the time of his death, Clarence was entitled to receive 20 percent of the income from the estate. However, the plaintiffs in the case, Edgar and Clarence's wife, asserted that Clarence was not receiving any income from his father's estate, and that in 1932 the estate, in fact, did not yield any income at all.[45]

In addition to managing their father's estate, Isabella's sons carried on with the management of the estate of her father, William Hardisty. This meant that they had to deal with the numerous appeals for money from Isabella's siblings, who had not transitioned as well into the new economy that replaced the fur trade. In fact, Isabella's mother and siblings receive rare mention in any of the documentation about the Lougheeds, making it difficult to discern how they adjusted to the new economy of the North-West. Yet it is clear that Isabella and James did maintain some contact with them. In 1897, at the height of gold rush fever, James reportedly "made arrangements to send a prospecting party to the Klondike by way of Edmonton—the all Canadian route. The party will be in charge of Frank Hardisty."[46] Isabella's brother Frank had been in southern Alberta earlier, in 1885, when he served with the Rocky Mountain Rangers. This group was tasked with keeping the peace when Louis Riel led the Métis to challenge the government and incoming settlers from overtaking their ancestral lands.[47] There was no further information in the local newspapers regarding how successful James and Frank's gold-prospecting venture was. However, it does not appear that Frank realized much wealth from it, or, if he did, he was not able to retain that wealth. Nor did Frank retain any of the wealth from his father's estate, which was eventually the subject of some dispute by family members. These disputes demonstrate that Isabella's brothers, particularly Frank, were not as financially successful as she was. In fact, it would be fair to conclude that some of her siblings and her mother were destitute for some of their lives after William Hardisty had died.[48]

There are many who believed that Peter Lougheed "came from money," and there is no doubt that there were instances in which his ancestors would have been considered wealthy in comparison to other Métis and mixed-race couples. Yet both Isabella and James Lougheed clearly experienced times of privation, and both were equally involved in establishing themselves as what we would now term a "power couple." Despite the fact that Isabella and James Lougheed were clearly strong partners who both contributed to their success as Calgary's "First Couple," archival records at the University of Alberta (which houses the political and personal documents of Peter Lougheed and the records of the Progressive Conservative Party) reference only the accomplishments of James Lougheed as inspiration for Peter's political success. Noting that James Lougheed was knighted in 1916, the summary of archival holdings states that it was perhaps the example of his grandfather which inspired Peter Lougheed to believe in the importance of service to the community and to commit such a significant part of his life to that vocation.[49]

Not only do the archival records tend to reference only the success and contributions of James as inspiration for Peter's success, but historians have continued to do so. In one example of the enduring focus by historians on James Lougheed, Peter C. Newman noted only Lougheed's ancestry as the grandson of Sir James Lougheed, a "lawyer and businessman who arrived in Calgary on a railway-construction handcart in 1883 and stayed to prosper as a lawyer and investor, a founder of the city's social and political life."[50] These are indeed facts. However, Newman either is not aware of or regards it as insignificant that James Lougheed, the son of poor Irish immigrants, who grew up in Toronto's Cabbagetown district, had first tried his luck in Winnipeg and Medicine Hat before he was able to "prosper" in Calgary. It is a fact that key to his ability to prosper in this pioneer community was the quick connections that James had made with the Hudson's Bay Company elites—the Hardisty family and Peter's grandmother Isabella in particular.

Indeed, Peter Lougheed himself, perhaps not as fully aware of his grandmother's own contributions, most often referenced the success of his grandfather and how that may have influenced him. When Lougheed considered the offer of becoming chancellor of Queen's University in 1996, he initially objected because he had never attended

51

that university, although both of his sons had. Yet, upon completion of the post that he did in the end accept, Peter Lougheed drew the connection between his grandfather James and the Ontario city where Queen's University is located. In addition to the appeal of the fact that Queen's viewed itself as a national university,

> on the personal side, serving as chancellor allowed Lougheed to spend a great deal of time in Kingston, the home of Sir John A. Macdonald. Lougheed's grandfather, Sir James Lougheed, the first-ever lawyer in Alberta, happened to be forever indebted to Kingston's most famous son.

As Peter told the *Kingston Whig-Standard* upon the completion of his six-year term as chancellor, "John A. Macdonald appointed my grandfather who was only 35 years of age at the time, as a senator ... And he rose to be leader of the government in the Senate."[51] In reality, James Lougheed may have been appointed to the senate by Macdonald, but the senate seat he occupied had just been vacated by Isabella's uncle Richard Hardisty, and there is ample evidence that lobbying by the Hardisty network influenced that appointment for James.[52]

It is indeed difficult to uncover references, either in the archives that house his papers or in the history texts of that time, to Peter Lougheed's family history while he was in office that would confirm that his grandmother was the daughter of a Métis Chief Factor of the Hudson's Bay Company's northern fur trade district and the member of such an influential network. Yet, in later years, Peter became involved in the Historica Foundation, serving on its board, while his grandmother's beloved mansion, Lougheed House National Historic Site (originally Beaulieu House), became "one of his primary charitable and historical concerns."[53] Peter's grandmother had herself demonstrated interest in preserving the history of the West when she served as president of the Women's Pioneer Association. Indeed, Peter remained a member of the parent association, the Southern Alberta Pioneer Association, his entire life, as has his son Joe.[54] According to Joe Lougheed, Peter was "profoundly proud to be the grandson of pioneers as I am proud to be a great-grandson. He was a member all his life of the Southern Alberta Pioneers ... and I am a member now."[55]

Indeed, in his 1998 address to the Churchill Society, Peter noted that he would "continue to make the need for history teaching one of the priorities of my life."[56] In another address, which seemed to surprise Peter Lougheed for the attention it garnered, when speaking on the occasion of the end of his term as chancellor of Queen's University in 2002, he noted that there was an issue in Canada at the time that "absolutely distress[ed]" him. That issue was that

> only half of our nation can identify our first prime minister ... We have to think about that, about what, about how, we teach the history of our country and the low priority we give to the teaching of our history.[57]

Peter Lougheed took the opportunity to call on every province to mandate the teaching of Canadian history at all three levels: elementary, junior high and secondary. Peter also took the opportunity to explain why he was so emotional about this, specifically noting that it was a major regret for him: "I fouled up. I was premier for 14 years and I was wrapped up in energy and the constitution and I didn't really take a good look until the last two years on what we teach in our school system and curriculum."[58] In a letter to the *Globe and Mail* in 2001, Peter made an impassioned plea to recognize that history was as critical to the education of students as mathematics, science and grammar. As he wrote:

> A good history education will reveal that the historical narratives we grew up with are dynamic, multidimensional and always open to being recast and re-examined in the context of the present.

Among topics of importance to learn in Canadian history listed by Peter were "the Iroquois Confederacy, the Winnipeg General Strike, the Patriotes rebellion, the construction of the CPR." In conclusion, he noted that "Canada's history, our collective memory, must reflect the diversity of our past and of our present."[59] He repeated what he had previously noted in a 1996 interview in response to the question of where Canadians might look in order to hold the country together:

> I will answer this question simply. I think they have to look over the back fence. They have to meet

their neighbour, understand where their neighbour comes from and what their neighbour looks like, and appreciate the neighbour for the neighbour's differences. If Canadians take their holidays in Florida or Arizona, how are they going to know about Atlantic Canada? If they don't study the history of the West, how are they ever going to understand the West? Canadians have to learn more about their own country, its people, and particularly its history. It's the key to staying together. [60]

It is perhaps only coincidence, but the man who would become mentor to Peter Lougheed was Fred C. Mannix, himself a descendant of Red River homesteader Frederick Stephen Mannix. The Mannix empire had humble beginnings, as Fred Mannix used a team of horses and a dirt scraper to fulfill contracts to build Canadian Pacific branch lines as they "bristled out across the Prairies," stopping in Calgary to establish a construction company that built roads, irrigation ditches, hydro dams, and coal-strip mines.[61] As mentor to Peter Lougheed, and according to his recollections upon his retirement from public life, Fred Mannix had impressed upon Peter that he should not be fearful of any challenge, telling him, "If you think you are right ... take it on."[62]

Like Fred Mannix, Peter Lougheed had a rather humble beginning in the sense that the Lougheed family had lost a good part of the estate that James and Isabella Lougheed, Peter's grandparents, had amassed as two of the first pioneers in what would become Alberta. As pioneers, there is ample evidence that Isabella and James relied on the support of their families and community members—illustrating the reality that "it takes a village" to succeed.

Indeed, Isabella Hardisty Lougheed's contemporaries acknowledged the link between the old economy of the North-West and that which eventually replaced it. In 1922, the periodical *Saturday Night* featured "Lady Lougheed" in its series entitled "Canadian Women in the Public Eye." The article noted that

> thirty-nine years ago a young girl came to visit her uncle, who was a Hudson Bay factor, and who had been sent by the great Hudson's Bay Co. to establish a trading post, at the Junction of the Bow and the Elbow rivers ... Her uncle whom she visited was the late Senator Hardisty, the first senator of the North West Territories, and of the well-known family of Hardisty that had been so intimately connected with the Hudson Bay development in the McKenzie and Saskatchewan river districts ... At that time a new country was just awakening ... And the young girl who visited her uncle in that unpretentious log home in the summer of '83 was destined to see an amazing feat of civilization.[63]

The article went on to say that the story of Lady Lougheed's life had "all the background of romance, adventure and hardship of the pioneer life of the frozen north—on down to the comforts and civilization of the 'Boom Days.'"[64] There is no doubt that this article romanticized Isabella's early life. Yet it does demonstrate that even her contemporaries believed that she, much like Indigenous women who lived when the fur trade economy dominated, was destined to serve as an agent of transition. For Isabella, the transition was from the fur trade to a sedentary agricultural economy increasingly reliant on paper transactions. In fact, as the article pointed out, the transition period was very short:

> From the humble first home of her married life she has lived long since in one of the most beautiful homes of the West, in a decade the flat stoney [sic] prairie "Yard" was changed into beautiful terraced grounds where Calgarians are proud to entertain many official visitors.[65]

In this case, the newspaper identified Isabella not as an Indigenous woman but as a pioneer who had survived hard times to now enjoy civilization and "Boom Days." No doubt her membership in the Hardisty family, which continued to be important in the transitional society of Calgary where she lived her adult life, enabled this pioneer persona.

In Isabella's case, she appeared equally at ease hosting in her stately home the aristocracy of Europe, while they enjoyed the strains of classical piano, as she did hosting the pioneers of southern Alberta, with whom she enjoyed the tunes of the Red River Jig and reputedly may have gladly shared the smoking of a pipe.[66] Yet while on the one hand explaining the privations that she, as a daughter of the fur trade, endured at northern posts, Isabella could just as quickly express disdain that the only hired help available to her as she managed her stately mansion were "Halfbreeds," who were none too reliable.[67] Isabella's classification of the Indigenous women who did manual labour in her home was indicative of the class system that emerged during the fur trade, in which Métis women who had access to Euro-Canadian education were deemed to be of higher status than Indigenous women who continued to rely on more traditional lifestyles.

When Peter Lougheed was interviewed in 1996, the remarks that he made about the "rugged and 'un-Canadian' individualism" that he felt was becoming more prevalent in Alberta were reminiscent of the beliefs of the early pioneers, and indeed of Métis society. As he noted,

> The pioneer nature of the Canadian West, where I come from, necessitated helping one's neighbour. We always had a strong sense of community. We didn't sit there on our part of the land and let the other fellow suffer if his plough broke. We would go over and help him to fix it, or we would lend him ours. We had a real sense of community.[68]

It may be an indication of Peter Lougheed seeking to learn more about the history of his own Métis grandmother, given that she passed away when he was eight years old, that led him, after he left public life, to state:

We have to do better in what we teach ... I will continue to make the need for history teaching one of
the priorities of my life.[69]

Son Joe Lougheed notes that Peter's interest in history
only continued to grow after he left public office, observing that if it might appear at times that his father was more
aware of James Lougheed's contributions than those of
Isabella, this was

> simply a reflection of the times—prominent men
> got the attention ... My father was very proud of
> his grandmother ... My father and uncle did have
> memories of her and the "big house" ... To my
> father, as he got older, I believe he realized she was
> a true pioneer woman of the West, a leader before
> her time, who sought to make her city a stronger
> place in her own way, as society then allowed and
> promoted. She was no doubt a trailblazer.[70]

It does appear that Peter Lougheed had a genuine
interest in learning more about his own Indigenous ancestry—
that much is clear from the documents that remain in his
personal files held by various Alberta archival collections.
Indeed, when he was recognized as Humanitarian of the
Year by the Calgary Legal Guidance in 1987, the narrative
of his life noted Peter's grandfather Sir James Lougheed had
married the "daughter of an English army officer and Metis
woman," meaning that Peter had "a portion of native ancestry—a heritage in which Mr. Lougheed takes great pride."[71]

It Takes a "Historical" Village

Yet we know that Isabella's father was not an "English army officer" but, rather, a Métis man.

While Peter may not have known this at the time, he did become more involved in the preservation of his own family's history when he supported the designation of national historic site to what had started out as Beaulieu House, but which became Lougheed House National Historic Site in 1977. While it has not been clearly confirmed why Isabella and James chose the name Beaulieu House for their grand mansion at the height of their importance as first couple of the North-West, the Beaulieu name is very significant to the Métis people in the northern district where Isabella spent her formative years. Indeed, François Beaulieu II has been recognized as a national historic person for his position as a "founding father of the Métis of the Northwest Territories."[72] While James may not have been as aware, certainly Isabella knew the significance of the Beaulieu name to the Métis people.

Despite her early acculturation as a Métis living in the North, Isabella's mother, Mary Anne Allen Hardisty, once claimed she was French,[73] perhaps partly due to William's apparent need to explain his marriage choice. Indeed, the choice to identify as French is one that some Métis continue to make even today. Regardless, there appears to be only one photo of Mary Anne Allen Hardisty that was preserved, and that photo, along with her documented history, belies her claim of French ancestry.[74] This photo, held by the University of Calgary Digital Collections, is also found among Peter Lougheed's personal papers at the

University of Alberta Archives, suggesting that he may have wished to learn more about this Indigenous member of his family. Indeed, according to Joe Lougheed, the photo of Mary Anne Allen Hardisty

> was proudly displayed in our living room growing up—a photo I have today in my home next to a Métis sash I was given by the Métis Nation of Alberta. He spoke of her and her history . . . he was clearly proud of his heritage.[75]

With the preservation of history as a motivator, in addition to his work with the Historica Foundation, and in the year 2000, both Peter and Jeanne Lougheed were honorary co-chairs of the Calgary Foundation's "Our Millennium."[76] According to Joe Lougheed, his father was

> a student of history all his life. He was keenly interested in Western Canadian history and that of the fur trade and the HBC, knowing his family had a deep connection to that history I suspect. I now own most of his historical library—it is fascinating to see how many books touched on Western history, Métis and First Nations history and the role of the HBC in opening up the West. His library also contains books of his distant relatives . . . Senator Richard Hardisty, Métis, to Donald Smith, later Lord Strathcona, who married his great aunt . . . Books also touch on early Canadian political history, the Riel Rebellion, the CPR—all connected historically to his, and our,

family. He clearly studied the history and was very interested in it. My father (and our family) are also blessed that so many have done research into our family. As premier, numerous citizens would offer items and stories or articles concerning his grand-parents. Much of this would likely have educated him further into the Métis connection.[77]

In terms of his own family history, Peter Lougheed did undertake a tour of the Northwest Territories in 1975, making stops at various locations. At that time, his papers indicate that he was briefed on the economy of Fort Resolution, the post where his grandmother Isabella was born in 1861. At the time of his visit, the community relied on trapping, fishing, hunting (much as they would have during Isabella's time there), but had now ventured into mineral exploration and a sawmill.[78] According to son Joe, who, along with his siblings and his mother, accompanied Peter on that trip, they travelled extensively in the North but not directly to Fort Resolution. However, they were able to

learn first-hand much of the North and the HBC fur trade. We did make a special trip to Lougheed Island, named after Sir James. I am sure that trip was no accident. Again, a connection to, and paying respects to, the past.[79]

Although, as stated earlier, there are not many recorded comments made by Peter Lougheed in regard to his Métis grandmother and her Métis parents, he confirmed in a 1976 newspaper article by Eva Reid the importance of this ancestry to him. Speaking about the restoration of Government House, after it had been closed in 1938 (serving other purposes such as housing wounded veterans), he noted that

> the test of the significance of restoration is the response of the pioneers ... There was a great cross section of Alberta in the some 40 groups who came from as far north as Peace River and as far south as the border. Many of them knew my grandparents (Senator and Lady Lougheed) and I was so happy to be the grandson of pioneers; it was most gratifying.

In fact, when Peter Lougheed decided to seek public office, there was much debate about how to portray him when he set about to revive the Conservative party. Should they downplay his connection to an "Old Alberta family," or would this lead to resentment from some sectors of the population? Given that he would be challenging an elder statesman such as Ernest Manning, there was concern that Peter's youth might be held against him. In the end, many concluded that the best approach would be to promote Peter Lougheed as the first "Alberta-born premier."[80] The consensus seemed to be that belonging to an "Old Alberta family" might work to his advantage if "voters believe[d] that background and resources are being used for the benefit of the province."[81] In fact, in the end, relying on his history and the community-building activities

63

of his grandparents would serve Peter Lougheed well, and there was the sense that Peter appreciated the historical significance in assuming some of the same ideology as his ancestors in the political choices that he made. The cultivation of Peter's image as an Alberta-born premier, something that he was genuinely proud of, would also come to serve him very well as he was determined to maintain Alberta's independence from the federal Conservative party and to pursue policies that were independent from the "federal spectrum."[82]

In the end, and despite debates about how to portray him to voters, Peter Lougheed remained committed to that vision of the Alberta pioneer. Indeed, when he announced his intention to lead a revitalized Progressive Conservative Party of Alberta, the party's news release referred to Peter as "Alberta's youngest political leader," who "is a chip off the pioneer block with a western Canadian family background going back to the days when Calgary was a cluster of houses on the banks of the Bow and Elbow rivers." Featured prominently was a reminder that Peter was the grandson of "Calgary's first lawyer Senator James Lougheed," along with the history of James's arrival in Calgary "fresh out of Toronto law school." Claiming that James had actually walked to Calgary from Medicine Hat, it was noted that he arrived in a Calgary that boasted "about 100 citizens, and eggs sold three dollars a dozen." The brochure went on to say that James had married "Belle Hardisty, niece of Alberta Senator Richard Hardisty and daughter of a pioneer Hudson's Bay Company trader who spent 36 years in the MacKenzie River district." In one of the few public recollections of his grandmother Isabella Clark Hardisty's role in the social organizations of Calgary, the press release noted that

> Belle Lougheed, or Lady Belle as she was known after her husband became Alberta's first and only citizen to be knighted prior to Canada opting out of the British honors system, was the city's first hostess. Her guests included the Duke of Windsor, Governor General Byng and Princess Patricia. Their old home is today Red Cross House on 13th Avenue. S.W.[83]

According to Peter's son Joe, this would have been no accident, as Peter was

> not afraid to embrace his past—in fact he campaigned on it. I think he was saying, "I am from here; our family has been part of building this city and contributing to the West for over 100 years and I would like to continue that tradition."[84]

Although he was speaking of Government House in the earlier reference to historic buildings, Peter's comments might as easily have been made of his grandparents' residence, Beaulieu House, when, according to Eva Reid, he "noted the acoustics of the 'old Sandstone Lady' were excellent, another tribute to the craftsmanship of her day."[85] It was customary, when Isabella and James built their grand home, for the leaders of Calgary to build and name their homes as a way to signal their importance to the community. The architecture followed the fashion of the grand Victorian homes found in Europe. Trudy Cowan, the first director of Lougheed House National Historic Site, wrote that the nineteenth century, when the nouveau riche were overtaking the gentry, was a time of great contradictions, when architects combined many styles. Not long after such displays of wealth and status were apparent in the East, they appeared in the new North-West.[86] While Isabella was not really a member of the nouveau riche, certainly James was, and Beaulieu House did combine many architectural styles. Indeed, the at times ostentatious and garish displays of wealth in the transitional North-West elicited the following observation by one researcher:

> Calgary's elite were forever revealing telltale signs of their humble origins ... Calgary's Edwardian mansions were an ostentatious mishmash of freely borrowed and poorly interpreted styles from many historic periods. They possessed little continuity of style and exhibited little aesthetic taste. The interiors were cluttered with incongruous objects.[87]

As pioneers of the West's great chapter, James and Isabella Lougheed earned significant wealth, but as noted earlier, during the Great Depression of the 1920s and 1930s the family also suffered losses alongside other pioneers who had ventured west in the early days. It is that hardship to which Peter Lougheed harkened when he presided over another major period of growth for Alberta.

For Peter, the prosperity of the oil boom was to be enjoyed by all Albertans, if not monetarily then certainly through access to quality basic services in education, health care and retirement. As an editorial in the *Calgary Herald* noted in 1994, this prosperity for citizens was not a given in other oil-rich jurisdictions. For the *Calgary Herald*, the difference in Alberta was due to Peter Lougheed himself. Why was that? According to the editorial,

> Lougheed himself says it was because of what he experienced, as a child in the Great Depression. His family, among the most prominent in Alberta, was bankrupt and dispossessed. They watched the family home and contents fall under an auctioneer's hammer. Lougheed resolved, not to become rich, but to do his best to make Alberta a place where things like that didn't happen. "Even at that age (he was eight) it made me understand that the Depression had an impact on everybody."

The editorial continued:

> Peter Lougheed did more than preside over a prosperous economy while he was premier of Alberta. His Progressive Conservative government over 16 years in power, set a standard for equity and fair play unequaled anywhere in Canada.[88]

Whether we agree with this assessment or not, Peter Lougheed's vision for his "village" of Alberta in the 1970s was influenced by his own political and economic times, but clearly shaped by the historical village of Calgary, which welcomed his Métis grandmother, raised in northern fur trade country, and his Irish grandfather, raised in Toronto's poor Cabbagetown district. The village that contributed to the shaping of Peter Lougheed was the village that had provided the opportunity for Sir James and Lady Belle, first couple of the North-West. This mixed-race couple were ancestors to a man who, by many accounts, remains one of the most impactful Canadian leaders of the twentieth century. This impact was, indeed, despite the fact that Peter Lougheed was of Métis ancestry, but not at all involved in Métis activism. Yet, unlike his grandmother Isabella, who at times appeared to disparage her own Indigenous ancestry, and unlike Isabella's own mother, who referred to herself as French, Peter Lougheed did not deny that Indigenous ancestry. This was true of his time in office, during the 1970s and 1980s, when it was not politically expedient to acknowledge one's Indigenous ancestry. Regardless, it is fair to say that some today might argue that Peter Lougheed's legacy was not, in the end, as helpful to Métis activism as some may have wanted.

three

Métis Activism in Alberta

The first and only Metis self-government in Canada, recognized constitutionally as a distinct and pro-tected people, the Metis Settlements are a vital and rich part of our Canadian cultural identity.[1]

W HEN THE MÉTIS HAD TRAVELLED across the prairies during the fur trade era, they commonly established winter *hivernant* settlements. In Alberta, the historic Buffalo Lake Métis Settlement in the east central area of the province was strategically important for the Métis. It allowed them to access bison as a food source and to supply the commercial trade along the Saskatchewan River Basin. Estimates are that the population and use of this settlement at its peak was as high as 1,200 to 2,000 people. While it served as a seasonal settlement at its peak, for a time Buffalo Lake served as a permanent settlement as many of the Métis left the Red River after the fighting in 1877. Recent archaeological work provides more concrete evidence of some

1,700 to 2,000 Métis residing in this settlement during the 1870s. The evidence also speaks to a rich social history for the Métis families who resided here on a seasonal basis.[2]

Also centrally located, Tail Creek Métis Settlement served as a staging area for Métis from as far north as Lac La Biche, Lac Ste. Anne, St. Albert, Edmonton and east to Batoche. It was a major distribution point for free traders, and mule trains often extended two miles in length and travelled from Tail Creek to Fort Benton, Montana. Estimates are that 1,500 to 2,000 Métis used this settlement between 1870 and 1879. Known as François Gabriel Dumont's wintering place, Boss Hill and Tail Creek Settlements reportedly consisted of approximately 400 dwellings, with Métis scrip documents confirming the kinship networks that continued to rely on this settlement as Euro-Canadian settlers increasingly encroached on Métis land in the Red River Settlement.[3] Today, the Tail Creek Cemetery has been preserved and is the final resting place of many members of these early Métis families.

Also known as Laboucane Settlement, the Battle River Métis Settlement in the central part of Alberta was settled by several Métis families in the mid-1800s, including the Laboucane and Salois families. Reportedly, in the winter of 1874–75, Abraham Salois, described as "the most successful of the half-breed hunters … made a kill of six hundred [buffalo]."[4] From this location, the Métis established a trade route to transport merchandise by Red River cart, providing Fort Edmonton with buffalo meat and supplies. Part of the Métis economy also included raising livestock and horses,[5] as many of the

Métis had followed the retreating buffalo herds to this area. When Euro-Canadian settlers arrived in larger numbers beginning in 1896, many of the Métis moved their livestock and settled in communities such as St-Paul-des-Métis in northeastern Alberta. Eventually, the Battle River Métis Settlement was renamed Duhamel Settlement after the Roman Catholic bishop.[6]

Roman Catholic missionaries often travelled with the Métis brigades, and one of the better known is Father Albert Lacombe. Ordained in 1849, Lacombe spent a brief period of time in Red River before being posted to the Lac Ste. Anne Mission. With this mission serving as his base, Lacombe travelled extensively throughout the district and into Montana. Familial connections for the Métis in Lac Ste. Anne extended not only to Red River but also to St. Albert, Buffalo Lake, Baptiste River and Tail Creek.

In 1861, the Métis community at St. Albert worked with Father Albert Lacombe to build the church at the St. Albert Mission Settlement. At that time, the settlement was said to have become the centre for a thriving French-speaking Métis community.[7] The mission grew quickly, with the parish listing "600 Metis Catholics" in 1868. The Sisters of Charity had arrived in 1863 to establish a hospital and school.[8] In 1983, during Premier Peter Lougheed's time in office, the church was recognized by Alberta as the oldest remaining building in the province.[9] In 2006, the Father Lacombe Church was added to the registry of Canada's Historic Places.[10]

It was after the transitional period, when the fur trade had waned and many had left the Red River area, that the

Fleury family settled in Baptiste River Métis Settlement near Rocky Mountain House. The settlement was occupied between 1930 and 1945, and represents an example of the economic and subsistence strategies unique to a Métis extended family at that time. In 1997, this settlement was preserved and recognized as a historically significant place by the province of Alberta, with artifacts now housed at the Royal Alberta Museum. As was the case for so many Métis during the transitional period, the Fleurys had settled on Crown land and were forced by government policies and incoming settlers to leave the settlement in the late 1940s.[11]

Earlier, in the 1930s, Wolf Lake Métis Settlement, in northeastern Alberta, once a wintering place, had become a permanent settlement as Métis mobility was increasingly challenged. When oil and gas exploration expanded into this area in the 1950s, pressure mounted once again on the Métis. Extraction of other resources, such as timber, and the establishment of the Primrose Lake Air Weapons Range in 1956 led to the disbandment of the settlement in 1960. In her discussion of this Métis settlement, Chantal Roy Denis argues that the colonial approach to the Métis settlements was to view land as a "thing," demonstrating a disregard for the connection that the Métis had to the land. Roy Denis writes that, for the Métis, it was the land that "fostered their political, economic, and social traditions" through daily activities that recognized "reciprocity with all living and non-living relations." As Roy Denis concludes, "Wolf Lake serves as an important reminder of the existence of Métis territory, and the importance of

Métis places."[12] Clearly, these Métis places of significance extended well beyond the Red River area and into many of the early Métis settlements in Alberta.

In an example of the complexity of Métis identity, the self-identified "Mountain Métis," which today count among their members 200 people living in Grande Cache, Alberta, differed from the Red River Métis. These self-identified Métis are descendants of Iroquois and European free traders who travelled west with the Northwest Company and the Hudson's Bay Company during the early eighteenth century, settling in the Athabasca Valley. "The origins of these Metis are contemporary with, but quite independent of, the métis groups at Red River."[13] While unique, these Métis faced similar challenges with their homeland, and in the early 1900s were also forcibly removed from their settlement when the federal government created Jasper National Park, with many of them resettling in Grande Cache. This event is referred to by current-day Mountain Métis as the "Jasper Exodus." Community representatives note that they were forcibly removed by government officials who "sealed their guns, leaving them with no means of survival." Despite the forced relocation, the Mountain Métis note that they "continue their close connection with the land and follow traditional practices such as hunting, trapping, fishing and gathering of plant medicines and berries."[14]

Indeed, displacement was a common theme of Métis history after 1885, and concern for the condition of the Métis prompted Father Albert Lacombe to petition the federal government for land to establish a Métis settlement.

In 1896, Lacombe was granted a ninety-nine-year lease for 92,160 acres of land in northeastern Alberta at a cost of one dollar per year, and St-Paul-des-Métis was established. The Métis soon built a school, church, sawmill and gristmill, and many Métis from the earlier east central settlements moved to this settlement.[15] However, the colony has a tragic history, and some still debate the original intent of the Roman Catholic Oblate missionaries in its establishment.[16] With little experience in farming, the missionaries were in no way prepared to assist the "landless Métis" to become successful sedentary farmers. When a group of Métis children set fire to the residential school in an apparent act of defiance in response to their poor treatment at the hands of church officials, the focus reverted to establishing a French-Canadian community. Scholars such as Heather Devine have speculated that there was "some debate over whether the colony was a 'planned' failure" from the very start.[17] Regardless, when the lease with the federal government was terminated at the request of the Oblates, a significant number of French-Canadian claims were soon registered on former Métis leases.[18]

One of the early settlers to St-Paul-des-Métis was Laurent Garneau, for whom the Garneau District of Edmonton is named. An ardent supporter of Louis Riel, Garneau, his wife and nine children arrived at Fort Edmonton in 1874 to settle on River Lot 7. Garneau subsequently became a successful farmer and entrepreneur. However, much of his farmland was "annexed" (some might argue stolen) by Edmonton in 1907, prompting Garneau to relocate to the new settlement of St-Paul-des-Métis in northeastern Alberta. In 1953, a stone cairn was erected in the Garneau District of Edmonton in recognition of the contribution of the Garneau family to the early settlement of that community.[19] The significance of Garneau's contribution to Métis heritage and history in the Edmonton region was again recognized in 2017. A ceremony was held to mark the removal of a 143-year-old Manitoba maple that was planted by the Garneau family in 1874. The symbolism was noted in that the typical lifespan of these trees is fifty years. Attendees, including some of the Garneau descendants, shared stories and traditional music.[20] Scholar Nathalie Kermoal, organizer of an earlier Garneau Conference held at the University of Alberta in 2008, noted that the intent was to "build stronger connections between today's francophone and Métis communities," while also celebrating what the "Métis have done, not only in Edmonton but also for Canadian history ... Laurent Garneau's life illustrates the challenges that the Métis had to deal with in the 19th and 20th centuries."[21]

Indeed, as noted, many of the early winter settlements in Alberta that the Métis had long used seasonally, such as Tail Creek and Buffalo Lake in east central Alberta, and Lac Ste. Anne and Lac La Biche in north central Alberta, became somewhat permanent settlements following the exodus of the Métis from Red River. However, just as had occurred in Red River, the Métis were often forced from these Alberta settlements as more new settlers arrived. Being "forced" from the land can refer to anything from racist policies and actions on the part of incoming settlers and governments to outright theft of previously settled Métis lands. An example of this is the settlement of St-Paul-des-Métis, discussed earlier. As noted, many Métis had moved to this new settlement from earlier settlements such as Tail Creek and Buffalo Lake. However, with no Métis input into governance, and the change in 1907 that opened the land in the St-Paul-des-Métis area to settlers from other parts of Canada, many of the Métis were forced off their land to, once again, become landless. According to Métis activist James Brady, an early resident of the area, and drawing from a letter from the Half-Breed Claims Commissioner to Frank Oliver, minister of the interior, in 1909 "Many Metis were comparatively well to do" with some possessing "large herds of cattle and horses and other holdings of a comfortable nature."[22] When they were forced off their farms, the Métis often had to leave all of their possessions behind, and new settlers availed themselves of these items. In a recently published book by some of the descendants of the St-Paul-des-Métis families, oral history confirms that some Métis returned from hunting trips to find new settlers, who had been encouraged to "squat" on land occupied by Métis families, already living in their homes. With no means of redress for the Métis, who were blamed for the failure of their settlement by Roman Catholic clergy, the descendants of these earlier families contend that there remains today a divide between the French and Métis families in this area.[23] Indeed, many of the early Métis activists had roots in this early settlement of St-Paul-des-Métis, and the first organizational meeting of L'Association des Métis d'Alberta et les Territoires du Nord-Ouest was held in what was by then referred to as St. Paul in 1932. The minutes of that first meeting noted that:

> Our first objective and the one in which we have our deepest interest the one which more than anything else called our movement into being, is to see that adequate provision is made for homeless and destitute families.[24]

As in other prairie provinces, the Métis in Alberta often found themselves landless, settling where they could, including along road allowances. As Lawrence Barkwell notes, in this instance discussing some urban road allowance communities in Manitoba:

> In the early years of the depression of the 1930s a number of homeless families, many of whom were destitute Metis built small shacks illegally on the Canadian National Railway property adjoining city owned land.[25]

Of course, living along road allowances deprived the Métis of physical addresses required to allow them to attend schools. This fuelled the cycle of poverty and discrimination that continued to plague the Métis People long after their forced exodus from the Red River area.

Indeed, the exodus of the Métis from their own lands that followed the *Rupert's Land Act* of 1868 meant that for many decades to follow the Métis fled to points west and north, relocating their families on Crown land on undeveloped road allowances.[26] Increasingly, rigid racial boundaries meant that survival for the Métis, including those who were born in or who had settled in Alberta, involved disguising their Métis identity, if that was possible, and choosing to publicly identify as either Franco- or Anglo-Albertans. Many of Alberta's early Métis political actors, who had a tremendous impact on Métis political activism throughout Canada, had ancestral connections to these settlements and to the landless Métis. Respected Métis elder Maria Campbell was herself a descendant of "landless Métis," and her family had settled along the road allowances in Saskatchewan. Later moving to Alberta, Campbell joined early activists in working for Métis rights. Her 1973 book entitled *Half-Breed* contributed to the "Indigenous rights case" alongside Harold Cardinal's *The Unjust Society* (1969). Some regard the political activism of the 1960s and 1970s, of which Campbell and Cardinal were a part, as the "golden era of Métis grassroots activism."[27]

The fact that a pride in Métis ancestry remains "hidden" in the private realm for some Métis even today gives some sense of the need for the Métis who lived on the prairies early in the twentieth century to obscure their own ethnicity. Indeed, it also gives a sense of the challenges in tracing one's Métis ancestry to a historic Métis Nation. This obscuring of identity presents further challenges in fully understanding the history of the "Alberta Métis." Yet the survival strategies of the Métis in being able to publicly obscure their identity, all the while privately nurturing that Métis identity, for those who were able to do so, meant that some of them emerged as community builders of the Prairie West. This was possibly the case for Peter Lougheed's grandmother Isabella Hardisty, given that Peter did not deny his own Indigenous ancestry, suggesting that his father Edgar Lougheed also did not deny that ancestry. Yet the ability of some Métis to publicly obscure their Métis identity afforded them a heightened sense of their own uniqueness as they helped to construct their new communities. Nonetheless, the reality is that many Métis did not wish to, or were simply not able to, obscure their identity, and thus the survival stories and the history of the Métis in Alberta remain complex.

As noted earlier, the continuing displacement of the Métis also led to political activism, often by people whose families had experienced that displacement. In the 1920s and 1930s, five men, who have come to be known as the "Big Five," worked to establish provincial organizations in Alberta that served as the precursors of the modern Métis organizations throughout Canada. Joseph Francis Dion, Malcolm Frederick Norris, James Patrick Brady, Peter Tomkins Jr. and Felix Calliou were among those involved in the formation of L'Association des Métis d'Alberta et les Territories du Nord-Ouest in 1928, the first politically active Métis organization in Alberta, and indeed in Canada.

Activism on the part of the Big Five and others through L'Association des Métis d'Alberta et les Territoires du Nord-Ouest and the Métis Association of Alberta eventually led to the appointment of a provincial Royal Commission on the Condition of the Half-breed Population of Alberta, which came to be referred to as the Ewing Commission. The report of the Ewing Commission recommended that the government set aside lands for the purpose of addressing the abject poverty in which many of the Métis in Alberta lived at that time. In 1938, the *Metis Population Betterment Act* was enacted by the government of Alberta. While the original intent of the legislation for the government was primarily to address the abject poverty of many of the Métis people living in Alberta, for the Métis at the time it represented, and continues to represent, attempted redress for the historic wrongs, as well as a way to preserve their culture and identity. Of historic significance is that the *Metis Population Betterment Act*, by setting aside a land base for Métis people, served as the impetus for further political activism by the Métis in Alberta and across Canada. This early activism eventually contributed to the current acknowledgement by Canada of the Métis as distinct Indigenous Peoples with a right to self-determination. It is significant that the *Metis Population Betterment Act* represented the first time in Canada that land would be set aside as Métis land.

Indeed, land was inextricably linked to self-determination for the Métis. As Dorion and Prefontaine note, in a fifty-year period between 1874 and 1924, the Métis lost the land base that they had enjoyed during the fur trade era, and which was so critical to their own culture and identity. The loss of land was due to several factors including an influx of new settlers, the scrip system poorly managed by the federal government and the corruption of some of the Indian Agents. While the Métis were promised protection of their land base in the *Manitoba Act of 1870*, the *Dominion Lands Act of 1879* did not stipulate any land guarantees for the Métis. Beginning in 1879, and managed outside of the *Dominion Lands Act*, the federal government issued either money or land scrip to the Métis as a way to extinguish their land rights. The general consensus by historians is that the scrip system was deliberately complex and disorganized, and that it subsequently failed to compensate the Métis adequately, leaving many of them with few options except to abandon their traditional lands and fall into destructive cycles of poverty, distrust and abuse.[28]

The loss of their traditional land base for the Métis coincided with the agricultural settlement of the region by newcomers. However, given that settlement by newcomers was not uniform across the prairies, the Métis were sometimes able to establish settlements in new areas, either where they had pre-existing kin connections or where they managed to forge new connections. Yet, increasingly, the Métis connections did not prove as advantageous as they had once been. Gerhard Ens, in editing the memoir of Johnny Grant, a Métis man born at Fort Edmonton in 1833, concludes that Grant's racial identity was fluid and situational and that, in fact, it was not of benefit to him during the transitional period after the end of the fur trade.[29] There is no doubt that it was not advantageous for many Métis to claim a Métis identity, particularly as the primarily French-speaking Métis continued to be held responsible by many for the fighting that erupted in 1885 in Batoche, and which impacted other parts of the West.

However, some English-speaking Métis, who had fared better during the fur trade by way of their association with the Hudson's Bay Company, like the ancestors of Peter Lougheed, continued to be successful as the fur trade waned. This was particularly so in parts of the prairies in the period between 1885 and 1925 when, for example, many of Alberta's business community continued to have ties to the Hudson's Bay Company. In fact, two of the wealthiest men in the North-West during this period were the Métis HBC Chief Factor Richard Hardisty, Isabella's uncle, the district's first senator, and the man who married Richard Hardisty's Métis sister, Donald A. Smith. In 1971, Parks Canada recognized Smith, also known as Lord Strathcona, who was great-uncle to Peter Lougheed, as a person of national historic significance.[30] Smith had risen through the ranks of the Hudson's Bay Company, in some part due to his connection through marriage to the Métis Hardisty family.

Yet for those many Métis who could no longer rely on previous fur trade connections, the struggle to survive in a changing economy was exacerbated by social conditions that saw racial boundaries solidify in the Prairie West with the arrival of more new settlers. The displacement that resulted from the defeat in Red River and Batoche in the late 1800s continued to be a common theme for the Métis in the early 1900s, with many of them landless and without a traditional means of subsistence in the changed economy. The plight of many Métis was also exacerbated by the Great Depression that ravaged the prairie landscape and economy in the 1920s and 1930s, which also left many of its new settlers destitute and landless. For many of the Métis this only intensified the extreme poverty in which they had lived since the turn of the century. It is significant that at the height of the Depression in 1933, when the government of Alberta was focused on the devastation of its economy as a whole, it agreed that a Royal Commission should examine the conditions for the Métis in particular. Indeed, it was the activism on the part of the Big Five and others through L'Association des Métis d'Alberta et les Territoires du Nord-Ouest and the Métis Association of Alberta that prompted the government in 1933 to "make enquiry into the condition of the half-breed population of the Province of Alberta, keeping particularly in mind the health, education, relief and general welfare of such population."[31]

The Métis Association of Alberta (MAA), formed in 1932 from an earlier political lobby,[32] had been successful in pressuring the government to establish the Royal Commission on the Condition of the Half-breed Population of Alberta (the Ewing Commission). The MAA strongly advocated for land to be set aside so that the Métis could "pursue their traditional economic livelihoods of hunting, trapping, and fishing."[33] The report of the Ewing Commission recommended that the government set aside lands, but as alluded to earlier, it was for the purpose of addressing the abject poverty in which many of the Métis in Alberta lived at that time, and was not intended to recognize the Métis historic right to land. Regardless of intent, as recommended by the Ewing Commission, in 1938 the *Metis Population Betterment*

Act was enacted by the government of Alberta. Despite the agenda of the government at the time, this remains the first and only time in Canadian history that a provincial government set aside land in response to Métis claims.

The success of the Métis political organizations in pressuring the Alberta government to act at a time when it was not in a good financial position itself has been attributed to the political acumen of the Métis Association of Alberta and of the "Big Five." By utilizing a labour union organizational model, which included area locals overseen by a central executive, the MAA achieved a historic win for the Métis. From the perspective of the government at the time, which did not recognize the historical and rights-based arguments for land put forward by the MAA, land was cheap and an expedient way to address the social welfare needs of the Métis. However, as noted earlier, the land had tremendous historical significance for the Métis in terms of past wrongs,[34] and also because it had been used by generations of Métis as hivernant and permanent settlements. Even more importantly from a historical perspective, the land base set aside by the *Metis Population Betterment Act* represented a means for the Métis to protect their cultural identity as a result of unified political action, while also setting the stage for future political activism across Canada.

While not intended to grant the Métis the right to self-determination, and still from the perspective of assimilationist ideology, the land base that was set aside as a result of the Ewing Commission and the *Metis Population Betterment Act* was the precursor for the eventual establishment of twelve Métis settlements, with eight of those remaining today. While the land was not set aside to acknowledge historical wrongs, some of the original twelve settlements were located where the Métis had traditionally settled during and immediately following the end of the fur trade. The settlements were Buffalo Lake, Cold Lake, East Prairie, Elizabeth, Fishing Lake, Gift Lake, Kikino, Marlboro, Paddle Prairie, Big Prairie, Touchwood and Wolf Lake. While a paternalistic structure was in place in the settlements with government and church officials having a majority say in governance, the Métis originally had "limited self-governing authority relating to hunting, fishing, and trapping." Four of the settlements—Cold Lake, Marlboro, Touchwood and Wolf Lake—were eventually dissolved, leaving the eight that remain today. With political activism on the part of the Alberta Federation of Métis Settlements, formed in 1975, the Métis were successful in gaining control of 512,121 hectares of land.[35] After Peter Lougheed retired in 1985, it was his successors in the Conservative government who carried through with a series of motions and legislation that led to the 1989 signing of the *Alberta-Metis Settlements Accord,* making Alberta the only province in Canada with a recognized Métis land base. The 1990 *Metis Settlements Act* established the Métis Settlements General Council, with a mandate to deal with matters that affect the collective interests of the eight Métis settlements.

The progression toward self-determination that was inspired by the 1938 Alberta legislation represents not only provincial significance for the Métis in Alberta, but

85

also national significance, evidenced by the signing of the *Canada-Métis Nation Accord* in 2017. See Appendix II for more information.

In addition to the Big Five of political activism, countless Métis people have made significant contributions to the history and survival of the Métis in Alberta. Some of those discussed here were either born in Alberta, came to Alberta to work during the fur trade era or moved west as part of the Métis diaspora from the Red River or other points east and north. Given the difficulty in identifying sources on the history of the Métis in Alberta, those who are highlighted are meant to serve as examples only of the Métis culture, kinship networks, identity and history that experienced periods of *Le Grand Silence* and periods of triumph in Alberta.

86

Victoria Belcourt Callihoo was an author, farmer, freighter and hunter who was born in 1861 at Lac Ste. Anne, and who died in that same settlement in 1966. Living for over a century, Victoria freighted for the Hudson's Bay Company between Edmonton and Athabasca Landing. Her mother was a medicine woman who shared her knowledge with her daughter, while Victoria retained vivid memories of the time she spent as a young girl on the buffalo hunts. When Callihoo was ninety-one years of age she dictated her memoirs, some of which were translated and published by *Alberta Historical Review*.[36] In her oral and written accounts, Victoria described the roles that Métis women assumed on those hunts. There are also hours of audio recordings by Callihoo in a St. Albert archive that serve as important historical records of Métis

THE PREMIER AND HIS GRANDMOTHER

culture and history in Alberta. It was Victoria's uncle
Michel Callihoo who signed Treaty 6 on behalf of his band
of Cree, Iroquois and Métis kin. This band was given a
reserve northwest of Edmonton on the Sturgeon River.[37]
Indeed, Victoria Callihoo witnessed the transformation
of the North-West from a time when buffalo hunts ended
as the big herds disappeared, when many Indigenous
Peoples were relocated to reserve land, and when travel in
Red River carts was replaced by automobiles. According
to Cora Taylor, author of Callihoo's biography, Victoria
celebrated her hundredth birthday in 1966 by dancing the
Red River Jig.[38]

Another Métis woman who left a record of her experiences as an early pioneer of Alberta during the transitional
period, and who lived for almost a century, was Marie Rose
Delorme Smith. Marie Rose was born in the Red River
area and recalled traversing the plains with her father,
who was a buffalo hunter and trader. Marie Rose's grandfather was Urbain Delorme Sr., known as "le Chef Des
Prairies," and who served as captain of hunting and trading brigades. The senior Delorme settled near Cuthbert
Grant, recognized as an important Métis leader of his
time, on the White Horse Plains (Saint François Xavier) in
what is now Manitoba. Marie Rose spoke French, English
and Cree (the language of the fur trade), and she gained
recognition as a southern Alberta pioneer for her roles as
medicine woman, author, homesteader and rancher, and
for her traditional skills, which led some to refer to her as
"Buckskin Mary." Marie Rose left behind manuscripts that
speak to her early experiences as a pioneer of the plains,

and she published a series of articles in the prairie periodical *Canadian Cattlemen*. She was a friend of Father Albert Lacombe, as well as a friend and neighbour of prairie characters such as John George "Kootenai" Brown, Sir Frederick Haultain, William Gladstone, Lord Lionel Brooke and Colonel James Macleod.[39]

An example of the role played by Métis men in the Alberta fur trade and into the transitional period is provided by Louison "Captain Shot" Fosseneuve, born in 1844 at Red River. He died in 1914 at Athabasca, Alberta. Fosseneuve is representative of the boatmen and voyageurs who were so critical to the success of the fur trade. For fifty-two years, Louison worked as a boatman and guide who piloted flotillas of heavy-laden scows from Athabasca Landing through the Athabasca River's Grand Rapids and to northern destinations, transporting goods, missionaries and Klondikers. It is said that until he conquered the Grand Rapids, thus establishing a much shorter route, supplies for the north country were taken in by the Hudson's Bay Company from the east by way of Portage la Loche (the Long Portage), then down the Clearwater River to Fort McMurray and to the hinterland beyond. Some say that he received the nickname "shot" in recognition of being the first to establish a new trade route by "shooting" the Grand Rapids, while others say that he was a "sure shot" at buffalo hunting.[40] It is likely that both accounts bear some truth.

A more contemporary Métis figure who contributed to the preservation of Alberta's Métis culture and history is Dr. Anne Anderson. Born on a river lot farm east of St. Albert in 1906, Anne Anderson was often referred to as the "Grand Lady of the Métis." With over one hundred publications on Cree language and Métis history, she is most recognized for her 1975 project, in which she translated a 38,000-word English dictionary into a Cree Michif dictionary. While Anne was educated at a Grey Nuns convent where she was taught in English, her mother insisted that the children speak Cree at home. As an adult, Anne taught for sixteen years in the public school system, as well as teaching Cree at Grant MacEwan College (now University). In 1984, she opened the Dr. Anne Anderson Native Heritage and Cultural Centre, where Cree lessons were taught, and where First Nation and Métis arts and crafts were sold.[41] Dr. Anderson passed away in 1997.

In 2018, Edmonton Public Schools announced that they would name two of their new schools in honour of two prominent St. Albert Métis women, Dr. Anne Anderson and Thelma Chalifoux. Born in 1929, Chalifoux returned to school in 1960 as the single mother of seven children. She became the first Indigenous woman to broadcast on commercial radio on CKXL Radio Peace River. She later worked as a land claims negotiator, social worker, educator and founder of the Slave Lake Native Friendship Centre. Chalifoux was appointed in 1997 as the first Métis (Indigenous) woman to serve in Canada's senate. Thelma Chalifoux leveraged that role to draw attention to the challenges for Indigenous women residing in northern Canada.[42] Later in life, she founded the Michif Cultural

Institute (Michif Cultural Connections) in St. Albert.[43] Thelma Chalifoux passed away in 2017.

As noted earlier, in 1938, Métis activists such as Jim Brady, Joe Dion and Malcom Norris saw the results of their work in part through the enactment of the *Metis Population Betterment Act* by the government of Alberta. Despite its inherent problems, the Act, in addition to setting aside a land base for the Métis, was the first step in Alberta's recognition of Métis rights, and the first acknowledgement of their rights anywhere in Canada. Along with acknowledging a need to formulate "one or more schemes for the purpose of bettering the general welfare of the Métis population of the Province, and for the settlement of the members of such association on lands set aside for that purpose by the Province," this Act defined Métis as meaning a "person of mixed white and Indian blood" which did not include "either an Indian or a non-treaty Indian as defined in *The Indian Act*."[44] This attempt, and many others, to define the Métis along the lines of blood quantum (something that Peter Lougheed himself referenced, as we will see later in this chapter), is fully rejected by Indigenous people in Canada today. As Jean Teillet, a lawyer and great-grandniece of Louis Riel, writes, the Métis battled continuously for recognition as distinct people, for their lands and for their freedoms.[45] Nonetheless, *at the time*, the definition put forward by the Alberta government, as ill informed as it was, did serve to acknowledge that the Métis were unique and entitled to recognition. It is of note that, according to Stan Daniels, one-time president of the Métis Association of Alberta, who was speaking in 1977 to a small rural newspaper, that "Premier Lougheed has often reminded Native leaders, myself included, that he is one-eighth Indian, but he does not know which one-eighth."[46]

Clearly, and as alluded to earlier, along with the assimilationist ideology assumed by the *Metis Population Betterment Act*, another problem was the very definition of Métis People as those with "mixed white and Indian blood." In his 2014 publication *"Métis": Race, Recognition and the Struggle for Indigenous Peoplehood*, Chris Andersen notes what he refers to as the

> simplistic tropes of mixedness and hybridity that seem to fascinate so many scholars who write of Métis histories, literatures and politics. Not a vision that seeks to deny our mixedness but rather a vision premised on the notion that all Indigenous peoples are mixed ... understanding Métis nationhood or peoplehood can never begin or end with a discussion of hybridity.[47]

With a view to the current situation, some in the Métis community would argue vehemently against this definition of Métis as "mixed." Rather, as Brenda Macdougall has stated, "There's a misperception that Métis means mixed." While Macdougall argued in 2019 that this misperception was fairly recent, Alberta's 1938 legislation demonstrates that has not always been the case. In her argument in support of Métis uniqueness, Macdougall cites the fact that "the State itself goes to war against the Métis twice. Once in 1869–70, and another in 1885. I don't think you can be confused about a people when you're willing to fight them."[48] Whether one can use the case of the fighting in 1869–70 and 1885 to argue that the government at the time acknowledged the Métis as a "distinct People" is debatable. However, it is absolutely the case that many Métis understood themselves then to be a distinct people, and that they understand that to be the case today.

In her publication *One of the Family: Metis Culture in Nineteenth-Century Northwestern Saskatchewan*, Brenda Macdougall demonstrates that a distinct Métis identity emerged in one northern Saskatchewan community, and this serves as an example of the same situation for many communities. Further, Macdougall argues that the

> idea of Metis cultural and economic solidarity, values embedded in wahkootowin, itself a worldview linking land, family, and identity in one interconnected web of being, appears to have been ubiquitous in Metis communities across Canada, and it continues to be a theme commonly pursed in studies of Metis society.[49]

Despite documented cases of the Métis viewing themselves as a distinct people, such as that highlighted by Brenda Macdougall, there are many examples that speak to the challenges in asserting that identity at different times in Canadian history. Tracing her own Métis ancestry after her mother, who had been adopted by a non-Indigenous family, discovered her own personal history, scholar

Heather Devine went on to publish *The People who Own Themselves: Aboriginal Ethnogenesis in a Canadian Family*. In the introduction to her book, Devine noted the many questions that her own personal history elicited for her, such as why her great-grandmother had not taught "Cree and Saulteaux to her children, when she spoke those languages herself? Why had she sought to distance herself from her own background during much of her life?"[50] It was her journey to an appreciation of her own Métis identity that led Devine to graduate work in Métis studies, and to the eventual publication of her book. In 2004, Nicole St-Onge offered case studies of particular communities as evidence of varied and changing identities. For example, in the community of Saint-Laurent, Manitoba, between 1850 and 1914, there had emerged a class system that led some families to publicly abandon their Métis identity altogether from one census period to another.[51]

The struggle for Métis identity that was experienced by some was not aided by the regulations that were imposed on the Métis People by the Canadian government in the form of various initiatives, such as the scrip system that intended to extinguish land title. While the *Constitution Act, 1982* finally acknowledged the Métis as "Aboriginal" People, it did not offer any insight into who could rightfully identify as Métis. Over a century earlier, the French version of the *Manitoba Act, 1870*, used the distinction "des Métis residents," while the English version described the residents as "Half-breeds," demonstrating that it was felt that there were two separate and distinct groups. From that point on, references in Canadian legislation no longer made the distinction between the two groups. In Alberta, no distinction between the two groups was made, as the first political body organized by the Métis, in 1932, bore the name "L'Association des Métis d'Alberta et des Territoires de Nord-Ouest." That name was later changed to the Métis Association of Alberta, and then to the Métis Nation of Alberta.

Yet the struggle for Métis identity continues to be complicated. In his influential book "*Métis*," published in 2014 and referenced earlier, scholar Chris Andersen noted:

> From my perspective, whether or not an Indigenous individual or community self-identifies as Métis today, and whether or not the Indigenous community is "older" than Red River, if the individual or group lacks a connection to the historical core in the Red River region, it is not Métis.[52]

At the same time, Andersen acknowledges that many Métis continue to view themselves as "outsiders." Thus, one wonders how to reconcile Andersen's view with those of the Métis whose identity formation was experienced in one of those "older communities," or in communities far removed from Red River. It should also be noted that, prior to the encroachment on Métis lands by incoming settlers, there were divisions in the Red River region, sometimes between the French- and English-speaking Métis. A more unified Métis community emerged in Red River due in part to the racism and persecution by the incoming settlers.

Indeed, in a 2020 exhibition launched by Library and Archives Canada, "Hiding in Plain Sight," the national archive acknowledges that

> identifying Citizens of the Métis Nation in the archival record collections of Library and Archives Canada can be problematic. While there are portraits of well-known leaders and politicians, images depicting Métis Citizens are difficult to find. Adding to this challenge are the archival descriptions, which were mostly created over a century ago and exemplify colonial views of the "other" culture. As a result Citizens of the Métis Nation have often been misidentified or incorrectly described and, in some cases, completely omitted from the historical record.[53]

The recognition by the national archives that identifying the Métis "can be problematic" is a reality that the Métis themselves have long recognized. The path to official recognition in the *Constitution Act, 1982* was a long one, begun by activists such as Louis Riel, continued by those who gained recognition through Alberta's *Metis Population Betterment Act* of 1932, taken up by those such as Jim Sinclair and the Native Council of Canada in the 1970s and 1980s, and explored again by the 1996 Royal Commission on Aboriginal Peoples. This commission acknowledged that many Canadians have Aboriginal and non-Aboriginal ancestry, but this fact alone does not make them Métis. The report continued that those who identify as Métis associate distinctly with a Métis culture. So could we make this argument when we examine the exponential growth in the Métis population in Canada 2016 through 2019? According to Statistics Canada, in some areas of the country, most evident in Nova Scotia, Quebec and New Brunswick, those choosing to publicly identify as Métis at that time grew by 204.8 percent, 149.2 percent and 140 percent respectively.[54]

While this growth in self-identification has led to some controversy and ambiguity about Métis identity, there was no ambiguity in a 2016 decision by the Supreme Court of Canada when it ruled in *Daniels v. Canada* that the Métis and non-Status Indians were considered "Indians" under section 91(24) of the 1982 Constitution. The Supreme Court ruled unanimously that the federal government has jurisdiction for all Indigenous Peoples, including Métis and Non-Status people. While the decision did not grant "Indian Status to Métis and non-Status Peoples," it did clarify that these groups could expect that the federal government, and not provincial governments, were responsible for providing programs and services, such as education, housing and health care, to the Métis.[55]

Inspired by the work of early Métis political activists, and strengthened by the victory for Daniels in 2013, the Métis Settlements of Alberta, serving as the governing council of the remaining eight Métis settlements, is "the first and only Métis self-government in Canada." This governing council today oversees the management of 1.25 million acres across the Métis communities, each connected by the vision for self-government and self-determination. The first and only Métis self-government in Canada, recognized constitutionally as a distinct and protected peoples, the Métis Settlements are a vital and rich part of our Canadian cultural identity.[56]

The political momentum continued in 2019 when the Métis Nations of Ontario, Alberta and Saskatchewan signed the *Canada-Métis Nation Accord*, effectively establishing principles of self-government for Métis People. At the time, Métis Nation of Alberta president Audrey Poitras noted, "It's not an exaggeration to say the agreements signed today are something we've been fighting for for close to a century."[57]

Given that Peter Lougheed led the province of Alberta as its tenth premier from 1971 to 1985, the Métis did gain recognition of their status as Indigenous Peoples in the Canadian Constitution during his tenure. As a leader with Indigenous ancestry, one might have assumed that Peter Lougheed would have been a strong proponent of that recognition. Yet we must remember that his great-grandmother publicly identified as French, and that there is no evidence of his grandmother publicly identifying as Indigenous. In the end, Peter Lougheed did not initially support Section 35—the clause in the *Constitution Act, 1982* that recognizes Aboriginal rights and defines "aboriginal peoples of Canada" as including "the Indian, Inuit and Métis people of Canada"—as it was first drafted in the 1982 constitutional negotiations, and Indigenous people and their supporters subsequently judged him harshly for his position in his own province. One can only surmise whether Peter Lougheed, a man with Indigenous, and specifically Métis, ancestry, were he leading the province of Alberta in 2023, might be more publicly supportive of the long struggle on the part of the Métis to gain recognition of their cultural identity as a distinct people and their right to self-determination. However, Peter Lougheed was not socially Indigenous; thus, his approach may have remained in 2023 as it was in the 1980s.

four

A Woman and a Man of Their Times

He was a man of his times—and the
times are not ours.[1]
—DONALD B. SMITH

ISTORIAN DONALD B. SMITH NOTES in his discussion of Canada's first prime minister, John A. Macdonald, that

depressing though it is from today's vantage point, the reality remains that in Canada in the 1870s, 1880s, and 1890s assimilation, or "civilization" as it was termed at the time, was the universally accepted approach. Macdonald and his non-Indigenous political contemporaries did not understand that the First Nations had different cultures that they were determined to retain. Their ancestors had lived in what is now Canada for five hundred or so generations at the moment of the Europeans' arrival, and despite the newcomers' intense pressures, the Indigenous people had no desire to disappear.[2]

While it is certainly true that Indigenous Peoples had no desire to disappear, from the historian's perspective in Canada, they did disappear in the sense that until the 1970s, their presence in the dominant written historical record was that of a commodity of a Euro-Canadian–controlled fur trade. It is a fact that the historiography of a nation both shapes, and is shaped by, its scholars. Until approximately the 1970s, the dominant theme in the writing of Canadian history was the triumph of colonialism. The work of scholars such as Harold Innis in 1930, who popularized the "staples theory,"[3] influenced the study of the fur trade, and the study of the development of the nation of Canada. Although Indigenous Peoples were integral to the success of the fur trade, and of course to the development of Canada, little attention was devoted to exploring their history and culture until after the 1970s. In 1936, F.G. Stanley's *The Birth of Western Canada: A History of the Riel Rebellions*, which garnered six reprints, noted that the western Canadian frontier was peopled by "peaceful, law-abiding ranchers, farmers and government-encouraged colonists ... obliged to improvise for themselves the institutions of law and order." In 1961, Stanley, the man credited with designing the Canadian flag,[4] noted that things had not changed much since the original edition of his book, so that, in regard to the Métis, there was little difference between them and the First Nations. Even more telling, in Stanley's perception, "By character and upbringing the half-breeds, no less than the Indians, were unfitted to compete with the whites ... or to share with them the duties and responsibilities of citizenship."[5]

Indeed, for Alberta in particular, there emerged, almost from its inception as a province, a persona of the maverick and the prairie populist, fiercely independent and agrarian by nature, and certainly not at all Indigenous in identity or culture. In an award-winning literary study, which subsequently became a museum exhibit at Calgary's Glenbow Museum, Aritha Van Herk fuelled the maverick persona to argue that as "bronc-riders of boom and bust, Alberta's people are a beguiling mix-ture of opinionated extremists, hardy pioneers and gentle sinners."[6] While other provinces were influenced by different immigration settlement patterns, Alberta was most influenced by the "Last Best West" boosterism campaign, which saw an influx of land seekers from the American Midwest. Indeed, beginning in the late 1890s until the beginning of the First World War in 1914, the western prairies were marketed by the Canadian Interior Department to prospective immigrants and to eastern Canadians as the land of opportunity. More importantly, the Canadian prairies increasingly attracted settlers from the United States, where free, arable land was becoming scarce.[7] American-born and agrarian thinkers such as Henry Wise Wood would assume a significant role in the prairie populist persona that rose to prominence with the election of the United Farmers of Alberta as leaders of the province in 1921.

It was in this tradition of prairie populism that Peter Lougheed was able to revive a flailing Conservative party to become what historian Brad Rennie terms a "managerial-type premier."[8] First elected to office in 1971, this grandson of a Métis woman would, as a man of his times, be viewed by the majority of his constituents as a non-Indigenous former lawyer and businessman who embraced, and indeed cultivated, the prairie populist persona. In fact, Peter Lougheed's own entrepreneurial grandfather, James Lougheed, supported the "Last Best West" ideology that inspired the boosterism and marketing of the West,[9] and that was later expounded upon by many historians who would argue that this mythological West had no place for Indigenous Peoples.[10]

If we are to understand how the majority of Canadians, including Peter Lougheed, viewed the history of Indigenous Peoples as it was presented to them, it is important to explore the perspectives of some of the most influential scholars in early Canadian historiography. In terms of the Métis, to which Peter Lougheed owed some of his ancestry, they were a people born of the fur trade that operated in Canada, and particularly in the North-West, for over 150 years. Yet the long struggle to gain recognition as Indigenous people culminated as recently as 1982, by way of Section 35 of the *Constitution Act.* The lengthy road to recognition was in part due to the portrayal of the Métis in Canadian historiography. The first scholar to conduct an in-depth study of the Métis People, Marcel Giraud, helped to create (in historiography) a stereotypical Métis character unsuited to function in the new economy,[11] and a belief that deficiencies in Métis culture were a result of miscegenation.[12] In the same way, W.L. Morton, often seen as the first regional historian of the Canadian prairies, believed that

> when the agricultural frontier advanced into the Red River Valley in the 1870s and the last buffalo herds were destroyed in the 1880s, the half-breed community of the West, *la nation métisse*, was doomed, and made its last ineffectual protest against extinction in the Saskatchewan Rebellion of 1885.[13]

Despite viewing the Métis as doomed people, Morton saw what he believed to be the "two strongly defined currents" emanating from unions between HBC men and Indigenous women, and those between the French traders and Indigenous women. However, Morton also acknowledged a sense of unified identity, in that "the children of both streams of admixture had bonds of union in a common maternal ancestry and a common dependence on the fur trade."[14] Nonetheless, for Morton, there was a clear break between fur trade society and that which replaced it, and there was really no place for the Métis in the new society and economy.

Beginning in the 1930s with the work of Harold Innis, discussed briefly earlier,[15] through to Arthur Ray's work in the 1970s,[16] the economy of the fur trade and company corporate cultures were the primary focus for historians, with

Indigenous people often viewed as commodities of that trade. In the transitional period of Métis historiography that began in the 1970s, John Foster's work explored the emergence of the Métis as a distinct cultural group.[17] Scholars such as Sylvia Van Kirk,[18] Jennifer Brown[19] and Jacqueline Peterson[20] expanded Indigenous history to focus on the role of Métis women who lived during the fur trade era. The important work that these scholars initiated inspired many subsequent scholars to explore the concept of "being and becoming Métis."

If we are to understand how the majority of Canadians, Peter Lougheed included, learned about the history of Indigenous women, then it is equally important to briefly explore how that historiography evolved to demonstrate the critical role that they played in the development of the North-West. The focus on the economy of the fur trade evolved to examinations of kinship links for Métis people, with work by scholars such as Lucy Eldersveld Murphy,[21] Tanis Thorne[22] and Susan Sleeper-Smith, who also expanded the geographic focus from Red River to the Great Lakes area of what is now northwestern Indiana and southwest Michigan.[23] Sleeper-Smith explored the thesis that Indigenous women who married French men actually assumed a role as cultural mediators and negotiators of change when they established elaborate trading networks through Roman Catholic kinship connections that paralleled those of Indigenous societies.[24] To Sleeper-Smith it was evident that these women did not "marry out," but rather that they incorporated their French husbands into a society structured by Indigenous customs and traditions.[25] Thus, these Métis women did not reinvent themselves as French but rather enhanced their distinct Métis identity, while expanding their family networks. Van Kirk also argued that, from an Indigenous perspective, the process of women marrying fur traders was never regarded as marrying out.[26] Rather, these marriages were important means of incorporating traders into existing kinship networks, and traders often had to abide by Indigenous marital customs, some of which, at times, included the payment of bride price.[27]

These scholars were able to demonstrate that Métis women made significant contributions to the fur trade. However, there have yet to be a significant number of studies that examine the important roles that both Métis men and women played in the transitional period from the fur trade economy to the industrialized sedentary economy that replaced it in the Prairie West.[28] This lack of significant studies of the Métis experience is also evident in Alberta. Peter Lougheed's own family history serves as one example of the pattern identified by Van Kirk and Brown, and as an example of the limited research conducted on the Alberta Métis. While James and Isabella, significantly supported by her Métis network, went on to become among the wealthiest residents of the new settlement of Calgary, and among the leaders of the community, it is James Lougheed's name that is most recognizable by historians and by the general public today. Yet it was Peter's grandmother Isabella who was raised in northern fur trade country and who was sent to live in the early community of Calgary with her HBC Chief Factor uncle after her father died.

While there had not yet been much research conducted on the Alberta Métis when Peter Lougheed served as premier, more recently, scholars of Indigenous ancestry, such as Heather Devine[29] and Brenda Macdougall,[30] used genealogical reconstruction and biographical methodologies to examine Métis identity formation in geographic areas that expanded beyond the Red River area. While not mentioning Isabella Clark Hardisty Lougheed, Macdougall's work examines the Métis identity of Hudson's Bay Company men who served in northern fur trade country, as did Isabella's father. Martha Harroun Foster, whose research also expanded beyond the traditional fur trade era that had previously been studied by many historians, noted that some Métis in the Spring Creek community of Montana used kinship networks as a way to consolidate more recent trade relationships in order to ensure their families' prosperity and, in essence, to reaffirm existing Métis networks.[31] The Spring Creek Métis, former fur traders, became business people in the new economy and tended to extend their kinship networks through such practices as asking non-Métis associates and neighbours to serve as godparents for their children.[32]

Significant for the study of Métis people today, and for the matter of Métis identity in the context of the times, is that the more extensive the kinship network became for the Spring Creek Métis of Harroun Foster's study, and the more that it included non-Métis people, the more complex became the terms that the Spring Creek Métis used to identify themselves. Thus, terms like "breed," once common, became more private, so that few Métis people remembered using the terms "Half-breed" or "Métis" outside of the family. Yet self-identification as Euro–North American could, but did not necessarily, represent a rejection of a Métis identity or Métis kin group.[33] For this group of Montana Métis, although a private Métis identity survived, that identity became increasingly complex, multilayered and situational, but nonetheless remained rooted in the kinship networks first established as part of fur trade culture.[34]

In reality, for families of the fur trade north of the forty-ninth parallel that might have various "tribal relatives," as well as Euro-Canadian family members, Métis ethnicity was historically often inclusive enough to encompass and to accept all members of the family. Kinship links between culturally distinct groups enabled accommodation and subsequently influenced survival strategies in many geographic areas when larger-scale settlement by Euro–North Americans occurred.[35] Because there was very little opportunity on the prairies between the late 1890s and the 1920s to publicly identify as Métis due to increasingly rigid racial boundaries, it was not unusual for many Métis during that time to identify as either First Nations or non-Indigenous, while privately nurturing a Métis identity. History confirms that it has always been an integral aspect of the Métis culture to allow a web of kinship ties to enrich rather than to destroy a sense of unique ethnicity.[36] In fact, kinship systems often allowed the Métis to sustain their identity in a safe, supportive atmosphere, even if those identities had to be enjoyed only in the private realm at particular times in our collective history. Again, this reality was evident in the ancestry of Peter Lougheed. While her contemporaries certainly knew that she was Métis, Isabella cultivated a public persona as a non-Indigenous "First Lady" of Calgary and of Beaulieu House. Contemporary newspaper articles featured pictures of Isabella in Euro-Canadian ball gowns and included elaborate descriptions of her grand home and of the high-society balls and gatherings at which she hosted community leaders and British royalty, all the while not acknowledging her Métis ancestry.

In Canada, the fact that the Métis were often forced at various times in history to enjoy their identity in the private realm was due, in part, to the fact that Métis identity has not always been open to individual choice. As alluded to earlier, at various times in Canadian history, by way of the *Indian Act*, treaty negotiations and enforcement, and scrip regulations, the government determined who was "Status Indian" and who was Métis. It is entirely possible that some Métis in Canada, as in the United States, found at times in their history that they could be "white and Métis or Métis and Indian with sincerity and apparent ease."[37] In a study of her own "French-Indian" ancestors who settled in the Willamette Valley, Melinda Jetté concluded that

> they were not exclusively American, Indian, French-Canadian, or métis, but were all of these things at

different times and in different places ... there was
a process of negotiation that went on throughout
their lives ... the family navigated a place for itself
amidst a unique set of cultural traditions.[38]

Indeed, while examining the ethnogenesis in her
own Métis family, historian Heather Devine noted that,
within one family, children could assume dramatically
different identities based on their life experiences.[39] In
Isabella Hardisty Lougheed's case, her mother, Mary Allen
Hardisty, applied for and received Métis scrip, while her
grandsons, Peter Lougheed and his brother Donald once
mused in a newspaper interview that Isabella would likely
be most disheartened by the talk of pardoning Louis Riel
in recognition of his role as a leader of the Métis People.
If anything, this observation by grandsons who had very
little memory of their Métis grandmother, speaks to the
complexity of Isabella's own history and identity. While
there was certainly continuity between her early upbringing by Métis parents in northern fur trade country, her
identity as a Métis woman in the early 1900s was no doubt
situational and complex, in line with what societal norms
permitted at the time.

Despite observations, such as those by Harroun Foster
and Jetté, regarding the complexity and continuity of Métis
culture and identity, as noted earlier, historians and scholars argued that fur trade society was abruptly replaced by
a new economy, just as they continue to debate who can
rightfully identify as Métis today. In reality, research confirms that not only does Métis identity remain complex

and situational, but that there was distinct and identifiable continuity from the fur trade economy to the new sedentary agricultural and commercial economy throughout the prairies. Yet despite the fact that the Métis established themselves throughout fur trade country, given the historic events that occurred in Red River, understanding the history of the Métis in any of the prairie provinces necessitates an understanding first of the social and cultural complexities of the Red River Settlement. It is plausible that many who have in the past been referred to as the "countryborn," and who may not have had close connections to Red River, such as Peter Lougheed's Métis grandmother, increasingly internalized a distinctly Métis identity in the same way as did French- and English-speaking Métis with clearly identifiable ties to Red River.

Still, many currently subscribe to the argument that a distinct Métis identity and nationalism emerged in response to conflicts with outsiders, specifically in the Red River area, such as those in 1816 (referred to by some as the Battle of Seven Oaks), in 1869–70 (referred to as the Resistance by some) and in 1885 (referred to by some as the Northwest Uprising or Rebellion). This focus on Red River and the historic conflicts has fuelled the notion of a "singular Métis consciousness and national identity."[40] For many, the Métis are those who can trace their history to the

buffalo hunting and trading Métis of the northern Plains, in particular during the period between the beginning of the Métis buffalo brigades in the early nineteenth century and the 1885 North West Uprising.[41]

This view would actually negate Isabella Hardisty Lougheed's claim to Métis ancestry had she made one then, or particularly if that claim were being made in 2023. Yet this categorization of Métis identity as linked to historic events disregards the connection of many Métis to the earlier fur trade, and to those Métis who were born and spent their entire lives in other areas in which the fur trade was active, such as Alberta. Some historians, such as Nicole St-Onge and Carolyn Podruchny, argue that

> definitions of Métis that rely on the ingredients of buffalo hunting, practicing Roman Catholicism, speaking French, and wearing woven sashes imply that Métis cultural traits are static, exclusive, and singular, thus precluding cultural change and the creation of diverse ranges of Métis cultural expression.[42]

According to the Manitoba Métis Federation in 1983, Métis culture and identity was formulated by way of a wide variety of commercial and domestic forms of living, such as those listed by St-Onge and Podruchny, as well as on "historical knowledge."[43] In a more recent article, Adam Gaudry presents three distinct arguments in regard to Métis identity: 1) Métis are not defined by mixedness, but by their collective history;

2) Métis understand their origins are in the West; 3) Métis already have an agreed-upon definition of who they are, which needs to be respected. This perspective establishes geographic parameters for Métis identity.[44] From another perspective, Denis Gagnon points to the 1996 Royal Commission on Aboriginal Peoples, which stressed in its report that it was important to respect "the name that a people chooses to give itself and the legitimacy of using the term Métis to refer to communities in Labrador, Quebec, Ontario, Nova Scotia, New Brunswick, British Columbia and the Northwest Territories." Gagnon writes that it is of note that the *Powley* decision in 2003 granted Aboriginal Rights to the plaintiffs of a Métis community who lived in the Sault Ste. Marie area of Ontario. As Gagnon continues, the *Daniels* decision in 2016, which recognized Indigenous status for the Métis, noted that "there is no need to define the word Métis, because it is an ethnic and cultural label with no neat boundaries."[45]

Respecting the diversity of opinion, we should acknowledge that historical knowledge, most often connected to the fur trade, may be very different for a Métis person born in Red River than for one born at a fort in the northern Mackenzie River District, or at a settlement in what became Alberta, but may be no more or less indicative of the retention of Métis culture and identity. Although there are not many produced by Métis people, biographies can offer insights into the self-identification process. It is helpful at this point to acknowledge what Theda Perdue has argued; specifically, that "biographies can, in fact, serve as sifters that both separate individual women's lives and distinguish women's experiences."[46] Sarah Carter and Patricia McCormack's *Recollections: Lives of Aboriginal Women of the Canadian Northwest and Borderlands* is a recent example of assuming a case study approach to share the stories of Indigenous women not accessible in traditional archival sources.[47] In the same way, biographies (now viewed as a more common and acceptable form of Métis historiography) and close case studies, which permit comparative analysis of Métis people in different geographic locations, suggest that retention of culture and identity occurs equally on an individual basis as it might on a collective "Nationhood" basis.[48]

In fact, it is the view of scholars Christopher Adams, Gregg Dahl and Ian Peach, editors of a recent collection of essays, that "Métis" is not a "signifier of a particular population situated in a specific time or place."[49] In another recent publication, noting a focus on ethnic groups rather than way of life, historians Gerhard Ens and Joe Sawchuk concur with an analysis of Métis ethnicity that does not focus on geography. The authors argue that ethnicity is culturally constructed, and that ethnic groups, particularly in modern settings, are "constantly recreating themselves and ethnicity is continuously reinvented in response to changing realities."[50]

Regardless of how a study of the Métis People is approached, it is difficult to understand the retention of culture and identity during the transitional period after the fur trade for both men and women and in areas that currently have higher populations of Métis people than are found in Manitoba, such as Alberta. Yet it is evident that by way of their contribution to the family economy, Métis women, like Peter Lougheed's grandmother, often continued to rely on their cultural knowledge as they had during the earlier period when there was a vibrant trade in items produced by women.[51] Given the slower pace of settlement in areas beyond the Red River, such as Alberta, the traditional work that Métis women had undertaken in the fur trade continued to contribute to the subsistence economy. More importantly, the contributions of women helped to preserve the Métis culture and identity, even if that might be in the private realm when circumstances necessitated it. In fact, family narratives reveal that the ability of women to continue to rely on their traditional skills gave them a sense of continuity with their past in ways that were perhaps not always afforded to Métis men as racial boundaries solidified.[52] Not only did the practical skills of Métis women to allow them that continuity, but their skills, and indeed their Métis kinship networks, also helped their families to transition to the new economy.

Further, when Métis women participated in the shifting economy in ways such as providing traditional clothing to newcomers, they assumed roles as cultural brokers, just as they had during the height of the fur trade.[53] The roles of Métis women, their skills and their elaborate kinship networks that facilitated trade in the earlier period later served to transform the impersonal exchange process characteristic of capitalism into a socially accountable process.[54] Yet it remains that few women who contributed the unpaid labour vital to the success of both the fur trade and the transitional economies of the North-West viewed their own roles as significant enough to record details of their lives with the intention of passing them on to a public archive. This is certainly the case with Isabella Lougheed, with only one letter found to date that is written by her. Indeed, few Métis men left archival records of their experiences during the transitional period either. This means that we must often rely on sources such as oral history and material culture in order to gain a better understanding of the emergence and retention of Métis identity and culture in areas removed from Red River, such as in Alberta.

The permeable boundaries of identity, established during the fur trade era, remained for many Métis people during the transitional period after the fur trade, and indeed in contemporary society, as there is no consensus on the "idea of being Métis in Canada today."[55] Some of the contemporary narratives by the Métis note that there was a silence about Métis identity in their own lives,[56] just as *Le Grand Silence* impacted Métis in general near the end of the fur trade. This makes it difficult to gain a full understanding of the Métis story as the fur trade transitioned, not only for non-Indigenous people but also for some Métis themselves, and as many Métis settled in new geographic areas across the prairies. And it is important to remember what many scholars have noted; specifically, that Métis identity was never static. Rather, it was (and continues to be) negotiated and renegotiated, attesting to the "diversity, fluidity, resilience and [often] silence of Métis identities."[57]

If we were to rely on the "Red River" definition of one who could rightfully identify as Métis as it is described by Chris Andersen,[58] then, as noted earlier, Peter Lougheed's grandmother, Isabella Clark Hardisty Lougheed, would not be considered Métis. This despite the fact that her mother and at least two of her brothers applied for and received Métis scrip, certified because both parents were listed as Métis and because both were born at Fort Simpson, nowhere near the community of Red River, where the historic Métis Nation is said to have its origins. This is also despite the fact that the Gabriel Dumont Institute's Virtual Museum acknowledges Peter Lougheed as the "first person of Métis ancestry to become Premier of the Province of Alberta."[59] Indeed, it was clear to her contemporaries that Isabella was a "Half-breed," a term more commonly used at that time than it is currently. As mentioned earlier, Sylvester Clark Long, a man, who was himself familiar with attempted assimilation, confirmed Isabella's ancestry as a "Half-breed" in a very public way when he stated it in the *Mentor*. It should also be noted that there are ongoing debates and discussions about the right to self-identify as Métis. Some argue that the narrow definition of Métis, put forward by those such as Andersen, demonstrates a "limited understanding of Métis history." For communities in Ontario and Eastern Canada seeking official recognition as Métis, the argument is that "mixed-descent families and communities existed since the 18th and early 19th century Great Lakes fur trade, before the establishment of the Red River Settlement."[60]

As evidenced by Long's words, Peter Lougheed's Métis grandmother was forced to establish a public persona for herself in a society that was becoming increasingly racialized. Indeed, Isabella's Métis aunt, married to Donald A. Smith (Lord Strathcona), was on at least one occasion referred to as his "squaw wife," and Smith himself was criticized for having married her. The fourth Earl of Minto, serving as Governor General to Canada in 1898, wrote in a letter to his brother about what had long been the custom during the fur trade era—the practice of taking a country-born wife. He referred to Donald Smith's Métis wife Isabelle, saying, "Poor old Strathcona attempting to lead society, the ways of which he is ignorant of, with a squaw wife who is absolutely hopeless what could he expect."[61] Despite the lack of regard paid her by Canada's Governor General, Lady Strathcona was, in fact, quite successful at social networking, as was her niece Isabella.[62] However, this success still did not prevent Lord Strathcona from "legitimizing" his marriage later in life by arranging a quiet ceremony in New York when he and his wife were in their seventies.[63]

The disparaging remarks made about Isabella's aunt were a result of changing times. Indeed, those same comments were made about Isabella herself, according to Allan Hustak, who wrote an unauthorized biography of Peter Lougheed. Hustak wrote:

> In the homogeneous nature of frontier society at the time, there was nothing unusual about the interracial marriage. But later as James Lougheed's position

grew, he had to face taunts of discrimination about his "Indian" wife. If it ever bothered them they never let it show.[64]

As noted by Digital Museums Canada, "Like many Métis people of the time across Canada, Belle's Indigeneity became invisible as Anglo-domination flourished."[65] However, the Métis were not always held in such low regard on the prairies. Indeed, the Métis, including those who were born or settled in Alberta, as a people born of the fur trade, were often referred to as "wardens of the plains." At the height of the fur trade and of Métis ethnogenesis, the Métis referred to themselves as *les gens libres* (the people who own themselves). The Plains Cree referred to the Métis as *Otipemisiwak* (those that rule themselves).[66] Over time, the agency of the Métis changed drastically, influenced by conditions such as waning supplies of pelts, territorial clashes between both Europeans and Indigenous Peoples, the increasing access to guns and horses, and the eventual influx of settlers. Historian Gerald Friesen argues that there were four eras of "post-contact native experience." He identifies them as: 1) the era of equality; 2) the period of time when that equality was destroyed; 3) the era in which Indigenous people existed in a "plain of inequality"; and 4) the period of cultural and political resurgence. Friesen views the era of equality as enduring between the 1640s and the 1840s, while the period of inequality began in the 1890s and ended in approximately the 1940s.[67]

While some may dispute his timelines, particularly as they apply to the Métis in some parts of the prairies, it is so that the period between approximately 1640 and 1840 saw the relationships between Indigenous and non-Indigenous people evolve into trading partner and military ally. It was also during this period that Métis ethnogenesis emerged and solidified. This was when the Métis with ties to the Red River area emerged as the "wardens of the plains," largely led by Cuthbert Grant, a man now recognized as a person of historic significance in Canada.[68] From their summer homes on river lots along the Red River, the Métis travelled throughout the northwestern prairie region, hunting and trading.

The prairies extend west and north from the Red River toward the Rockies and the Arctic, and include parkland, boreal forest, native spruce and pine. Seasonal movement between these landscapes served as the natural cycle for the European fur trade. At the beginning of the fur trade, Europeans relied on Indigenous middlemen and their existing vast travel and trade routes to supply them with pelts. Competition between European fur traders soon led labourers and free traders to venture in-country, where they forged relationships with Indigenous Peoples. These relationships occurred throughout fur trade country, resulting in the birth of the Métis People. At the height of the era of equality identified by Friesen, the Métis enjoyed roles as mediators, hunters, traders, freighters, labourers and company officers throughout the territory in which the fur trade operated.

119

A Woman and a Man of Their Times

It was during the period of inequality, beginning in approximately 1890, but which one could argue began at varying times on the prairies given the settlement patterns, that the Métis diaspora led many Métis from the Red River area to push further west and north, where they had either pre-existing kin connections or where they managed to forge new connections. There is no doubt that, as noted earlier, it was not advantageous for many men to claim a Métis identity, particularly as the primarily French-speaking Métis continued to be held responsible, alongside Louis Riel, for the fighting that erupted in 1885 in Batoche. Yet well before this time, the French-speaking Métis (who often referred to themselves as *bois-brule*) increasingly encountered challenges to their livelihood, while some English-speaking Métis (who often referred to themselves as Half-breeds) were able to establish themselves in the Hudson's Bay Company. Indeed, and as noted earlier, by the end of the fur trade, those English-speaking Métis associated with the Hudson's Bay Company fared much better. This was particularly so in Alberta during the period between 1885 and 1925, when Alberta's business community continued to have ties to the Hudson's Bay Company. As noted earlier, two of the wealthiest men in the North-West during this period were Richard Hardisty, the Métis HBC Chief Factor, the district's first senator and the uncle of Peter Lougheed's grandmother Isabella, and Donald A. Smith, Lord Strathcona, who married Richard Hardisty's Métis sister.

While there is evidence that Métis women continued, out of necessity, to rely on the skill sets that they had learned as children, it is also clear that they were active agents in the formation of new settler communities as the fur trade transitioned. In fact, as new settlers arrived in the Prairie West during the last half of the nineteenth century and the early part of the twentieth century, racial boundaries remained fluid, often out of necessity, despite the fact that both Canada and the United States were intent on establishing separate and distinct countries and linear boundaries.

Despite the desire to establish boundaries, settlement of the prairies was not immediate or consistent; thus racial boundaries remained fluid for some time. For example, on the one hand, Mary Inderwick, a newly arrived settler to southern Alberta, was "pleased to note" in 1883 that "squaws were not allowed" to attend the ball at the North-West Mounted Police (NWMP) barracks at Fort Macleod. On the other hand, Inderwick noted that "Half-breeds" were allowed to attend,[69] suggesting that the class distinctions that emerged in the latter part of the fur trade persisted in some parts of the prairies.[70] It is perhaps significant that Inderwick's often racist comments regarding Indigenous people were made in documents that were intended for her audience of family members and acquaintances in the East. In the privacy of her own diary, Inderwick revealed little of either racism or admiration; she simply recorded the fact that she shared her space with Indigenous people.[71]

In fact, the presence of so many people of Métis ancestry made it difficult to maintain the boundaries that newcomers in the emerging society of the North-West might have sought to establish. Yet, for many newcomers, ethnic boundaries were increasingly maintained in other ways by reinforcing the social distance, and by coming to view Indigenous people as "other." This is especially so given that the arrival of more Euro–North Americans in the North-West coincided with treaties and the growth of ranching, which led to the establishment of more Euro-Canadian institutions.[72]

Yet, until the late nineteenth century, the Euro–North Americans who arrived in Alberta were, for the most part, "spatially isolated on ranches." Given this isolation, it is debatable the degree of social change that Euro–North Americans could effect during the late 1800s if it was "rare to see two or three together at one time."[73] In 1882, former Red River resident Alexander Begg (by then a southern Alberta rancher) reported that he had seen "scarcely a house between Fort McLeod and Fort Calgary."[74] When Mary Inderwick arrived in Calgary in 1883, she wrote that the town was "very nice but it is a village of tents framed in Indians and squaws in plenty."[75] It was not until the 1890s that federal officials started actively encouraging agricultural settlers to southern Alberta in order to replace the large land lease companies.[76]

The slow settlement in Alberta was no doubt due to the fact that the region seemed farther from "civilization" and remained difficult to access until the Canadian Pacific Railway was completed.[77] Indeed, while the last spike that connected Canada "from sea to sea" was driven in 1885 by Isabella's uncle Lord Strathcona, and boosterism promoted the West's wide open spaces and limitless land,[78] the fighting in Duck Lake between the Métis and government troops continued for some time to give the impression that the North-West was a harsh and inhospitable place.

By the time Euro–North Americans had established a permanent and more visible presence in the larger centres of Alberta in the early twentieth century, many Métis women had already relied on the skills they had acquired in the fur trade to establish themselves as matriarchs of their own extended families. Generally, they were especially successful in this if they had married non-Indigenous men. In fact, their roles as matriarchs represented an important aspect of the building of the Prairie West. Researchers Judith Hudson Beattie and Helen M. Buss used the example of the Métis woman Mary Allen Hardisty Thomas (Peter Lougheed's great-grandmother) to argue that her situation "illustrates an important part of Canada's settlement. The line of succession from Indigenous and European grandparents to Canadian prairie dweller is not an unusual one."[79] In this regard, Beattie and Buss astutely identify the continuity from fur trade society to sedentary industrialized agriculture and commerce in Alberta. Mary Allen was an orphaned daughter of a Euro–North American man and his Indigenous wife, and she spent the bulk of her life at northern posts living one of the traditional fur trade lifestyles. However, her daughter Isabella Hardisty Lougheed, based in Calgary, Alberta, went on to become one of the most influential women in the new society of the North-West, not only for her role as Lady Belle of Beaulieu House but also for her leadership in many new community groups.

Two of the social factors that, in fact, contributed to the ability of some Métis families to successfully establish themselves in Alberta were the custom of the Métis in which they traditionally lived close to kin groups and the custom in which they incorporated outsiders in a way that would enrich the web of kinship. For many Métis, the period after 1885 afforded them the opportunity to stake homesteads in southern Alberta because that district was slow to attract newcomers. It is Diane Payment's conclusion that when they established communities in new geographic areas such as Alberta and Saskatchewan, for the Métis at the "turn of the twentieth century, family, culture, and lifestyle" continued to "shape and distinguish Métis society." Relying on interviews with Batoche Elders in this case, Payment identified what she called an "enduring hidden pride in their Métis heritage."[80]

In an article perhaps appropriately entitled "Private & Enterprising," reporter John Portwood noted in the 1980 publication *Calgary* that Peter Lougheed's grandmother "was a Métis, the daughter of a Hudson's Bay Company employee."[81] This statement was indeed more private than it was public, certainly while Isabella Hardisty Lougheed was establishing a position for herself in the early 1900s, and even to a degree while Peter Lougheed served as premier of Alberta, from 1971 to 1985. Indeed, according to Peter's son Joe, even today he encounters people "all the time" who are surprised to learn that Peter Lougheed had an Indigenous grandmother. As Joe says, his father "did not in many people's eyes fit the mold of what they define or see as 'Métis' or even of Métis heritage." Yet, Joe continues, "As the Métis Nation of Alberta confirmed/confirms today, Peter Lougheed was of Métis heritage, hiding in plain sight. As he did not speak of it publicly that often, it was not widely known." And Joe Lougheed points out

> Richard Hardisty, when appointed to the senate by John A. Macdonald ... as a Métis, would have been the first person of Indigenous ancestry to serve in the Canadian Parliament. I believe the records of the Library of Parliament back this up. Later, Peter Lougheed was the first person I believe of Indigenous ancestry and Métis heritage to serve as premier of Alberta.[82]

The fact that Peter Lougheed did not often speak of his Indigenous ancestry is not to say that he deliberately did not share publicly the fact of that ancestry. Indeed, embracing one's Indigenous ancestry was not as prevalent and openly acceptable in the 1970s and 1980s. However, as one spends time going through the archives that hold both his personal and political documents, there is a sense that Peter was interested in learning more about his ancestry. Certainly, that is the strongly held belief of his son Joe. However, there is also the sense that, while in public office, Peter Lougheed was not actively engaged in learning more about that ancestry. This would not have been unusual at the time—the desire to learn more about Indigenous ancestry has grown well beyond what was seen in the 1980s.

Whether or not he was actively engaged in learning more about his Indigenous ancestry, it is clear that Peter Lougheed was deeply honoured when the Kainai People bestowed upon him a Kainai Chieftainship in 1974. Nominated by Second World War veteran Pat Eagle Child, Peter was welcomed with a ceremony at Stand Off, Alberta. His face "smeared with yellow paint (for wisdom), Premier Peter Lougheed became Chief Crop Eared Wolf" in a ceremony "during which a person considered a friend of the Blood Indians is made an honorary chief." As the ceremony continued, "the medicine man also put red paint on the premier's face—a sign of trust."[83] Noted as one of the "great leaders of the Blood Reserve," Crop Eared Wolf, whose name Peter Lougheed was honoured to receive, was the Head Chief from 1900 until his death in 1913.

He was the leader at a time when the Kainai defeated a government-mandated vote on land surrender, voting by a majority of three to one against such a surrender. In recognition of his own leadership, Peter Lougheed accepted the name in memory of this beloved Chief.[84]

One reporter who witnessed the honouring ceremony mused, "Whether or not the name will have significance for Premier Lougheed and his fight with the federal government over oil policy is yet to be seen."[85] Regardless of whether there was any significance in future negotiations with the federal government, it seems that the honour was an important one to Peter Lougheed. In a letter to Chief Jim Shot-Both-Sides of the Blood Tribe in July of 1974, Lougheed wrote that the honour bestowed upon him at Stand Off was "indeed one of the highlights of my life and one which I will not take lightly but with great bid and abiding desire to acknowledge through service the aspirations of all our native people." In regard to the name that was bestowed upon him by the Kainai, Crop Eared Wolf, Peter noted that this was "a most meaningful name to me and I will strive to perpetuate many of the great qualities of leadership shown by him." He concluded by thanking the Chief "most sincerely again for the trust shown me by including me in the Kainai Chieftainship."[86]

It was perhaps only coincidental that a member of Peter's family had earlier received a similar honour. Richard Hardisty, brother of Peter's great-grandfather William Hardisty, received the name of Red Head from the Blackfoot Nation.[87] There was another connection between an honorary chieftainship and the Hardisty-Lougheed family. In 1919, Edward, Prince of Wales, was the recipient in the first recorded instance of the Blood Tribe conferring an honorary Chieftainship.[88] Edward was a frequent guest of Peter's grandparents, Isabella and James Lougheed, Beaulieu House, where he was often the dance partner of their daughter Dorothy. It is not clear if Peter Lougheed was aware of this connection between the honour that had been bestowed upon him and that bestowed upon a frequent guest of his grandparents.

In his files, Peter kept a copy of the draft notes that would become a history of the Kainai Chieftainship and those honoured to belong to it, written by Hugh Dempsey.[89] Dempsey was the grandson by marriage of the Indigenous senator James Gladstone, who served as president of the Kainai Chieftainship at the time of Peter Lougheed's induction. Peter also retained a copy of the memo detailing the "actual ceremony itself where you will be required to strip to the waist and later dance with one of the Indian ladies. You will also be required to respond very briefly after your head-dress has been presented," concluding with "tea at the teepee of Medicine Man Manz Grey Horse."[90]

Dempsey's history tells us that the Kainai Chieftainship was established in 1951 with a goal in part to "render assistance toward a wider and higher system of Indian education." In order to be recommended one must demonstrate "past and present interest, sympathy and assistance towards progressive endeavour to the Indian's welfare in general" or be of "recognized standing."[91] The dispensation of Kainai Chieftainships was not without its controversies. In 1957, Bishop H.R. Ragg, Anglican bishop of Calgary from 1933 to 1943,[92] noted that "those selected for this honour ... should be persons who are interested, really interested, in the Indian Peoples, and more especially in the Blood Band."[93] While this may not have always been the case, in 1960 a prominent figure who had demonstrated an interest in the rights of Indigenous Peoples was honoured with a Kainai Chieftainship.

In fact, it was Kainai inductee Prime Minister John Diefenbaker who had appointed James Gladstone of the Blood Tribe to the senate of Canada. It was also Diefenbaker who had enacted legislation granting Indigenous people the right to vote in federal elections without fear of losing Treaty Rights. Diefenbaker had proclaimed that never again will [Indians] be second class citizens, as they have been in the past. Nor will this mean that they will suffer any loss of hereditary or treaty rights, as long as the rivers flow and the mountains stand, so long will their rights, privileges, and treaty prerogatives be respected and upheld.[94]

Interestingly, Diefenbaker was the only Canadian prime minister that Peter Lougheed noted was a leader who he viewed as a good role model and who he hoped to emulate. His reason? Because it was Diefenbaker who "did so much to make new Canadians feel part of our nation."[95]

Shortly after Diefenbaker's honour in 1962, and prior to Peter's own naming ceremony, the Kainai Chieftainship is said to have "finally" returned to the place of honouring people who were important to the Blood.[96] Yet there was a discussion at the meeting of the Blood Tribal Council in February of 1975 that might have foretold the future rescinding of the honour to Peter Lougheed. At that meeting, while it was noted that honorary Chiefs were appointed for life, it was also noted that this honour was intended to be apolitical. An example was used of a member of Parliament who, while being an honorary Chief, "took an opposite stand to the Bloods on Sec. B-12 of the *Indian Act*." Yet, and despite the claim of being apolitical, there was a suggestion made at this meeting that Chieftainship members who held political office should be approached for their support when "Indian business" came before the House of Commons or provincial legislatures.[97] It is not clear if this type of political activism was ever undertaken by the council members.

Any good relationship between Peter Lougheed and those who honoured him with a Kainai Chieftainship did not shield the premier from political activism on the part of those who voted to strip him of the honour, something that reportedly greatly bothered Lougheed.[98] As Hugh Dempsey, the former secretary-treasurer and president of the board of the Kainai Chieftainship, describes the "Lougheed Affair," it was the first time that an honorary Chieftainship previously bestowed was rescinded. Indeed, the council itself had stated that the honour was intended as a lifetime one. The Lougheed Affair resulted after Indigenous people across Canada mounted an opposition to the patriation of Canada's Constitution because it lacked clarity on the protection of Indigenous Rights as they were guaranteed by the Royal Proclamation of 1763. Led by Peter Lougheed in 1981, premiers from across Canada expressed concern that the proposed new clause recognizing "Aboriginal and Treaty Rights" did not itself provide clarity on what specific rights were recognized and the financial implications for provinces. It was at Peter Lougheed's insistence that the word "existing" be added to the clause guaranteeing Treaty and Aboriginal Rights. According to one account, Lougheed would later be astonished that governments and the courts ignored the term "existing" and, rather, redefined Indigenous Rights as "inherent" rights, thus, he felt, raising a "whole new set of legal questions."[99] According to son Joe Lougheed,

The addition of the word "existing" I think is misunderstood ... Various premiers, notably my father and Premier Blakeney of Saskatchewan, were concerned that the Charter of Rights would lead to an increase in judicial interpretation, intervention ... in Canada ... The addition of "existing," I suggest, was not meant to freeze rights as some have suggested; it was intended however, I believe, to restrict who could extend those rights—Parliament or the Courts.[100]

Nonetheless, at the time, Lougheed's insistence on the addition of the word "existing" in Section 35 (1) damaged his relations with Alberta's Indigenous people.[101] It was during a demonstration at the Alberta legislative grounds that a public announcement was made by the Blood tribal administrator that Peter Lougheed was being stripped of his honorary Chieftainship. It would not suffice for Lougheed to reassure Indigenous people that their "existing" rights were protected, nor would it be when that word was included in the Constitution Bill. Regardless of any protests, the amended bill became law on April 17, 1982, and Peter was indeed stripped of his Chieftainship. There is evidence in the historical account of the events at the time that the act of stripping Lougheed of his honorary Chieftainship was an unsanctioned political act on the part of those who declared it publicly. At the time, Hugh Dempsey, serving as secretary-treasurer to the Kanai Chieftainship, noted that it fell to him to "carry on the communication with the tribal council."[102] No communication was ever formally sent to Peter Lougheed to advise him of the rescinding of the honorary Chieftainship. Although the tribal constitution and bylaws were later amended in order to prevent any such incident in the future, the Chieftainship was never reinstated for Peter Lougheed, and he remains as the only person to have it removed.[103]

The fact that he continued to display the headdress suggests that this loss was significant for Peter Lougheed. This assumption might be further supported by the fact that Peter's son Joe does not recall any discussions with Peter about the actions of the members of the Kainai Chieftainship who, according to Hugh Dempsey, acted unilaterally at the time with their public announcement, without any formal support of the tribal council.[104] Indeed, according to Joe, the honorary headdress always remained prominently displayed in their family home, as did the photo of Chief Crop Eared Wolf, and they continue to hold a place of prominence in Joe's home today.[105]

Another honorary headdress also continued to be displayed in Peter's home, according to son Joe. In 1971, Peter Lougheed was honoured with the name Chief Thunderbird by the people of what was then referred to as Hobbema (now Maskwacis). As Peter noted in his letter to Chief Norman Yellowbird, "I am honoured by you making me Honourary Chief Thunderbird. It was a day and an occasion that I will never forget … You can be assured that I will do everything I can to help promote the rights of the Indian People of Alberta in every way possible."[106]

While there is no way to definitively conclude how Peter felt about his own Indigenous ancestry, there were certainly instances when the matter of Peter Lougheed's Métis ancestry was discussed, both privately and publicly. In documents held by Lougheed House National Historic Site Archives, there is a copy of a letter written to Peter Lougheed when he served as premier. Dated May 6, 1975, the letter from Jean Johnston of Kitchener, Ontario, inquired about his ancestry. Johnston wrote that, while in Edmonton, "I was in a hotel lobby of the MacDonald, someone told me that you are of mixed blood—Métis. As I am researching for a book about Indian integration in Canadian society, I felt that I should ask you direct." She continued by asking "Would you be kind enough to confirm this, and if so, would you mind me using your name as an example of successful integration?"[107] It is not clear if or how Peter Lougheed responded to this inquiry. However, were this inquiry made today, the recipient might well find the request to "use" any Indigenous person as an example of successful integration offensive.

Certainly, in the early 1900s, when Peter Lougheed's Métis grandmother was establishing a position of importance for herself in Calgary society, there were those who desired to present examples of successful integration by Indigenous people. In Isabella Lougheed's case, we can see the manipulation of her persona, both on her part and on the part of the media, who were always intent on covering every aspect of life at Beaulieu House. Contemporary publications paid Peter's grandmother attention in large part because of her position as the wife of the area's senator. A great deal of space was devoted to elaborate descriptions, often made by male journalists, of Isabella's

133

clothing and her hostess skills. Pictures and descriptions of Isabella as a gracious Euro–North American lady, while most were aware of her Indigenous ancestry, suggest that she may have been viewed as a commodity of boosterism and of successful assimilation, or "integration." However, it also suggests that Isabella not only allowed herself to be such a commodity, but that she manipulated the management of her own image. During the few public interviews she granted, while dressed as a gracious woman, Isabella ensured readers were aware that she had endured many "privations" at a northern fur trade post but that she had successfully transitioned.

In the early 1900s Prairie West, it was not altogether unusual for people to adopt a public persona that would help them to survive, and in some cases thrive, in a society that was becoming increasingly aware of racial boundaries. People such as Grey Owl,[108] Chief Buffalo Child Long Lance[109] and Onoto Watanna,[110] an acquaintance of Isabella, embellished or even invented personal lineages in ways that they imagined would render them more interesting, yet "palatable," to the emerging society, while allowing them to profit from the new economy.

On the other hand, some individuals of Indigenous ancestry simply were not fully aware of their own family history, even into the 1970s and 1980s. There is some evidence that, for his part, Peter was interested in learning more about his Métis grandmother. On one occasion, a researcher in the Office of the Premier, wrote a memo for the files on the subject of "Re: Premier Lougheed's Native Heritage." The memo noted that Peter Lougheed's family

could be traced through his grandfather Sir James
Lougheed and Lady Belle (Hardisty) Lougheed

to one of the early pioneer families of Western
Canada. Lady Lougheed was a Hardisty, daughter of William Hardisty, the chief factor of the
Mackenzie district for the Hudson Bay Company
and of Mary (Allen) Hardisty. Mary Allen was
born in Fort Dunvegan in 1846. Her father was a
white man named Robert Allen, and her mother
was a Métis woman named Charlotte Scarborough.
Unfortunately we do not know anything more about
them. So we could say then, that Premier Lougheed's
grandmother's grandmother or great-great grandmother was the earliest person we know of to have
native heritage in the Premier's family history.[111]

135

Of course, this conclusion is not fully accurate.
Isabella Hardisty Lougheed's father was William Hardisty,
and his father was Richard Hardisty Sr. who married
Marguerite Sutherland, both of Métis ancestry.[112] As noted
earlier, Richard Hardisty Sr. always worked in the North-
West with the HBC, as had three generations of Hardisty
before him. For his part, William Hardisty was an officer
for thirty-six years, rising to the position of Chief Factor
for the vast Mackenzie River District.

This oversight on the part of Peter Lougheed's
staff might be forgiven, as even current historians fail
to acknowledge the Métis ancestry of both his great-
grandmother and his great-grandfather. In his book *The*

A Woman and a Man of Their Times

Lougheed Legacy, published in 1985 and sanctioned by Peter Lougheed, David Wood wrote that his book was based on numerous interviews with Peter himself and members of his government. In the book, Wood wrote that "the claim to some native ancestry is one in which Peter Lougheed takes great pride." Yet Wood also wrote that James Lougheed married "Isabella Christine Hardisty, the daughter of an English army officer and a Métis woman,"[113] while not acknowledging the Métis ancestry of Isabella's father. Even more recently, in 2009, historian John English, while acknowledging the Métis ancestry of Peter Lougheed's grandmother's mother, Mary Allen Hardisty, neglected to note the Métis ancestry of his grandmother's father, William Hardisty. In this instance, English was discussing the challenges when Pierre Trudeau's Liberal government was determined to repatriate the Constitution. As alluded to earlier, there was much debate about the inclusion of Indigenous Rights, with Peter Lougheed and other premiers raising concerns regarding the recognition of "Aboriginal Rights" and how future courts of law would interpret such recognition. While the final version of the Constitution included Section 35 (2), which did recognize the Métis as Indigenous, Peter Lougheed was able to convince his fellow premiers to include a recognition only of "existing Aboriginal Rights." Not only did this insistence garner much criticism of Lougheed by Indigenous Peoples across Canada and particularly in Alberta, but English noted the "Canadian press, astonishingly, missed the irony of his [Peter's] opposition to the extension of Aboriginal status to Métis people: Lougheed's great-grandmother was Métis."[114]

In regard to the Hardisty men, English did not acknowledge that they were also Métis, writing only that Richard Hardisty had "nobly fought for the rights of the Métis in the Northwest a century before."[115] In actual fact, Richard Hardisty had not "nobly fought" for the rights of the Métis. Rather, this Métis man was himself sent as a representative of the central Canadian government to try to quell the activities of the Métis in 1869. Nonetheless, English was correct to note the irony that Lougheed would oppose recognizing Métis People as Indigenous People, given that his great-grandmother Mary Allen Hardisty was Métis.[116] Certainly, if we are to view Peter Lougheed as a leader through the lens of today, we might argue that, as a man with Indigenous ancestry, he should have done more to ensure justice for Canada's Indigenous Peoples. While one of his fellow premiers, Quebec's René Lévesque, paid Lougheed homage when he noted that "this Albertan, by far the most remarkable man on the Prairies in his time, is so passionately concerned about sovereignty in his own way, that even though he opposes us he can understand our position."[117] This is indeed an interesting observation from a man who many might have viewed as Lougheed's adversary, so focused was Lévesque on the sovereignty of an independent Quebec. This is ironic in itself in that Peter Lougheed appeared to respect Quebec's desire for sovereignty, but appeared not to be concerned, at this stage, about recognizing the sovereignty of Indigenous Peoples.

Clearly, Peter Lougheed was a "man of his times," and his history is indeed complex. This is perhaps nowhere more evident than in some of the policies that he initiated and supported as they impacted Indigenous Peoples. As noted earlier, Peter Lougheed remains the only person in history to have been stripped of the honorary title of Chief by the Kainai People, perhaps speaking to the complexity of not only his history but also the expectations that some had of Alberta's first Indigenous premier when they hoped that he might be more vocal in his defence of Indigenous Rights, and perhaps more vocal about his own ancestry.

Some time after Lougheed had left office, one Métis leader did note that Peter Lougheed was the "first person of Métis ancestry to become the Premier of the Province of Alberta." The BC Métis Federation noted, upon Peter's death, that "Peter was known to identity himself as Métis throughout his lifetime although the media of the day hardly identified Mr. Lougheed as such."[118] Whether it is true that Peter identified himself as Métis "throughout his lifetime," the Federation erroneously listed Isabella Clark Hardisty as Peter's mother, but we know that in fact Isabella was Peter's grandmother.

While having earlier introduced regressive legislation to amend the *Land Titles Act* in a way that would restrict Indigenous claims under provincial legislation, and perhaps indicative of the changing times, in the final years of his premiership, Peter Lougheed did introduce a motion for Métis betterment, amending the *Alberta Act* of 1905 to provide constitutional protection of the Métis Settlement Legislation with the intention that it would be "for the benefit of Alberta's Métis people for future generations."

In 1985, Peter Lougheed's minister responsible for Native affairs, Milt Pahl, explained that this legislation was an important first step that arose as a result of the "stated desires and aspirations of the Métis people of Alberta for protecting lands ... It indicates the desire of the Alberta Government to work cooperatively with Métis Albertans toward this end."[119] As Peter Lougheed said to the Legislature when he introduced this bill intended to grant control of existing Métis lands to the Métis People, his belief was that

> they would be able to do so well with this land base ... and that not only will they have the strength that goes with the ownership rights to the land but the strength that will flow from that to being in control of their own destiny.[120]

He continued:

> I realize that there are others involved that look on this and say, "When is our time?" Yet, that's fair. But let's get this one done, and let's get it done well. I haven't any doubt, Mr. Speaker, that in the time I've been in this position, in attempting to read the public about a bold move, whether it's a grain elevator in another province or it's a move with senior citizens or it's this one, Albertans are essentially very fair-minded people. They will say this is the right

139

A Woman and a Man of Their Times

course. It's at the forefront of action in this nature in Canada, and it should be. We're in a position to do it. We're in a position to take this historic first step. I believe we'll all be very proud that we're party to it. I personally wish the people in the settlements the very best in the future.[121]

As noted at the time by Ray Speaker, a member of the Opposition, when he responded to the motion by the premier,

> I certainly am willing to extend my appreciation to the government in that type of action ... there was consultation at every level and the federation is very pleased with the resolution as a first step toward Métis self-government.[122]

This initiative to acknowledge the Métis right to self-government on the part of Peter Lougheed's government represents a significant shift from his earlier insistence on the insertion of "existing rights" into the Constitution. For the Métis, existing rights in 1985 would in fact not acknowledge their historic connection and their right to their land located throughout the North-West.

As stated earlier, one's self-identity is often complicated, and for Métis people it can be especially complex. This is particularly so for those whose identities are manifested in the "public view," such as it was for Peter's Métis grandmother, Isabella Clark Hardisty Lougheed, and for Edgar Lougheed, Peter's father, and, indeed, for

Peter Lougheed himself. It is incumbent upon society to recognize that our public figures are rounded characters, characters whose private persona, while it may inform their public persona, is often more complex, than we sometimes wish to believe. Indeed, it is incumbent upon society to appreciate and to understand that the boundaries of identity are often as blurred as they are complex, and that they are inextricably linked not only to ethnicity, but also to the context of the times.

▲ Peter Lougheed participating in the ceremony when he was granted the
honorary Kainai Chieftainship. THE UNIVERSITY OF ALBERTA ARCHIVES ACCESSION
#UAA-2012-046-013-1979 F22.

▶ Another moment from
the ceremony in whcih Peter
Lougheed was honoured with
the Kainai Cheiftainship.
THE UNIVERSITY OF ALBERTA ARCHIVES
ACCESSION #UAA-2012-046-013-1979 F22

▲ *L–R, back row:* Joe Healy interpreter, Running Crane; *L–R, front row:* Blackfoot Old Woman, Day Chief, Crop Eared Wolf. When Peter Lougheed was honoured with the Kainai chieftainship, he was given the name of Crop Eared Wolf. PHOTO COURTESY OF LIBRARIES AND CULTURAL RESOURCES DIGITAL COLLECTIONS, UNIVERSITY OF CALGARY NA-201-1

▶ Mary Thomas, photographed in Calgary, Alberta, ca. 1880 by Notman and Sandham. She was the mother of Isabella Clark Hardisty (the future Lady Lougheed) and great-grandmother of Peter Lougheed. The Premier retained a copy of this photo in his personal papers. LIBRARIES AND CULTURAL RESOURCES DIGITAL COLLECTIONS, UNIVERSITY OF CALGARY. NA-2758-1

◀ Isabella Clark Hardisty Lougheed, Lady Lougheed (1859–1936). Calgary, Alberta, ca. 1920s–early 1930s. LIBRARIES AND CULTURAL RESOURCES DIGITAL COLLECTIONS,UNIVERSITY OF CALGARY. NA-3232-5

▲ Southern Alberta Pioneer and Oldtimers women's group at Lougheed House, Calgary, Alberta Ladies dressed in traditional clothing and displaying their handicrafts—*L–R:* Ruth Irwin, Elizabeth McDougall, Annie McDougall, Nettie Wright. See Calgary Herald July 12, 1923 by Oliver, W.J.

Elizabeth McDougall was the wife of Methodist missionary John McDougall. She was the first white woman to arrive in the Alberta foothills, moving to Calgary in 1898 where she became president of the Southern Alberta Pioneer Women and Oldtimer's Association, an organization in which Isabella also served. Annie McDougall, also pictured here, was the wife of David McDougall, who maintained a business partnership with Isabella's uncle Richard Hardisty. LIBRARIES AND CULTURAL RESOURCES DIGITAL COLLECTIONS, UNIVERSITY OF CALGARY. ND-8-408

▼ Mount Lougheed, Alberta. Photo by W.J. Oscar. LIBRARIES AND CULTURAL RESOURCES DIGITAL COLLECTIONS, UNIVERSITY OF CALGARY. ND-8-418

▲ John Diefenbaker at Indian Village on Stampede grounds, Calgary, Alberta. Prime Minister Diefenbaker being made an honourary Chief. Diefenbaker at this time had already been named an honourary Kainai Chief on June 27, 1960. Photo by Rosettis Studio. LIBRARIES AND CULTURAL RESOURCES DIGITAL COLLECTIONS, UNIVERSITY OF CALGARY. NA-5093-850

▼ Lieutenant Governor R. Steinhauer, with Peter Lougheed and other dignitaries in the background, at the opening ceremonies of the Lethbridge Winter Games, photographed by Bob Matula on February 11, 1975. PROVIN-CIAL ARCHIVES OF ALBERTA. GR1989.0516/1838 #1

▲ Long Lance on horseback, Calgary, Alberta. 1923. For a time Chief Buffalo Child Long Lance was well-known and highly regarded in Calgary as an
honourary member of the Kainai people. Actually the descendant of enslaved
Black people, but presenting himself as a Cherokee, Long Lance had gained
entry into the Carlisle Indian School in Pennsylvania. His education gained
him some fame as he starred in picture shows and wrote for the *Calgary
Herald*, where he once reminded readers that Isabella was a "half-breed."

► Lady Lougheed in ball gown, ca. early 1900s. Society pages of local newspapers often featured stories on Isabella as she assumed a role as hostess and First Lady of Calgary society. LIBRARIES AND CULTURAL RESOURCES DIGITAL COLLECTIONS, UNIVERSITY OF CALGARY. NA-3232-3

▼ James and Isabella Lougheed family photo. Undated. LOUGHEED HOUSE ARCHIVES. LHCS 2-1

▲ Peter Lougheed at the ceremony where he was named Honorary Chief Thunderbird in the Indigenous communities known as Hobbema at the time, on August 6, 1971. Hobbema is now known by its traditional name of Maswacis and is the traditional territory of the Samson, Louis Bull, Ermineskin and Montana Cree nations. PROVINCIAL ARCHIVES OF ALBERTA J.682

▲ Lieutenant Governor Ralph Steinhauer entering the Legislature to deliver the Throne Speech at the Legislature. February 25, 1977.
PROVINCIAL ARCHIVES OF ALBERTA J.3167/2

▼ Premier Peter Lougheed often wore the traditional colors of the Hudson's Bay Company, the fur trading company for which his Métis ancestors worked as Chief Factors. PROVINCIAL ARCHIVES OF ALBERTA PR19960383/5-40 UNIDENTIFIED

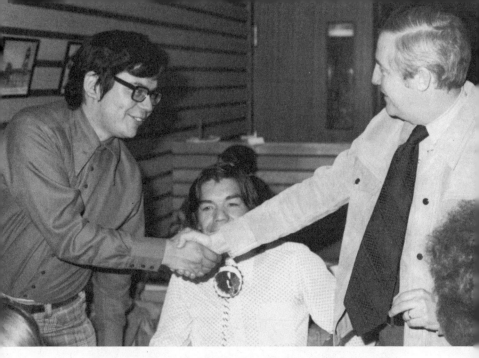

▲ Peter Lougheed with Harold Cardinal, the influential Indigenous rights activist who led the movement against the 1969 Statement of the Government of Canada on Indian Policy, also referred to by Indigenous Peoples as the "White Paper," which sought to do away with Indian Status and Treaty Rights. PROVINCIAL ARCHIVES OF ALBERTA PR19960383/5-42

◄ Stan Daniels, Métis Leader, July 30, 1974. In 1967, Stan Daniels assumed the leadership of the Métis Association of Alberta (MAA) and he oversaw tremendous growth in membership in the organization that had as its mission to advocate for the collective rights of the Métis. The MAA eventually became the Métis Nation of Alberta. PROVINCIAL ARCHIVES OF ALBERTA J1418

▲ Lieutenant Governor Ralph Steinhauer delivers the Throne Speech at the Legislature. February 25, 1977 PROVINCIAL ARCHIVES OF ALBERTA J.3167/4

clockwise from top left ◀ Hay Pitching contest between Peter Lougheed and Premier Harry Strom of the Social Credit on June 7, 1969. Two years later, Peter Lougheed and his Conservative Party swept into office by defeating the long-term Social Credits. PROVINCIAL ARCHIVES OF ALBERTA J346

▲ Hudson's Bay Company Chief Factor William Hardisty, Isabella's father and Peter Lougheed's great grandfather. LIBRARIES AND CULTURAL RESOURCES DIGITAL COLLECTIONS, UNIVERSITY OF CALGARY. NA-1030-18

◀ Lady Lougheed stands beside her vehicle, one of the first owned by a private citizen in Calgary. In the background is her grand home Beaulieu House. Now known as Lougheed House, in 1977 (while Peter Lougheed was premier) the family home was designated as a national and provincial historic site. LIBRARIES AND CULTURAL RESOURCES DIGITAL COLLECTIONS, UNIVERSITY OF CALGARY. NA-3232.6

▲ Peter Lougheed as a young boy in Calgary. JOE LOUGHEED

▼ Thought to be taken during the ceremony in which Peter Lougheed was honoured with a Kainai Chieftainship. JOE LOUGHEED

▲ Oscar Lacombe, a Métis veteran of the Korean War and several NATO and United Nations missions, and former Sergeant-at-Arms of Alberta's Legislative Assembly. Lacombe served in this capacity from 1974 to 1993, during the time that Peter Lougheed served as premier. He was also Lougheed's personal bodyguard. Upon his retirement, he was made a lifetime honorary Sergeant-at-Arms. He was the first Métis Sergeant-at-Arms for the Legislative Assembly and, at his passing in 2017, the last surviving member Charter Member of National Aboriginal Veterans Association of Canada. IMAGE COURTESY OF DELORES THERIEN-DEREN.

▲ Portrait of Premier Peter Lougheed by Yousuf Karsh. PROVINCIAL ARCHIVES OF ALBERTA. GR1989.0516.1675.0001

five

The Complexities of Leadership

The words of the schoolmaster charged with the education of Isabella Hardisty's children: "The "Red Men of the West" do not much care to work due to innate characteristics as "shiftless vagrants.""[1]

AT THE SAME TIME THAT Isabella Clark Hardisty Lougheed was maintaining an image and public persona as community leader and as Lady Belle of Beaulieu House, her son was attending a school at which the schoolmaster Archibald Oswald MacRae was publishing his beliefs on the inability of Indigenous Peoples to adapt to the new economy of the North-West. Though Isabella carefully managed her image to the point that there have been very few written records of her own thoughts, the fact that she must negotiate that image in an increasingly racist society would not have been lost on her.

It is interesting that the author of the first history of the province that Peter Lougheed would later lead, Archibald Oswald MacRae, served as the principal of

Western Canada College, a school that was attended by Isabella's son Norman, Peter Lougheed's uncle. What is equally interesting is that MacRae's views, as the author of Alberta's history, on people of Indigenous ancestry were not particularly complementary. While a more recent historian of western Canada, Doug Francis, provides a positive review of MacRae's history of Alberta for its inclusion of Indigenous people, even he concedes that MacRae's history is a "romantic" one, which praises the work of missionaries for "bringing civility to the province."[2] In fact, MacRae's own words on at least one occasion spoke to his belief in the need for civility to be inculcated into his students: "The Red Man of the West has always been a difficult individual, he does not care to work, to beg he is not ashamed. In consequence he tends to become shiftless and vagrant."[3] Peter's uncle Norman Lougheed was one of those students at Western Canada College, and it is reasonable to assume that Norman's parents, James and Isabella, were aware of Dr. MacRae's views. It is just as reasonable to assume that Dr. MacRae was aware, not only of the leadership roles of James and Isabella in Calgary society, but also of Norman Lougheed's Indigenous ancestry. Awareness of the views of leaders in Calgary at the time, such as Dr. MacRae, would undoubtedly influence Isabella's own public presentation of her persona as an elite English-speaking lady.

While there is no doubt that Isabella was a leading member of the new community of Calgary as it sought to establish itself as a centre of commerce in the early 1900s, it is her husband, James, who has garnered the most attention from historians for his leadership role. This is even though James Lougheed himself noted that he had become a "Company man" by marrying Isabella. When they were married, the Company—that is, the Hudson's Bay Company, still occupied an important position in the disbursement of wealth and patronage in the North-West. In marrying Isabella, James was able to forge business partnerships and gain political appointments that may not have been as easily accessible to him on his own, hailing as he did from the poor district of Toronto's Cabbagetown. Yet the North-West continued to be a diverse community in which newcomers such as James were able to forge important connections with other pioneers and to assume leadership roles in those communities.

When Peter Lougheed himself became a leader of one of the western provinces, he stressed that one needed a good understanding of the diversity of its people, and of its history. He identified himself as a Progressive Conservative with an ideology that is "socially conscious ... I am not on the right ... I'm in the middle of the road ... that is where the people are." When asked what influence his grandfather Senator James Lougheed had on him, Peter replied that he, in fact, had a significant impact: "as a young man I knew the role he had played—unelected Senator" who nonetheless assumed a major role in the province when it eventually gained control of its natural resources. In Peter Lougheed's view, if we understood our history, we would remain a united country. That understanding extended to a belief that smaller regions had the right to protect their culture, economy and way of life. Indeed, he stressed that he had always advocated for this during national discussions, whether those regions were in the west or the east.[4] Peter Lougheed was indeed a "man of his times" in that he strongly believed in regions protecting their rights at the same time that some in the Indigenous community were critical of him for seemingly challenging their inherent rights with the position that he had assumed during constitutional negotiations. It is a testament to the evolution of the discussion of inherent rights of Indigenous Peoples in that those rights are now more universally accepted.

Indeed, Peter Lougheed was always conscious of the role that his own ancestors had played in his success. When a mountain in Banff National Park was named in honour of Peter's grandfather James Lougheed in 1928, the family was mindful of the fact that the mountain chosen should be prominent and visible to travellers through the park. While he was not personally involved in the choice of the specific mountain, Peter Lougheed accepted an invitation from the Association of Mountain Guides to climb Mount Lougheed in commemoration of Alberta's seventy-fifth anniversary.[5] Along with his wife and children, the premier scaled the 10,200-foot peak of Mount Lougheed in August of 1980.[6] According to his son Joe, who joined his father on that climb along with his siblings and mother, it was particularly symbolic for Peter to climb Mount Lougheed as a way of connecting Alberta's history to his own.[7] In similar confident and assertive style, it is said that when Peter Lougheed was considering putting his name forward to lead and rejuvenate Alberta's struggling Conservative party, a task that many saw as insurmountable, he dismissed those who thought that his goal was unrealistic with the assertion that "the party is in such difficulty ... I have to win in an overwhelming way."[8]

When one considers the Indigenous ancestry of Peter Lougheed's grandmother Isabella and her union with a lawyer with no significant wealth or connections, and the fact that they were able to lead in the social circles and the politics of the early settlement of Calgary, one might also consider those accomplishments "overwhelming." Indeed, Mount Lougheed was one of the first of many public commemorations that would recognize the contributions of the Lougheed family to the growth of Alberta. Although climbing this particular mountain was no doubt a tribute to his grandfather James, most of the commemorations in Alberta would eventually not be in honour of James and Isabella Lougheed, but rather in honour of their grandson Peter. Those commemorations include hospitals, provincial parks, leadership institutes, awards, and community and performing arts centres.

Indeed, Peter Lougheed's accomplishments are such that at least one popular historian, Peter C. Newman, declared him to be Alberta's "most influential national icon."[9] On learning of the death of the former premier, Naheed Nenshi, who was mayor of Calgary at the time, said, "I, like every Albertan of my generation, am a Lougheed baby ... I have never known an Alberta or a Canada that did not benefit from his legacy." Quoting from the epitaph of Christopher Wren, Nenshi commented, "If you seek his monument—look around you."[10] In fact, when Peter Lougheed embarked on a trade mission to China, observers noted that the reception he received was comparable to that of a head of state. When Peter Lougheed undertook that trade mission, it was highly unusual for provincial leaders to do so, rather than the federal government leading such a mission on behalf of the entire country.[11]

Peter's knowledge of his grandmother's role in Calgary society may not have been as extensive as his knowledge of his grandfather's role, based in part on the greater attention paid by media and by historians to James's role. As Fil Fraser noted, those who knew Peter Lougheed well believed that "his grandfather's role in politics was never far from his mind." [12] The argument is that Peter chose the fledgling Conservative party as his best option for breaking into politics, at least in part because it was the party of James Lougheed. However, perhaps it was an equally important consideration that Peter Lougheed chose the Conservative party at that time based on pure pragmatism—the Liberals already had a leader in 1964 when he was considering politics, as did the Social Credits, while the Conservative party was without a leader and without a seat in the Legislature. Regardless, it was a political strategy well executed, as within three years, Peter was the leader of the Opposition with six seats in the Legislature. Pragmatism likely played a role in the political path that Peter's grandfather chose as well. In reality, some have noted that James would have had a difficult time had his political journey required election rather than appointment, in part due to his wife's Indigenous ancestry.

Indeed, Isabella's own leadership choices were equally "pragmatic." Despite her own Indigenous ancestry, she was a lifelong member of the Imperial Order Daughters of the Empire (IODE). While it may seem ironic given the mission of the IODE, Isabella assumed a leadership role, serving as first vice regent and hosting most of the meetings at Beaulieu. The IODE has evolved into a national women's charitable organization; however, its original mandate when founded in 1900 was to "promote and support the British empire."[13] Nonetheless, Calgarians seemed relatively enthusiastic about the arrival of the IODE to their community, and about the role of its first vice regent, as the *Morning Albertan* reported that a "strong chapter" was organized at the inaugural meeting held at Isabella's home.[14]

Leadership in early prairie communities necessitated a rather "broad" perspective in how people navigated their public persona, particularly if they were Indigenous. In addition to national organizations such as the IODE, Isabella was involved in many community-building initiatives. Some might argue that it was Isabella, with her love of the arts, who inspired James to establish Calgary's 1,500-seat Grand Theatre in the pioneer community. On opening night, February 5, 1912, hundreds of visitors converged on Calgary to view world-famous actor Johnston Forbes-Robertson, star of the English stage, in the play *The Passing of the Third Floor Back*. Reviews noted that no expense had been spared, with the actor himself observing that the Grand Theatre was "one of the finest and most commodious theatres in all of Western Canada," and others noting that "if one piled all the lighting features

The Complexities of Leadership

and stage accessories of the London theatres together, they would still be short of one or two stage accessories of the Grand Theatre."[15] It was clear that the Lougheeds, together, were sending a message that they were prepared to lead their adopted community of Calgary to greatness and were capable of the task.

While James Lougheed was of a strict Methodist upbringing which forbade dance, Isabella's time spent as a student at Wesleyan Ladies' College in Hamilton engendered a love of the arts. In one of the few surviving letters found written by Isabella, she wrote that she longed to return to piano playing after she rejoined her family in northern fur trade country. After having been away at school in Ontario, life was no doubt different for Peter's grandmother at the northern posts. Isabella expressed the sentiment in a letter to her aunt, Eliza McDougall Hardisty, that she wished to spend the next winter with her. As mentioned earlier, one of the reasons given by Isabella was that she found it "hard when I cannot practise my music. I will be glad when we go out, I am sure I will sit at a piano all day long if I get a chance."[16] Eliza McDougall would not have been familiar with the lifestyle at northern posts, so Isabella would naturally speak of something they might have in common, such as piano playing.

No doubt it was a great pleasure for the fun-loving Isabella when, in October 1912, a young Fred Astaire and his sister Adele introduced the tango to Calgary during a vaudeville act at the Lougheed's Grand Theatre.[17] Despite concerns expressed by local clergy[18] and the officials from the local university's administration, which forbade students to take part in the tango, it was rumoured that Isabella had organized a "dansant" at Beaulieu House for her daughter Dorothy on January 1, 1914, where guests reportedly partook in the tango.[19]

Clearly, Isabella, who likely did host the "dansant" for Dorothy and her friends, enjoyed playfully teasing the media. While many minute details were confirmed, such as the choice of "large yellow mums and yellow and white tulips ... tea was served at 4 o'clock," as far as the tango, the *Albertan* was forced to conclude, "Whether or not the tango was danced the young people had a merry time and are looking forward to another similar event this afternoon."[20] It appears that Isabella continued to host many "dansants" at Beaulieu, despite warnings such as that given by Rev. C.C. McLaurin in 1915, when he addressed a Baptist convention, warning that the West was "dance crazy," and that "such worldliness and pleasure-seeking" were a "curse to the community."[21] Peter's grandmother Isabella's networking skills must have been exemplary, for there is no evidence that her reputation as a community leader suffered, even though she enjoyed activities deemed a "curse" by some community leaders.

Indeed, rather than a tarnished reputation, increasingly Isabella was viewed as the First Lady of Calgary society. She assumed the official title of "Lady" when James Lougheed was knighted for his service as minister during the First World War. And this was not merely a symbolic title, as Peter's grandmother assumed an active role in the establishment of many cultural and community service organizations, such as the Victorian Order of Nurses, the local symphony and literary, skating and golf clubs. While for the most part remaining apolitical, Isabella did take part in the establishment of a Calgary chapter of the National Council of Women. In 1896, Isabella accepted the role of national vice-president for the District of Alberta, serving for two years.[22]

Given that Peter's grandparents lived in the "Big House," it was only natural that their home would be the venue where the new North-West welcomed not only community leaders but many visiting dignitaries. Given the importance of Beaulieu House to the boosterism of the West, Isabella assumed an important role in the marriage partnership, as it was she who managed the social capital that was Beaulieu House. There are many examples found in the local newspapers, reporting Isabella's superb "hostess" skills in particular. One such example was the occasion when Isabella and James hosted Nicholas Flood Davin,[23] at which time Davin delivered what was described as a "most eloquent speech." As well as commenting on the speech, the reporter noted,

A most enjoyable and instructive evening was wound up with a cordial vote of thanks, which called forth enthusiastic cheers to Senator and Mrs. Lougheed for the courtesy and hospitality shown by them to the members of the Liberal Conservative association.[24]

In fact, the *Herald* was clearly impressed, writing in its February 1, 1900, edition:

Beaulieu ... was last night the scene of a brilliant society event, when the Senator and Mrs. Lougheed were "at home" to their wide circle of friends and acquaintances. Entertaining at Beaulieu is the synonym for all that is best and most hospitable in Calgary's social history. Not even Government House at the territorial capital at its palmist could exceed Beaulieu as it appeared last night with its gay company of handsome women and their escorts. What less, indeed, could be expected? The appointments were in every respect perfect, the music bright and crisp, the supper unsurpassed, the dresses such as would have graced a London ballroom, and the host and hostess doing everything they could conduct to the enjoyment of their numerous guests. Dancing began shortly after 9:30 to the music of Mons. Augade's orchestra and was sustained with the utmost interest until an early hour. In the spacious billiard room, gentlemen who were no longer devotees of Terpischore enjoyed whist, billiards, cigars and mellow conversation. The spacious rooms, admirably designed for dancing, looked most brilliant in their floral decorations of pink and white carnations, white Roman hyacinths and palms.[25]

Readers could not help but be impressed by the transformation of former fur trade country by community leaders such as James and Isabella Lougheed into a space that now boasted venues equivalent to London ballrooms.

For the most part, the position of leadership that Isabella was able to forge for herself in Calgary was applauded by the media with little reference to her Indigenous ancestry. By the time Peter Lougheed became premier of Alberta, Indigenous ancestry of community and political leaders in Canada, while more acceptable, was still not celebrated. What was certainly celebrated were the many accomplishments of Peter Lougheed. He has been recognized for numerous examples of what has been referred to as visionary leadership, not the least of which was in 2001 when he was inducted into the Canadian Medical Hall of Fame. This recognition came in part due to the fact that, in 1975, when natural resource revenues were providing Alberta with a substantial surplus, Peter had demonstrated "visionary leadership" when he established the Heritage Foundation, which then endowed the Health Research Task Force with millions of dollars to conduct medical research that would, as noted by the Canadian Medical Hall of Fame, yield exponential benefits to the health care of not only Albertans but Canadians and beyond.[26]

We could argue that visionary leadership was apparent in James Lougheed as well. As mentioned earlier, it had not taken James Lougheed long to begin to think like a westerner after his marriage to Isabella Clark Hardisty. To that end, James Lougheed was one of the first members of the Provincial Rights Association, joining in the 1890s.[27] Not only was Peter's grandfather James a major advocate of provincial autonomy and control of natural resources, but he was also one of the first to invest in gas processing at Turner Valley, an investment that marked the beginning of the oil and gas industry in Alberta. In the end, James's campaign to secure natural resource control for the provinces was a profitable one for his adopted province and for his own finances. As most know, the discovery of oil at Turner Valley in 1914 became Alberta's first energy boom and would one day establish Calgary as a major oil and gas centre.

Yet it was Peter Lougheed's grandmother Isabella Clark Hardisty Lougheed who was a pioneer of the North-West, even more than was her husband, James. Isabella served as the first president of the Southern Alberta Pioneers Association, an organization which had established its mandate to record the "local history" of the pioneers, that group of people defined by the fact that they were living in the North-West prior to 1884.[28] It is clear that the pioneer association was not referring to the homesteading pioneer, but rather to the fur trade pioneer. The Southern Alberta Pioneers Association recognized Peter Lougheed's retirement with a letter of congratulations. As noted, Peter remained a member of that association his entire life.[29]

Beyond his membership in the Pioneers Association, Peter Lougheed remained committed to that vision of the Alberta pioneer. Indeed, when he announced his intention to lead a revitalized Progressive Conservative Party of Alberta, the party's news release referred to Peter as "Alberta's youngest political leader ... a chip off the pioneer block with a western Canadian family background going back to the days when Calgary was a cluster of houses on the banks of the Bow and Elbow rivers."[30]

The expectations were high for Peter Lougheed when he swept to power in 1971. He was young, energetic and very adept at the newly important medium of television. There have since been many assessments of his leadership of Alberta when it was staking its claim as an important contributor to Canada's national economy. Very few of those reviews of his leadership discuss in any detail the fact that he had Indigenous ancestry, and how that ancestry might have impacted his leadership or his policies. Given that Peter Lougheed did not often publicly discuss his ancestry, there is no way to reach any definitive conclusions about the impact, if any, on his approach to leadership and to the political issues that he dealt with.

Somebody who may have had some insight on Peter's approach to leadership was the man who wrote the only biography of Peter Lougheed, Allan Hustak. In his 1979 publication, Hustak stressed that his book was an "unauthorized biography." However, he does acknowledge that Peter read the book before publication and that he "objected to portions of it."[31] It is not clear what portions Peter objected to, but it is of note that Hustak's reference to Peter's grandmother as the daughter of a Métis mother and an "English Army officer" are incorrect. Further, Hustak does not really acknowledge Isabella's Métis ancestry, rather writing that "Belle grew up in the east."[32]

Even in the 1980s, as more people were publicly acknowledging their Indigeneity, when Peter was recognized as Humanitarian of the Year by the Calgary

Legal Guidance in 1987, the narrative of his life noted Peter's grandfather Sir James Lougheed had married the "daughter of an English army officer and Métis woman," meaning that Peter had "a portion of native ancestry—a heritage in which Mr. Lougheed takes great pride."[33]

In one of the few instances in which Peter's Indigenous ancestry was referenced publicly while he held office, an article in his personal files did just that, also making the claim that Peter happily shared that ancestry in discussions. The article, entitled "Lougheed is really an Indian," published in the *Castor Advance* on February 24, 1977, quotes Stan Daniels, then president of the Métis Association of Alberta. In the article Daniels made the public request that Peter Lougheed assume direct responsibility for the Native Secretariat. In a prepared statement released to the press, Daniels stated:

> The present living conditions of the Métis People are a cruel example of poverty in a land of plenty. The majority of the Native people struggle on the bottom [*sic*] of society to have adequate food, shelter, and jobs. With this in mind, it is ironic, that the two top Parliamentary officials in Alberta are both examples of . . . Native ancestry. Lt. Gov. Steinhauer and Premier Lougheed are both examples of the great contribution to this society that can be made by Native people.

Daniels continued:

It is time for a person, who has Native blood in his veins, to take over direction of Native Secretariat ... Premier Lougheed has often reminded Native leaders, myself included, that he is one-eighth Indian, but he does not know which one-eighth. I hope that part of the one-eighth includes his heart. For he will need great insight and compassion for his kinsmen, to lead our people from their present state to a decent and productive life within this society.

In conclusion, Daniels told the reporter that

I appeal to the Premier, as a brother, to examine and reject the half-hearted attempts by members of his government to help solve Natives [sic] Peoples' problems. I ask him as a brother, to create a policy, which will right the wrongs of 100 years, so that Native People can take their right place in a prosperous and productive Alberta.[34]

Of course, one can only speculate on the reason for retaining some documents and not others by those in public office. However, retaining the article in which Daniels made these comments might suggest a desire on Peter Lougheed's part to reflect about his ancestry and how that might impact his leadership approach in terms of matters of Indigenous Rights. Regarding the comments themselves, it is likely more a sign of the times than anything else that Peter Lougheed would make reference to "one-eighth" Indigenous ancestry in 1977, and that there appeared no rebuke for this on the part of Indigenous representatives such as Stan Daniels. Indeed, the same claim was made by some about Louis Riel as a way to discredit his identity as an Indigenous person. In an ironic coincidence, in the case of *Daniels v. Canada*, Jean Teillet, a descendant of Louis Riel's family, acted on behalf of the intervenor, the Métis Nation of Ontario. In that case, the original trial judge held that section 91(24) of the *Constitution Act, 1867*, was a "race-based" distinction, an analysis that the Federal Court of Appeal "failed to clearly reject." The argument was made by Teillet in 2016 (in advance of the Supreme Court's decision in *Daniels v. Canada*) that "using a race-based analysis for section 91(24) is a continuation of Canada's long history of systemic racism. The court's reliance on a racial analysis of section 91(24) led it into an inappropriate focus on Métis individual biological ancestry and hybridity."[35] Teillet continued:

> Focus on an individual's genealogy, bloodlines or race assumes that the only relevant fact is a genetic link to a fictional racial group: Indians ... In defining Métis in a manner that would include anyone with a drop of Indian blood, Phelan J [the trial judge] potentially creates a Métis out of a person who may not self-identify as Métis, may not be considered Métis by a Métis community, and may have no ancestral ties to a Métis community.[36]

It was in 1977, earlier than this particular case, when Stan Daniels made the comment about Peter Lougheed's Indigenous ancestry, that Lougheed was referenced by an Ottawa newspaper as being "completely within his rights [were he] to ask the federal government to put pressure on Lieutenant Governor Ralph Steinhauer to toe the line and not get involved in controversial issues, according to constitutional expert Senator Eugene Forsey."[37]

According to the Ottawa news article, Grant Notley, then leader of the New Democratic Party, suggested that Lougheed had indeed asked the federal government to "stop Steinhauer from making sensitive statements on a number of issues, particularly Indian affairs." The matter in question was in regard to a "controversial amendment" to the *Land Titles Act* that had been introduced by Lougheed's government in the current session of the Legislature, and which would restrict the filing of caveats on provincial land, a practice that had been used to protect from land claims by Indigenous groups. While Peter Lougheed did not confirm that he had contacted the federal government, Ralph Steinhauer ultimately said that he would sign the new legislation when approved.[38]

While this legislation may have caused Peter Lougheed some concern as premier and led to some strain on his relationship with his lieutenant governor, at the end of Ralph Steinhauer's tenure, Lougheed referred to him as a "very good friend," while Isabel Steinhauer noted, "We came to you as strangers, and you made us feel welcome."[39] In regard to the appointment of Steinhauer in the first instance, following tradition, it was Prime Minister Pierre

Elliott Trudeau who had made the call to Ralph Steinhauer offering him the role of lieutenant governor of Alberta. A former Liberal candidate in the 1963 federal election, Steinhauer initially responded to Trudeau's request by saying, "I'm not schooled for a thing like this ... You're plucking a person out of the farmyard and an Indian at that." Regardless of his own hesitation, Steinhauer, the founder of the Indian Association of Alberta, served as lieutenant governor of Alberta from 1974 to 1979, also becoming an officer of the Order of Canada in 1972.[40] Although the decision on who to appoint was officially made by the Governor General (at that time Jules Léger) on the recommendation of the prime minister, input would certainly have been sought from the premier of Alberta, Peter Lougheed. While the role of lieutenant governor is ceremonial, its functions include, among others, promoting a sense of identity and supporting social causes.[41] As an Indigenous person who was clearly proud of his own identity, the time of Ralph Steinhauer's service was a time when many Indigenous people in Canada were asserting their own identity. According to Peter Lougheed's son Joe, the premier was

> very proud of Mr. Steinhauer. I have no doubt he likely had a role in that appointment. While "reconciliation" as we know it today was not a driver of public policy at that time in Canada, I believe my father's actions and beliefs were very much part of his own reconciliation with his history and his past.[42]

While not fully responsible for the appointment of Ralph Steinhauer, Peter Lougheed did appoint a Métis woman, Muriel Stanley Venne, to the Alberta Human Rights Commission in 1973. It is said that Lougheed "recognized her strength and compassion" when he appointed her as one of seven commissioners. This appointment afforded Stanley Venne the public forum to continue advocating for the rights of Indigenous Peoples. Working throughout her life to bring attention to social justice, Stanley Venne was the first Métis person to receive the Order of Canada in 2005. In 2017, she also became the first Indigenous woman to have an Alberta government building named in her honour. Muriel Stanley Venne continued her work throughout her life to educate the general public about the sacred agreements between Indigenous Peoples and the Crown.[43] Ralph Steinhauer was also the first appointment of an Indigenous person, this time the first to serve as lieutenant governor of a Canadian province.[44]

In regard to his engagement with Indigenous people, in a 1999 interview, Peter Lougheed was clear about another matter that was, and remains, of great concern—the question of self-government and self-determination. His own concern was based at least in part on accommodating self-government when there were existing provincial and municipal governments and laws.[45] As referenced above, in an earlier move that might have been regarded by Alberta's Indigenous communities as even more detrimental to their land rights, Peter Lougheed's government passed retroactive legislation "making it impossible for anyone [whether Indigenous or not] to register a caveat against Crown lands ... This legislation meant that the Indians' court battle was effectively legislated out of existence." The court battle in question is that in which the communities of Chipewyan Lake, Long Lake, Loon Lake, Lubicon Lake, Peerless Lake, Sandy Lake and Trout Lake had filed a caveat in 1975 on the land registry of third parties, which had indicated an interest in 100,000 square kilometres in northern Alberta. This "undemocratic" legislation by the Lougheed government, as it was described by many, drew protests and the ire of opponents such as John McLaren, dean of the University of Calgary law school, who "blasted the bill as legislation which 'discriminates against the native people of this province.'" [46] Protests yielded no response as the bill successfully passed into law. Well into the 1980s, oil exploration continued in northern Alberta, sanctioned by the provincial government, led by Premier Don Getty (who served as minister of energy and natural resources in the Lougheed cabinet), without consultation with Indigenous Peoples. As historian Donald B. Smith noted in 1988, the government of the day continued in the tradition of some of the early fur traders. As an example presented by Smith, in 1786, Peter Pond had told Indigenous Peoples that "the country and the Indians belonged to him and he would do with them as he pleased and no other person should meddle with them." [47]

These examples demonstrate that the matter of identity and public versus private persona and how that impacts leadership decisions is a complicated one. It certainly was so for Peter, given some of these actions taken by his government, and also for his grandmother,

Isabella, particularly since they both lived during times when society had not yet transitioned to a time of "truth and reconciliation."

Perhaps the most important contribution that Isabella Clark Hardisty Lougheed made to the new community of Calgary was as an agent of transition.[48] Not only did she participate as a leader in most philanthropic and cultural activities in the new emerging economy, but her re-created persona was also used by many in the press to demonstrate the vitality of the transformed Prairie West. Attention to Isabella's European role as an English lady by the local and national press, when most knew she was Indigenous, served to demonstrate the economic integration of western populations and, to some extent, the successful assimilation of Indigenous people. No doubt when the City of Calgary allowed Isabella to remain in her stately home even after it had repossessed Beaulieu House for non-payment of taxes when she was widowed, and her estate had been decimated by the Great Depression, it was because the City appreciated the social capital that Isabella continued to contribute to the economy in the midst of the Depression era.

Although there was certainly a value to the social capital that Isabella contributed to Calgary's economy, that social capital also served the couple themselves well. It has already been established that Isabella's Métis kin network contributed to James and Isabella's success. Given this connection, it is of note that at least one author wrote of the possibility that James Lougheed may have dealt in Métis scrip. Journalist Allan Hustak, author of Peter Lougheed's biography, who unfortunately did not include much information on his sources, concluded that James Lougheed took unfair advantage of Métis scrip dealings, writing that there was "suspicion that not all of this wealth was earned legitimately."[49] Hustak intimates that some of James's wealth came not only from insider information about land deals but also from unscrupulous dealings in Métis scrip. While there is documentation that supports James Lougheed's extensive land holdings, there is no documentation that supports Hustak's claims.

Indeed, many historians have argued that the land and money scrip certificates that were issued to the Métis population through the *Manitoba Act* and later through the North-West Half-Breed Commission were often surrendered to unscrupulous entrepreneurs for very little in return.[50] When the practice attracted the attention of the federal government due to its alarming proportions, James did initiate a bill in the senate that imposed a three-year statute of limitations on any charges for unscrupulous dealings, a bill that likely ultimately protected a number of new western millionaires.[51]

One of those millionaires was Richard Secord, whose involvement in scrip dealing is supported by oral and written testimony. Reporter Graham Thompson referenced the oral testimony of descendants of Headman Moostoos and Richard Secord, both signatories to Treaty 8, and contemporary reports in the *Edmonton Bulletin* and the *Edmonton Journal*. According to Thompson, Secord had formed a partnership to operate a dry goods store with

John McDougall, "the richest man in Edmonton," who was, perhaps not coincidentally, a member of James Lougheed's extended family. Apparently Secord, armed with a suitcase

> stuffed with money … headed north with the government commissioners charged with negotiating the largest land deal in the history of the Dominion of Canada: the signing of Treaty 8.[52]

For three weeks in the summer of 1899,

> commissioners, policemen, secretaries, accountants, cooks, interpreters, and missionaries along with Secord spent three weeks on a gruelling 500-km journey by wagon, by boat and by foot into the heart of Canada's northwest interior.[53]

The report states that Secord, who later went on to become a member of the Alberta Legislature, bought

> an estimated 150,000 acres of Métis land at discounted prices which he, in turn, sold for a huge profit to incoming settlers. Twenty-two years later, Secord would be charged with fraud in connection with speculating in "script" [sic]—certificates for land and cash awarded to the Métis as a one-time compensation for giving up title to their traditional territory.[54]

Speaking to a newspaper reporter in 1999, Richard C. Secord, great-grandson of the scrip dealer, and an Edmonton lawyer who at that time defended Indigenous Rights, said of his great-grandfather: "It's hard to defend what he did … Nothing would surprise me in connection with my great-grandfather. He was quite a character."[55] According to the news report, the elder Secord was never convicted of fraud, the charge being

> conveniently quashed by sympathetic politicians in Ottawa who rushed into law a three-year statute of limitations on scrip cases. They applied it retroactively to Secord's case . . Then, in 1981, further scrubbing Secord's reputation clean, the province named a mountain in his honour as a "prominent Edmonton pioneer."[56]

One of the men who, like Secord, "followed the Scrip Commissioner through the North, buying scrip for himself and others," was Richard George Hardisty, son of the late Senator Richard Hardisty, and therefore Isabella's cousin.[57] Had James Lougheed dealt in Metis scrip, it might have been difficult to reconcile with the fact that his wife was of Indigenous ancestry.

In reality, leadership approaches are often complex, as are identities, and public and private personae. While mixed-race marriages were commonplace during the height of the fur trade, they became increasingly frowned upon in the early 1900s when James and Isabella were establishing themselves as leaders in the North-West.

James and Isabella clearly adjusted for this reality and made little public reference to Isabella's Indigenous ancestry. Peter Lougheed was clearly aware of his grandmother's Indigenous ancestry. There is no evidence he attempted to disguise that fact. Indeed, the opposite is true—Peter Lougheed acknowledged his Indigenous ancestry and there is evidence he sought to learn more about that ancestry. Yet from today's perspective, some of the decisions he made while in leadership roles in terms of Indigenous sovereignty appear contradictory, just as his grandfather James Lougheed's own decisions can now appear contradictory. At the very least, the leadership roles of James Lougheed, Isabella Lougheed and Peter Lougheed remain complex and situational, occurring as they did during times that were themselves complex.

six

Conclusion

SCHOLAR HEATHER DEVINE, WHO RESEARCHED the ethnicity of her own Desjarlais family only after learning as an adult that she had Indigenous ancestry, argued that, within one family, children could assume dramatically different identities based on their life experiences.[1] For the Métis in particular, that identity was often situational, inclusive, fluid and complex. Other scholars have argued that identification as a Euro–North American on the part of Indigenous people did not necessarily represent a rejection of a Métis identity or Métis kin group.[2]

In reality, for families of the northwestern fur trade that might have various "tribal relatives," as well as Euro–North American family members, Métis ethnicity was often inclusive enough to incorporate and accept all members of the family. Kinship links between culturally distinct groups enabled accommodation and subsequently influenced tribal politics in many geographic areas when large-scale settlement by Euro–North Americans occurred.[3] As Martha Harroun Foster wrote, because there was very little opportunity between the late 1890s and the 1920s to safely publicly identify as Métis, it was not unusual for most Métis during that time to identify as either "Indian or white," while privately nurturing a Métis identity. In fact, history confirms that it has always been an integral aspect of the Métis culture to allow a web of kinship ties to enrich rather than to destroy a sense of unique ethnicity.[4] Many have observed that kinship systems often allowed the Métis to sustain their identity in a safe, supportive atmosphere, even if those identities could only be enjoyed in the private realm.

There was indeed a place for the Métis in the new economy, and it was often the connections that the Métis had forged during the fur trade that enabled their successful transition and their roles as the nucleus of many of the early pioneer western communities. When Peter Lougheed referred to his grandfather James Lougheed as one of Alberta's early pioneers who contributed to the establishment of that province, the implicit reference must also be to Peter's Métis ancestors, who were those first pioneers with whom his grandfather forged important connections. Indeed, James Lougheed had himself confirmed that when he came west, he became a "Company man" by way of his marriage to a Métis daughter of the fur trade, Isabella Clark Hardisty Lougheed.

James Lougheed certainly knew that he was making a connection to an important Métis fur trade family when he married Isabella Clark Hardisty. Isabella's Métis identity and culture had been inculcated by her Métis mother and father in northern fur trade country. When James and Isabella married in 1884 in the pioneer prairie community that would eventually become the city of Calgary, marriages between Métis women and Euro-Canadian men were still common practice, as they had been during the height of the fur trade. Despite the fact that it was common knowledge that Isabella was of Indigenous ancestry, the social significance of the marriage was clear when the *Calgary Herald* reported that the principals James Lougheed and Isabella Hardisty had married. As the young couple settled into their new home, there were very few current-day amenities, so reliance on the Métis fur trade culture and kin networks would continue to be critical and of benefit. However, as more settlers arrived from eastern Canada and Europe, ethnic boundaries solidified. A woman of Isabella's status would have been astute enough to know that cultivating a public persona as a Euro-Canadian "lady" was key to maintaining the status that she had enjoyed as a daughter of fur trade aristocracy.

There is no way to know to what extent Isabella's public persona permeated her private persona, so there is no way to know how much awareness her own children had of their Métis ancestry and history. In the same way, in the case of Isabella's grandson Peter Lougheed, there is no way to determine with absolute certainty how much exposure he had to the Métis history and culture of his grandmother. Whether he knew much or little of his grandmother's Métis identity and history, there is certainly some indication that Peter Lougheed did not deny that Indigenous ancestry when he served as premier of Alberta. In fact, there is some evidence that he sought to learn more about his grandmother's personal history and identity. This was the case even though the matter of Indigenous history was only beginning to be an area of study in the 1970s when Peter Lougheed entered public office, and it was prior to the acceptance of oral history as a method of expanding our collective understanding. Indeed, when Peter Lougheed served as premier of Alberta, the matter of "Truth and Reconciliation" as we understand it today in regard to Indigenous Peoples was not something that would have been considered by politicians, educators or the majority of the general public.

There are some who speculate that by the time Peter Lougheed left political office in 1985, he had become more determined to learn about his Indigenous ancestry. It is the case that Peter devoted much time and effort to the restoration of Lady Isabella and Sir James's grand home, now Lougheed House. Peter supported the designation of this home as a national historic site. Indeed, he played an integral role in the designation and restoration of the building, known when Isabella lived there as Beaulieu House.[5] The Beaulieu name is synonymous with Métis identity in the northern fur trade culture from which Peter's grandmother internalized her own Métis history and identity. For many northern Métis, it is François Beaulieu who is the father of the Métis Nation, and not Louis Riel. Today, Lougheed House not only recognizes the importance of the Lougheed family in the building of the West, but also serves as a testament to the role of the Hardisty family—

one of the West's pioneer Métis fur trading families, who served as the bridge between the old and new economies of the West. It is perhaps fitting to include near the end of this study the words of Peter Lougheed's son Joe, who said, "My father was a pioneer in his own right. He never forgot where he came from and he never wavered on where Alberta should go. Respect the past. Honour and embrace the present. Plan for the future."[6]

Yet when Lougheed House was recognized for its historical significance by Parks Canada in 1992 as Beaulieu National Historic Site of Canada, there was no mention of the contributions of Isabella, a Métis woman of some note. Rather, it was more the elegance of the grand home that was recognized. As the plaque states:

One of the earliest surviving mansions on the Canadian prairies, this 1891 home brought a new elegance to its frontier town. Designed by Ottawa architect James R. Bowes for Senator James Lougheed and his wife Isabelle (née Hardisty), it hosted visiting royalty, travelling dignitaries and local society gatherings. An early domestic example of Calgary sandstone construction, the house combines historical styles in a robust Victorian Eclectic design. At one time, porches, carriageways and a terraced formal garden were edged by balustrades. Despite later uses, the grand interior is largely intact.[7]

While the official designation by Parks Canada acknowledges Isabella's link to the Hardisty family, there is no indication for those reading the plaque that Isabella was a member of a Métis fur trading family of some significance. This suggests that even in 1992, years after Peter Lougheed's time as premier ended in 1985, there was still hesitation to acknowledge the importance of the Métis identity and kinship networks that formed the nucleus of many of the pioneer communities in the West.[8] Only in the early twenty-first century did Lougheed House begin to share more widely the fact that Lady Belle was of Métis ancestry. In 2019, the site hosted a new exhibit that explored the Lougheeds' Métis history.[9] Lougheed House now features a page on its website entitled "Calgary Métis History," which provides a few details on Isabella's ancestry. Regardless of the slow pace of recognition, the history of Beaulieu (Lougheed) House confirms that the communities of the West were always more diverse than the history books acknowledged. In the words of Peter Lougheed,

174

> A good history education will reveal that the historical narratives we grew up with are dynamic, multidimensional and always open to being recast and re-examined in the context of the present ... Canada's history, our collective memory, must reflect the diversity of our past and of our present.[10]

Indeed, it is the nature of historical narrative that it must be revisited from the context of today, all the while recognizing that historical characters are always "people of their times."

Acknowledgements

I T HAS BEEN SAID THAT no person is an island—it can also be said that no author writes alone. Indeed, writing is a lifelong journey which crosses many paths. My previous books have provided the foundation for this work. I am ever grateful and humbled by readers of my books who have reached out to ask questions, to add stories, to offer suggestions for further research, and to express an interest in learning more about Métis People in western Canada.

Indeed, one's writing is enriched by the relationships that develop as we seek to learn more about the history, culture and experiences of Métis People—the people who own themselves. Most importantly, I acknowledge the generosity of countless family members of the Métis women whose lives I have been blessed to learn more about. These family members continue to offer support and insights as we work together to ensure that readers understand more about the important contributions that Métis People made, and continue to make, to the development of Canada.

Donald McCargar, great-grandson of Marie Rose Delorme Smith, remains a steadfast friend and supporter of my research and writing. His continued enthusiasm for learning and sharing the history of his great-grandmother was integral to the recent recognition of Marie Rose Delorme Smith as a person of national historic significance by the Historic Sites and Monuments Board of Canada, Parks Canada.

In the same way Joe Lougheed, great-grandson of Isabella Clark Hardisty Lougheed, son of Peter Lougheed, has been a committed supporter of initiatives to share the history of his Métis ancestors. His support and that of his father led to the designation of Lougheed House, Isabella's home in Calgary, as a National and Provincial Historic Site. Joe Lougheed's support in sharing stories, images and insights for this book added to our depth of understanding about the history of Métis people in Canada.

Keepers of stories including family members, as well as local, national and online archival databases are integral to the work of researchers and authors. Along with family members, there have been many archivists who have shared their knowledge of their holdings in support of my earlier books. This current book particularly benefited from the insights of archivists at, and holdings of, the University of Alberta Archives, the Provincial Archives of Alberta, the Glenbow Western Research Centre at the University of Calgary, and Lougheed House Conservation Society Archives.

There were some scholars who assumed the role of mentor as I began my journey of academic work, and who have continued to walk alongside me and to support my writing and research. Those include Dr. Heather Devine and Dr. Donald B. Smith, both now recognized as professor emeritus at the University of Calgary. I am forever grateful for the opportunity to learn from these dedicated and humble professionals who encouraged me to "dream big," despite very humble beginnings and late entry into scholarly research and the wonderful world of publishing one's projects fueled by a passion for learning.

Finally, the anonymous readers who read very early iterations of this work. Your honest and frank feedback was instrumental in the completion of this book all these years later. Sharon Anne Pasula, member of the Métis Nation of Alberta, who agreed to read a draft of this book —thank you! Your equally frank comments enriched this book. Editor Collette Poitras, also a member of the Métis Nation of Alberta, your incredibly supportive and kind comments about my book provided the important validation of the contribution this book makes to our collective knowledge.

I end by thanking my partner Alasdair—you walked alongside me on this incredible journey!

The woods are lovely, dark and deep,
But I have promises to keep,
And miles to go before I sleep.
And miles to go before I sleep.

ROBERT FROST, *Stopping by Woods on a Snowy Evening*

Acknowledgements

APPENDIX 1: The Hardisty-Lougheed Family

This is not a complete genealogical chart but is intended to complement the narrative as a way to provide clarity on the family members discussed in this book. To view an interactive version of this chart, visit https://www.mindomo.com/mindmap/richard-hardisty-b-1792-london-m-marguerite-sutherland-indigenousscottish-1e7d-c74296934e2fb2fe5b521d8a9b75.

Hardisty-Lougheed Family

Richard Hardisty (b. 1792 London) m. Marguerite Sutherland (Indigenous/Scottish)

Isabella Sophia Hardisty b. 1825 m. Donald A. Smith aka Lord Strathcona

William Lucas Hardisty

David Alexander Hardisty

Thomas Alexander Hardisty

William Lucas Hardisty b. 1822 Waswinipi House Quebec m. Mary Ann Allen b. Chinook People

Richard Charles Hardisty b. 1832 Ft. Mistassin Quebec m. Eliza McDougall f. George McDougall

Richard Robert Hardisty

Mary Louisa Hardisty

Frank Allen Hardisty

Isabella Clark Hardisty b. 1860 m. James Alexander Lougheed

Clarence Hardisty Lougheed b. 1885

Norma Alexander Lougheed b. 1889

Edgar Donald Lougheed b. 1893 m. Edna Alexandra Bauld

Dorothy Isabelle Lougheed b. 1898

Douglas Gordon b. 1901

Marjorie Yolande Lougheed b.1904

Donald Douglas Lougheed b. 1925

Edna Bliss Lougheed b. 1940

Edgar Peter Lougheed b. 1928 m. Jeanne Rodgers

Stephen Lougheed

Joseph Lougheed

Andrea Lougheed

Pamela Lougheed

APPENDIX 2: Métis Activism in Alberta

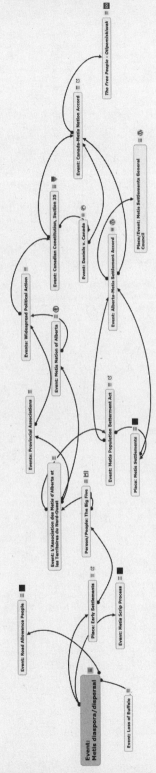

This mind map demonstrates how events in Alberta influenced the national story of the Metis culminating in the acknowledgement of the Metis self-determination with the Canada-Metis Nation Accord in 2017. To view an interactive version of this chart, visit https://www.mindomo.com/mindmap/the-people-who-own-them-selves-f4145382ae8e47a4968eb8e535582ca7.

Notes

INTRODUCTION

1. Donald B. Smith Collection, Beaulieu House File, Hardisty Box 2, Lougheed House Archive (LHA). Reference "A Daughter of the West Who Made a Difference," *Calgary Herald*, December 30, 2001.

2. Patricia Finlay, "Edgar Peter Lougheed," *The Canadian Encyclopedia* (2012; update June 16, 2022), thecanadianencyclopedia.ca/en/article/edgar-peter-lougheed.

3. Harold Innis, *The Fur Trade in Canada: An Introduction to Canadian Economic History* (1930; repr., Toronto: University of Toronto Press, 1999).

4. Arthur Ray, *Indians in the Fur Trade* (1974; repr., Toronto: University of Toronto Press, 1998). Also Carol M. Judd and Arthur J. Ray, eds., *Old Trails and New Directions: Papers of the Third North* American Fur Trade Conference (Toronto: University of Toronto Press, 1980). This anthology demonstrated the quickening pace of fur trade research, which was now becoming interdisciplinary, with studies in archaeology, economics, ethnohistory, geography, history and anthropology.

5. "Miscegenation," Britannica.com. britannica.com/topic/miscegenation. Miscegenation is defined as marriage or cohabitation by persons of different race.

It was believed that "anatomical disharmony" would occur in children produced by these unions. These theories were discredited by twentieth-century genetics and anthropology.

6.   Donald B. Smith Collection, Beaulieu House File, Hardisty Box 2, LHA. Reference "A Daughter of the West Who Made a Difference," *Calgary Herald,* December 30, 2001.

7.   Ibid.

8.   Linda Goyette, "Lougheed, Metis compromise," *Edmonton Journal,* November 21, 1981, Provincial Archives of Alberta (PAA), PR1985.0401/911 PR2207 1981–82, Box 78, Metis Association Meeting with Premier.

9.   Yvonne Zacharias, "Lougheed backs Metis," *Calgary Herald,* November 21, 1981, PAA, PR1985.0401/911 PR2207 1981–82, Box 78, Metis Association Meeting with Premier.

10. Robert Parkins, "Metis leader praises premier," *Calgary Herald,* March 17, 1983, PAA, PR1985.040/911 PR2207 1981–82, Box 78.

11. J.S. Sinclair, letter to The Honourable Peter Lougheed, Premier of Alberta, April 25, 1984, PAA, PR1985.0401/911 PR2207 1981–82, Box 78, Metis Association Meeting with Premier.

12. Chris Anderson, *"Métis": Race, Recognition, and the Struggle for Indigenous Peoplehood* (Vancouver: UBC Press, 2014), 24. Jean Teillet, a descendant of Louis Riel, also makes this argument in several of her publications.

13. Christopher Adams, Gregg Dahl and Ian Peach, eds., *Métis in Canada: History, Identity, Law and Politics* (Edmonton: University of Alberta Press, 2013), xv.

14. Joe Lougheed, interview by author, January 8, 2020.

15. Max Foran, "The Boosters in Boosterism: Some Calgary Examples," *Urban History Review* 8, no. 2 (October 1979): erudit.org/fr/revues/uhr/1979-v8-n2-uhr0895/1019378ar.pdf. As a way to promote the advances on the Prairie West, community leaders engaged in campaigns of boosterism relying on the "rhetoric of progress" to support expansionary policies.

16. This term came to represent the periods of time when many Métis chose not to identify publicly due to fears of danger and persecution after events such as the fighting in 1885 and repressive policies that ensued.

CHAPTER ONE: THE MAKING OF "LADY BELLE"

1. In order to provide context to further understanding of Peter Lougheed's ancestry, sections of this chapter that discuss his grandmother's ancestry and her role as first lady of the North-West draw on the author's earlier research, under copyright to Doris Jeanne MacKinnon, that supported and appeared in various publications including her Ph.D. dissertation, and articles and books with various publishers including University of Alberta Press, University of Toronto Press and *Canada's History*.

2. Richard Hardisty Fonds, Accession No. M477, File 137, #808, letter to My dear Hardisty, December 22, 1876, Glenbow Alberta Institute Archives (GAIA). As quoted in Doris Jeanne MacKinnon, *Metis Pioneers: Marie Rose Delorme Smith and Isabella Hardisty Lougheed* (Edmonton: University of Alberta Press, 2018), 68.

3. Donald B. Smith Collection, Belle Lougheed File, Hardisty Box 2, LHA. Trudy Cowan was the first director of Lougheed House National Historic Site and was instrumental in obtaining the designation as a historic site. Jennifer Bobrovitz was the first archivist and researcher.

4. Richard Hardisty Fonds, Accession No. M5908, Series 23-3, 1572, Bella Hardisty to Dear Aunt Eliza, December 10, 1877, GAIA.

5. It is not clear exactly how Mary Anne Allen ended up in northern fur trade country as a young child. There is evidence of her being baptized in the Mackenzie River District at the age of six, but it is not clear who cared for her until her marriage to William Hardisty. For a detailed discussion, refer to MacKinnon, *Metis Pioneers*.

6. Lougheed Family Bible, LHA. The Bible lists two different years for Isabella's birth, 1860 and 1861. Also Reel T6551, *Census of Canada, 1901*, Province of Alberta, District of Central Alberta, 13, Library and Archives Canada (LAC). This census lists Isabella's date of birth as April 18, 1861. Also Reel T6425, Census of Province of Alberta, District No. 197, 34, LAC, notes that Isabella's mother was born in British Columbia and her father was born in Quebec. Also Donald B. Smith Collection, the Lougheeds of Britannia File, James Lougheed #1 Box 1, LHA. This file contains documents stating that James's grandfather James Lougheed Sr. also married a "Miss Allen" when he immigrated to the United States from Ireland in 1804. Reference Jopie Lougheed, Viviane McClelland and Frank Ellis Wickson, *The Lougheeds of Britannia*, no publisher.

7. Beckles Willson, *The Life of Lord Strathcona and Mount Royal G.C.M.G., G.C.V.O., 1820–1914* (London: Cassell, 1915), 83. Willson wrote that Isabella's grandfather Richard Sr. married Marguerite Sutherland, a "dark, petite woman of remarkable beauty, undoubtedly derived from her mixed-blood or Indian mother." Willson also references Kipling Records 62. Also Donald B. Smith Collection, Hardisty Family File, Box 1, LHA. Reference Manuscript Group 25G vol. 14 Scrip certificate No. 734, application made in Edmonton in 1885, LAC. Scrip application references the marriage.

8. "Hardisty, William Lucas," Hudson's Bay Company Archives (HBCA), Biographical Sheets, www.gov. mb.ca/chc/archives/_docs/hbca/biographical/h/hardisty_william-lucas.pdf. Also Carol M. Judd, "'Mixt Bands of Many Nations': 1821–70," in *Old Trails and New Directions: Papers of the Third North American Fur Trade Conference*, ed. Carol M. Judd and Arthur J. Ray (Toronto: University of Toronto Press, 1980), 128. Judd notes that the exact meaning of the term "native" is not recorded, but she assumes that the word "parish" referred to the place from which the contracting employee derived his cultural traits. She continues that employees from Rupert's Land were almost always identified as native, an umbrella term that included "Indians, mixed bloods, and theoretically at least, also Europeans. Because very few natives of Rupert's Land at that time were of European descent, and fewer still probably worked for the Hudson's Bay Company, it is reasonable to assume that 'native' employees were either mixed bloods or Indians," 138.

9. Donald B. Smith Collection, James Lougheed #1 Box 1, Lougheed James Overview File, "James Alexander and Isabella Lougheed A Chronological History," LHA. Reference James Grierson MacGregor, *Senator Hardisty's Prairies, 1849–1889* (Saskatoon: Western Producer Prairie Books, 1978), 46–47. Reference Chief Trader William Lucas Hardisty to Sir George Simpson, Fort Yukon, November 10, 1857, D5/45, fo264d, HBCA. Also Judith Hudson Beattie and Helen M. Buss, eds., *Undelivered Letters to Hudson's Bay Company Men on the Northwest Coast of America, 1830–1857* (Vancouver: UBC Press, 2003). Reference D.5/45 Folder 263d-4d, HBCA.

10. Beattie and Buss, *Undelivered Letters*, 43. The editors offer no references upon which they base their conclusion.

11. Donald B. Smith Collection, Hardisty Box 2, Belle Hardisty Timeline File, LHA. Reference William Hardisty, Fort Simpson, to My Dear Miss Davis,

November 20, 1869, Davis Family Correspondence, General #22 Hardisty Family File 1, P1110-1122 (1869–70), Archives of Manitoba (AM).

12. Martha McCarthy, "Northern Métis and the Churches," in *Picking Up the Threads: Métis History in the Mackenzie Basin*, ed. Métis Heritage Association of the Northwest Territories (Winnipeg: Métis Heritage Association of the Northwest Territories and Parks Canada–Canadian Heritage, 1998), 135. Reference OAGP Faraud to Hardisty, July 8, 1863.

13. Charles D. Denney Fonds, W.L. Hardisty to Dear Sister, en Route to Portage La Loche, July 10, 1870, GAIA. Denney references Richard Hardisty Fonds Accession No. M7144 File #330000, GAIA.

14. MacGregor, *Senator Hardisty's Prairies*, 60. Reference Charles D. Denney papers, Marriage of Eliza McDougall and Richard Hardisty, September 20, 1866, GAIA. Richard no doubt met Eliza after providing travel accommodations for her father, George McDougall, and his son, John, on their early missionary trips as the Methodists struggled to keep up to Roman Catholic missionaries. As MacGregor writes, John McDougall, a "muscular young Methodist," was to give Father Lacombe a "hard race towards the pinnacles of fame . . . but also one whose family history was destined to run hand in hand with Richard Hardisty's," 44–45.

15. Richard Hardisty Fonds, Accession No. 5908-1458, Series 23-1, Richard Hardisty Sr. to Richard Hardisty, March 28, 1859, GAIA.

16. Richard Hardisty Fonds, Accession No. M5908-1469, Series 23-1, Richard Hardisty Sr. to Richard Hardisty, April 14, 1863, GAIA; Richard Hardisty Fonds, Accession No. M475, H264A, Richard Hardisty Sr. to Richard Hardisty, January 23, 1860, GAIA. In this earlier letter, Richard Sr. said of William that he did not "think that there can be any necessity for his sending

his wife to Canada to be educated, he is well enough able to educate her himself if he likes." Perhaps William took advantage of the educational material forwarded by England in order to do just that.

17. Donald B. Smith Collection, Hardisty Box 2, Belle Hardisty Timeline File, LHA. Reference William Hardisty, Fort Simpson, to My Dear Miss Davis, November 20, 1869, Davis Family Correspondence, General #22 Hardisty Family File 1, P1110-1122 (1869–70), AM.

18. Jennifer Bobrovitz, researcher, Lougheed House National Historic Site, interviews by author, Calgary, AB, 2007–2009.

19. Sylvia Van Kirk, *"Many Tender Ties": Women in Fur-Trade Society, 1670–1870* (Winnipeg: Watson & Dwyer Publishing Ltd., 1980), 97. Also Michael Payne, *The Most Respectable Place in the Territory: Everyday Life in Hudson's Bay Company Service—York Factory, 1788 to 1870* (Ottawa: National Historic Parks and Sites, Canadian Parks Service, Environment Canada, 1989), 108. Reference B.239/b/78, fol. 5, annual letter to York Factory, May 29, 1794, HBCA. It seems that the central office of the HBC in England had similar concerns. As early as 1794, London had shipped "one hundred Primers or Spelling Books for the use of the Children" to York Factory, and some were also shipped to other posts.

20. "Canadian Women in the Public Eye," *Saturday Night*, September 16, 1922, Newspaper Clippings File, LHA. In Lachine, as Isabella recovered from the illness that had forced her to leave Miss Davis's school, she would have worshipped at Saint Stephen's Anglican Church, which still stands today next to the cemetery, where, according to church records, her father is buried. Reference Quebec Family History Society, Burial 1881, St. Stephen Anglican, qfhs.ca. Also personal correspondence with St. Stephen Anglican. Unfortunately, the cemetery has fallen into ill repair and very few markers

are left to indicate the exact location of William Hardisty's burial (confirmed after a visit I made to Lachine, Quebec, in July 2009, and through correspondence with Bob Smith, church historian).

21. Research Files, Matilda Davis School Folder, Robert Hunter, Architectural History Branch, "Historic Sites and Monuments Board of Canada Agenda Paper," 253, LHA. Matilda was sent to England to be educated. When she returned to Red River, she was reportedly regarded as a "distinguished member of the community, invited to the governor's balls, complimented on the quality of her French by the Roman Catholic bishop and noted for her integrity."

22. Juliet Thelma Pollard, "The Making of the Metis in the Pacific Northwest Fur Trade" (PhD dissertation, University of British Columbia, 1990). Pollard wrote that the closest the Métis children ever came to an "all-Métis" education was when the HBC fort schools were established in the late eighteenth and early nineteenth centuries, 280–81. She refers to the journal of Reverend John West, who established the first Anglican school at Red River in 1820 and who wrote that the purpose was to maintain, clothe and educate a "number of half-breed children running about, growing up in ignorance and idleness," 281. Reference John West's journal, 12–13. Although most of the children were of mixed-blood heritage, Pollard argued that the goal was still to maintain a class system and to reproduce gentlemen and ladies in the children of officers, while the children of labourers were intended to become good Christians and useful labourers, 282. As to curricula, the HBC issued a directive that children be instructed in "A B C," and schools could be sanctioned for not doing so. As early as 1798 there is reference in post journals to children being "at their books" at Moose Factory, 284. Reference H.A. Innis, ed., "Notes and Documents: Rupert's Land in 1825," *Canadian Historical Review* 7, no. 4 (1926): 320.

23. Research Files, Matilda Davis School Folder, LHA. From Matilda Davis School Collection, MG2C24, Box 2 File 2, Notebook, 3, AM.

24. Richard Hardisty Fonds, Accession No. 5908, Series 23-2, 1489, Margaret Hardisty to Richard Hardisty, September 3, 1867, GAIA.

25. "Canadian Women in the Public Eye," Saturday Night, September 16, 1922, Newspaper Clippings File, LHA. Also Waymarking, waymarking.com/waymarks/ wm9XH_ONTARIO_LADIES_COLLEGE_Whitby. Whitby College was operated by the Methodist Church in the former residence of Nelson Gilbert Reynolds, a man appointed to serve as sheriff of Whitby, Ontario. Also Whitby Public Library, Online Historical Photographs Collection, images.ourontario.ca/whitby/43652/data. It is not clear if Isabella might have been referring to the son of the owner of the house, Reynolds, or to Rev. Dr. John James Hare, who served as the principal of the Ontario Ladies' College from 1874 to 1915.

26. Established in 1786, Fort Resolution was originally a Northwest Company post but was renamed after the amalgamation of the Hudson's Bay Company and the Northwest Company in 1821.

27. K.S. Coates and W.R. Morrison, "More Than a Matter of Blood: The Federal Government, the Churches and the Mixed Blood Populations of the Yukon and the Mackenzie River Valley, 1890–1950," in *1885 and After: Native Society in Transition*, ed. F. Laurie Barron and James B. Waldram (Regina: Canadian Plains Research Center, 1986), 255.

28. Jennifer L. Bellman and Christopher C. Hanks, "Northern Métis and the Fur Trade," in *Picking Up the Threads: Métis History in the Mackenzie Basin*, ed. Métis Heritage Association of the Northwest Territories (Winnipeg: Métis Heritage Association of the Northwest Territories and Parks Canada–Canadian Heritage, 1998), 63.

189

29. Donald B. Smith Collection, William Lucas Hardisty
File, Hardisty Box 1, William Hardisty to Miss Davis,
July 10, 1870, en Route to Portage La Loche, LHA.
Reference Barbara Johnstone Collection, prepared
by J. Pentland, August 1986, P2342 111, Davis Family
Correspondence General #222, 1 P1110-1122 1869–
1870, AM.

30. Donald B. Smith Collection, Belle Lougheed File, short
clip by Madeleine Johnson, reference April 1869, LHA.

31. For most of the girls at Red River, the goal was no doubt
that they would take their rightful place as wives of
officers and mothers of future officers and, in so doing,
increase the earning potential, strength and stability of
the extended family network.

32. Donald B. Smith Collection, William Lucas Hardisty
File, Hardisty Box 1, William Hardisty to Miss Davis,
July 10, 1870, en Route to Portage La Loche, LHA.
Reference Barbara Johnstone Collection, prepared
by J. Pentland, August 1986, P2342 111, Davis Family
Correspondence, General #222 1 P1110-1122 1869–
1870, AM.

33. Parish Records Saint Stephen's, F.39, p. 76, ACA.
William Lucas Hardisty was present and served as
witness to the burial.

34. George Heath MacDonald, *Edmonton: Fort, House,
Factory* (Edmonton: Douglas Print Company, 1959),
155. Reference Donald A. Smith to Richard Hardisty,
Montreal, December 27, 1872. The author
does not indicate where he accessed the letter.

35. Ibid., 193.

36. Hamilton Public Library Files, R376.8 W516 1871/72,
Wesleyan Female College, Tenth Annual Catalogue,
Wesleyan Ladies College Archives File, Hamilton
Public Library Archives (HPLA). The majority of
Isabella's schoolmates this year were from Ontario,
Quebec or the thirteen colonies.

37. Richard Hardisty Fonds, Accession No. M477-72, Series 6-7, W.L. Hardisty to Dear Sister, July 10, 1870, GAIA.

38. Ibid.

39. Richard Hardisty Fonds, Accession No. 5908, Series 23-2, 1505, Margaret Hardisty to Richard Hardisty, April 8,1872, GAIA.

40. Hamilton Public Library Files, R376.8 W518 WH, *Literary Club in connection with the Hamilton Ladies' College Alumnae Association*, 1, HPLA. The minute books of the Wesleyan Alumnae Association for the period prior to 1915 are missing, so I cannot confirm if Isabella was involved in any way after she left Hamilton.

41. Hamilton Public Library Files, R376.8 W518 WH, *Literary Club in connection with the Hamilton Ladies' College Alumnae Association*, Annual Report 1962–63, 1070, HPLA.

42. Hamilton Public Library Files, Hamilton Wesleyan College Archives File, Louise E. Purchase to Miss Waldon, October 26, 1962, "A Sketch of Janet (Nettie) T. Coatsworth Ramsey Mistress of English Literature, 1875–1879," LHA.

43. *Hamilton Herald*, June 29, 1927, 12.

44. Elizabeth Bailey Price Fonds, Accession No. M1000, File 2, "Lady Lougheed," 5, GAIA.

45. Arthur Ray, *The Canadian Fur Trade in the Industrial Age* (Toronto: University of Toronto Press, 1990), 26.

46. MacGregor, *Senator Hardisty's Prairies*. Members of Isabella's kinship network assisted the central Canadian government both in 1869–70 and in 1885. When fighting erupted in 1869 in Red River, Isabella's uncle, Donald A. Smith, was appointed by the Canadian government to travel to Red River in an attempt to resolve the dispute. Her other uncle, Richard Hardisty, interrupted his furlough and joined his brother-in-law

at Fort Garry, where he was promptly arrested by Riel's men, 70–71. Also Willson, *The Life of Lord Strathcona and Mount Royal*. While some accounts claim that both Donald A. Smith and Richard Hardisty were held prisoner when they arrived in Red River, Willson claimed that Hardisty, because he had "Indian blood in his veins," was allowed to consort freely with his Métis friends in the settlement. Willson continued that this freedom allowed Richard Hardisty to carry out Smith's mission to "secure partisans amongst the half-breeds" by offering them cash or promissory notes from the HBC, 327–28. Willson wrote that many old-timers later remembered that Donald Smith's life had been at great risk because he was an HBC man, 343. Also Gerhard Ens, *A Son of the Fur Trade: The Memoirs of Johnny Grant* (Edmonton: University of Alberta Press, 2008. Ens writes in the introduction that, according to Johnny Grant, who was in Red River in 1869–70, Richard Hardisty was not allowed to "consort freely," but rather his life was in as much danger as Donald Smith's, with violence only averted "through the mediation of the Catholic clergy," xviii.

47. Deborah Lougheed Research Disc, *Manitoba Free Press*, May 21, 1885, 1–4, LHA. Also McLaws Redman Lougheed and Cairns Fonds, Fond 37, File 173, Folder 2, William Lucas Hardisty Estate, certificate of death for Richard Hardisty, Province of Manitoba, Dept of Health and Public Welfare, May 12, 1885, issued April 12, 1930, the Legal Archives Society of Alberta.

48. Deborah Lougheed Research Disc, *Manitoba Free Press*, May 21,1885, 1–4, LHA.

49. Ibid., May 22, 1885, 5.

50. Ibid., May 28, 1885, 2.

51. Lougheed House Research Files, Chief Buffalo Child Long Lance, "Indians of the Northwest and West Canada," *The Mentor* 12, no. 3 (March 1924): 6, LHA. Also Donald B. Smith, *Chief Buffalo Child Long Lance:*

The Glorious Impostor (Red Deer: Red Deer Press, 1999). Smith explores Long Lance's real identity.

52.　Richard Hardisty Fonds, Accession No. M477, File 137, #808, letter to My dear Hardisty, December 22, 1876, GAIA. The author may have been R. MacFarlane, since other letters found in Richard Hardisty's files from the same location and with the same date are signed by MacFarlane.

CHAPTER TWO: IT TAKES A "HISTORICAL" VILLAGE

1.　In order to provide context to further understanding of Peter Lougheed's ancestry, sections of this chapter that discuss his grandfather's early life in Toronto and his arrival in the North-West draw on the author's earlier research, under copyright to Doris Jeanne MacKinnon, that supported and appeared in various publications including her Ph.D. dissertation, and articles and books with various publishers including University of Alberta Press, University of Toronto Press and *Canada's History*.

2.　Emil Longue Beau, "No. 45—Sir James Lougheed," *Star Weekly*, July 31, 1921, Newspaper Clippings File, LHA.

3.　David Bly, "Lougheed lists Alberta's key historic events," in *Calgary Herald*. Retrieved from IPL Exhibit Research, Box 1 of 3, Lougheed, Peter Speeches, LHA.

4.　Sir James Lougheed, Untitled, July 13, 1905, PAA, PR1997.0111 Lougheed Papers Box 8 111-121 Political Activities Lougheed Campaign, 1974-75.

5.　William Thorsell, "Straight from the feeling heart," *Edmonton Journal*, November 18, 1980. Retrieved from IPL Exhibit Research, Box 1 of 3, Lougheed, Peter Speeches, LHA.

6.　Donald B. Smith Collection, Lougheed James Biographical Dictionaries File, 31–40, LHA. Reference David J. Hall and Donald B. Smith, "Lougheed, Sir James Alexander," in *Dictionary of Canadian Biography* (DCB), vol. 15 (University of Toronto/

Université Laval, 2003–), http://www.biographi.ca/
en/bio/lougheed_james_alexander_15E.html. Also
J.M.S. Careless, "The Emergence of Cabbagetown in
Victorian Toronto," in *Gathering Place: Peoples and
Neighbourhoods of Toronto, 1834–1945*, ed. Robert F.
Harney (Toronto: Multicultural History Society of
Ontario, 1985), 25.

7. Hall and Smith, "Lougheed, Sir James Alexander."

8. Alan L. Hayes, *Holding Forth the Word of Life: Little
Trinity Church, 1842–1992* (Toronto: Corporation of
Little Trinity Church, 1991), 11.

9. Samuel's brother, Edward, later became premier of
Ontario and leader of the federal Liberals.

10. Donald B. Smith Collection, Lougheed James
1854–1925 Lougheed #1 Box 1, Newsletter Volume 4,
No. 2, November 1993, LHA. Also Donald B. Smith
Collection, Lougheed James Biographical Dictionary
File, 608, LHA. These reminiscences were reportedly
by cousins Jane and Elizabeth in 1936. Also Lougheed
Correspondence James & Bell File, Box 1, letter from
Donald Smith to Peter Lougheed, LHA. Smith writes
that Perkins Bull Papers Archives of Ontario inter-
viewed Jane Lougheed (1850–1939) and Elizabeth
Lougheed (1861–1947) in 1936. Reference Lougheed
Archives p36705. Also Donald B. Smith Collection,
Lougheed Toronto Trip File, Box 4, Lougheeds of
Britannia File, James Lougheed #1 Box 1, LHA.
Reference Ontario Archives Perkins Bull Collection
Series A. This file contains a copy of the interview.

11. J.R. Miller, *Shingwauk's Vision: A History of Native
Residential Schools* (Toronto: University of Toronto
Press, 1997), 140–41. Established in the 1880s, the
industrial schools aimed to assimilate Indigenous children in the classrooms, chapels, shops and farms. By
1910 the Department of Indian Affairs acknowledged
that there was no difference between boarding schools
and industrial schools.

12. Jennifer Bobrovitz Files, "James Lougheed Overview," James Lougheed #1 Box 1, LHA. Bobrovitz quotes Certificate, M4843, File 13, GAIA. Also Donald B. Smith Collection, Lougheeds of Britannia File, James Lougheed #1 Box 1, Correspondence of February 11, 1999, LHA. Correspondence dated March 2, 1999, notes that Sam continued in the family trade, becoming a carpenter and, for a time, teaching shop at residential schools established to house Indigenous students, both in Red Deer and Battleford. Also Donald B. Smith Collection, Samuel Lougheed File, LHA. Reference Walter J. Wasylow, *History of Battleford Industrial School for Indians* (Saskatoon: University of Saskatchewan, 1972), 346, 350, 354, 358. Wasylow writes that Sam Lougheed was a carpenter and Mrs. S. Lougheed the instructress at Battleford Industrial School from 1855 to 1897. However, these years may be wrong, as Charles D. Denney Papers, Richard Hardisty File M7144 #330,000 files 1 & 2, GAIA, indicates Sam Lougheed was transferred in the spring of 1895 to Battleford from Red Deer Industrial, where he had been since its opening in 1889.

13. Diary of James Lougheed, June 11, 1882, LHA.

14. Jennifer Bobrovitz Files, LHA. Reference Medicine Hat Archives, Thomas Tweed Family Fonds, 1884–1913.

15. Donald B. Smith Collection, Lougheeds of Britannia File, James Lougheed #1 Box 1, 35, LHA.

16. Marian C. McKenna, "Sir James Alexander Lougheed: Calgary's First Senator and City Builder," in *City Makers: Calgarians after the Frontier*, ed. Max Foran and Sheilagh S. Jamieson (Calgary: The Historical Society of Alberta, Chinook Country Chapter, 1987), 95–116. Reference Senate Debates, 15th Parliament, vol. 1 (January 12, 1926), 9. According to Senator G.D. Robertson, Lougheed's deskmate in the senate, James told him he arrived in Calgary on foot.

17. McKenna, "Sir James Alexander Lougheed." Although some accounts claim that James was the first lawyer to come to Calgary, McKenna writes there were at least three lawyers already in business in Calgary when James opened his practice, 98.

18. Donald B. Smith Collection, Lougheed Calgary 1883–89 File, LHA. Reference J. Fraser Perry, ed., *They Gathered at the River* (Calgary: Central United Church, 1975), 123.

19. Donald B. Smith Collection, Lougheeds of Britannia File, James Lougheed #1 Box 1, LHA. Reference newspaper article, no newspaper source listed.

20. Allan Hustak, *Peter Lougheed: A Biography* (Toronto: McClelland and Stewart, 1979), 12.

21. *Calgary Herald*, September 17, 1884. Also Jennifer Bobrovitz Files, chronological notes, 5, LHA. Reference McDougall Family Papers, Accession No. M732, File 12 or Folder 13, Methodist Church Mission, Morleyville, North West Territories, Marriage Register, GAIA.

22. George and John McDougall Fonds, Accession No. M729-74, GAIA. Also Donald B. Smith Collection, Calgary 1883–1889 File, LHA. Reference M485 Mrs. Wm Pearce, GAIA.

23. Donald B. Smith Collection, Lougheed James 1854–1925 File and Lougheed Drafts of Article File, Lougheed #1 Box 1, LHA. Reference James Grierson MacGregor, *Senator Hardisty's Prairies, 1849–1889* (Saskatoon: Western Producer Prairie Books, 1978), 194.

24. MacGregor, *Senator Hardisty's Prairies*, 223. While MacGregor does not provide footnotes for this, he does speak about a statement submitted by James Lougheed covering the period from May 1884 to April 1886, which lists several items that refer to debts owed to Richard Hardisty and to mortgages held on Calgary property.

25. Ibid., 137. Reference William Newton, *Twenty Years on the Saskatchewan* (London: Elliot Stock, 1897), 16. Given the partnership the McDougall family had with Richard on trading ventures, it is likely the Roman Catholic church was right to say that Richard Hardisty was influenced by the McDougall family to eject Roman Catholic missionaries from inside the Fort Edmonton palisades.

26. Donald B. Smith Collection, James Lougheed #1 Box 1, Lougheed Drafts of Article File, LHA. Smith writes, "In a statement submitted by his lawyer, James A. Lougheed, covering the period from May, 1884 to April, 1886, there are glimpses of some of [Hardisty's] personal dealings. Several items in Lougheed's statement refer to debts owed to Richard Hardisty and to mortgages he held on Calgary property." Reference MacGregor, *Senator Hardisty's Prairies*, 223.

27. McKenna, "Sir James Alexander Lougheed," 100.

28. Ibid., 101. *Calgary Herald*, March 13, 1936.

29. Emil Longue Beau, "No. 45—Sir James Lougheed," *Star Weekly*, July 31, 1921, Newspaper Clippings File, LHA.

30. *Calgary Tribune*, December 18, 1889, Newspaper Clippings File, LHA.

31. Ibid.

32. R.C. MacLeod and Heather Rollason Driscoll, "Natives, Newspapers and Crime Rates in the North-West Territories, 1878–1885," in *From Rupert's Land to Canada: Essays in Honour of John E. Foster*, ed. Theodore Binnema, Gerhard Ens and R.C. MacLeod (Edmonton: University of Alberta Press, 2001), 257.

33. Donald B. Smith Collection, James Lougheed #1 Box 1, LHA. Draft article for Online Dictionary August 1999, 3. Smith did not publish this comment in the online version of the biography on James. Also Donald B. Smith, Calgary's Grand Story: *The Making of a Prairie Metropolis from the Viewpoint of Two Heritage*

Buildings (Calgary: University of Calgary Press, 2005), 36. In this book, Smith spoke of this particular letter, writing that it demonstrated how well connected James now was. Just "three years removed from Toronto," James had a "surprising new acquaintance, his wife's uncle, Donald A. Smith."

34. Richard Hardisty Fonds, Accession No. M5908/1688, letter from James A. Lougheed to My Dear Mr. Hardisty, November 25, 1885, GAIA. Also Donald B. Smith Collection, Calgary 1883–1889 File, LHA.

35. Richard Hardisty Fonds, Accession No. M5908-1788, Series 23-7, GAIA. Edmund Taylor, "Ye Olde Tyme Tales and Valuable Historical Data," n.d. Also Shirlee Anne Smith, "Hardisty, Richard Charles," in *Dictionary of Canadian Biography*, vol. 11 (University of Toronto/Université Laval, 2003–), biographi.ca/en/bio/hardisty_richard_charles_11E.html. Smith writes that in January 1888, Hardisty was appointed acting inspector of the northern department of the HBC. Then in February 1888 he was appointed as the first senator for the district of Alberta, after having run unsuccessfully in the election of 1887 as an independent candidate.

36. Richard Hardisty Fonds, Accession No. M5908-1788, Series 23-7, GAIA. Taylor, "Ye Olde Tyme Tales"; Smith, "Hardisty, Richard Charles."

37. John Richards and Larry Pratt, *Prairie Capitalism: Power and Influence in the New West* (Toronto: McClelland and Stewart, 1979), 155.

38. Ibid.

39. Ibid., 154.

40. Hustak, *Peter Lougheed*, 22.

41. Ibid., 28.

42. Ibid., 25. Hustak speculates Douglas's death was a suicide but provides no references. Also "D.G. Lougheed Dies in City," *Calgary Herald*, October 16,

1931. Newspaper reports at the time simply stated that Douglas died in hospital "after an illness which had kept him in bed most of the summer."

43. "Clarence Lougheed, Prominent Native Calgarian, Is Dead: Son of Pioneer Family Expires in Bed Thursday Morning," *Calgary Daily Herald*, February 2, 1933; "Clarence Lougheed, Calgary Native Son Found Dead in Bed," *Morning Albertan*, February 3, 1933. Also *Morning Albertan*, February 6, 1933. Reportedly, "every walk of life" was represented at the graveside service held for Clarence, a man described as having a "warm heart and unselfish spirit."

44. Donald B. Smith Collection, Lougheed Box 1, Clarence Lougheed File, LHA. Reference David Mittelstadt, no book title.

45. *Morning Albertan*, October 14,1933.

46. *Calgary Daily Herald*, August 11, 1897.

47. Donald B. Smith Collection, Hardisty Box 1, Mary Hardisty 1840–1930 File, LHA. *Winnipeg Tribune*, May 1945, and Charles D. Denney Papers, GAIA.

48. For a comprehensive discussion of the challenges for Isabella's sons in managing her father's estate, see Doris Jeanne MacKinnon, *Metis Pioneers: Marie Rose Delorme Smith and Isabella Clark Hardisty* (Edmonton: University of Alberta Press, 2018).

49. University of Alberta Archives, "Peter Lougheed." Peter Lougheed fonds 2012-46, 4.

50. Peter C. Newman, *Titans: How the New Canadian Establishment Seized Power* (Toronto: Penguin Books, 1999), 453.

51. Arthur Mines, "Peter Lougheed, Up Close and Personal," *Kingston Whig-Standard*, May 10, 2002, 1, University of Alberta Archives, Peter Lougheed fonds 2012-46 Box 39 Lougheed File 2002-F-2.

52. MacKinnon, *Metis Pioneers*. The author explores the campaign that was launched to assure that James Lougheed would step into the vacant senate seat of Isabella's uncle.

53. University of Alberta Archives, Peter Lougheed fonds 2012-46, 17.

54. Joe Lougheed, interview by author January 8, 2020.

55. Ibid.

56. University of Alberta Archives, Peter Lougheed fonds 2012-46, 17.

57. Peter Lougheed, "Lougheed Laments Education Foul Up," excerpt taken from address to Queen's University Council, in *Edmonton Journal*, August 24, 2002, A17, University of Alberta Archives, Peter Lougheed fonds 2012-46 Box 39 Lougheed File 2002-F2.

58. Ibid.

59. Peter Lougheed, "Take Proud Aim on History," *Globe and Mail*, July 3, 2001, A11, in EPL Exhibit Research, Box 1 of 3, Lougheed, Peter Clippings, LHA.

60. "A Canadian Career: An Interview with Peter Lougheed," *Canadian Business Review*, Autumn 1996, 14, in EPL Exhibit Research Box, LHA.

61. Newman, *Titans*, 457.

62. Cam Morton, "Peter Lougheed: Public Lives and Private Moments," University of Alberta Archives, Peter Lougheed fonds 2012-46-T16.

63. "Canadian Women in the Public Eye," *Saturday Night*, September 16, 1922, Newspaper Clippings File, LHA.

64. Ibid.

65. Ibid.

66. While Trudy Cowan, the former director of the Lougheed House National Historic Site, once stated Isabella did smoke a pipe, archivist Amanda Kriaski noted this has not been confirmed in any documentation and may be an example of "folklore."

67. "Canadian Women in the Public Eye," *Saturday Night*, September 16, 1922, Newspaper Clippings File, LHA.

68. "A Canadian Career: An Interview with Peter Lougheed," *Canadian Business Review*, Autumn 1996,13, in EPL Exhibit Research Box, LHA.

69. Peter Lougheed, "Acceptance by The Hon. Peter Lougheed P.C., C.C., Q.C.," 1998, addressing the Churchill Society, University of Alberta Archives, Peter Lougheed fonds 2012-46 Box 36 Lougheed File 1198-F1.

70. Joe Lougheed, interview by author, January 20, 2020.

71. Calgary Legal Guidance Legal Humanitarian of the Year Award Dinner, 1987, University of Alberta Archives, Peter Lougheed fonds 2012-46 Box 29 Lougheed 1987-F1.

72. Parks Canada, "Beaulieu II, François National Historic Person," Directory of Federal Heritage Designations, pc.gc.ca/apps/dfhd/page_nhs_eng.aspx?id=1896.

73. Donald B. Smith Collection, Mary Allen Hardisty 1840–1930 File, Hardisty Box 1, LHA. Reference Charles D. Denney Papers, Richard Hardisty, Accession No. M7144, File 330,000 (1 and 2), Valerie Dartnell to unknown, September 11, 1973, GAIA. Dartnell wrote that Mary Allen "said she was French, but my mother didn't think so. She looked like a native."

74. Donald B. Smith Collection, Mary Allen Correspondence File, LHA. Reference McCord Museum, Notman Collection, catalogue number NA-2758-1, source Mrs. L. Morrison, Calgary.

75. Joe Lougheed, interview by author, January 8, 2020.

76. University of Alberta Archives, Peter Lougheed fonds 2012-46, 17.

77. Joe Lougheed, interview by author, January 8, 2020.

78. "Fort Resolution," University of Alberta Archives, Peter Lougheed fonds 2012-46, Box 8 Lougheed, File 1975 – F4.

79. Joe Lougheed, interview by author, January 8, 2020.

80. Alan Hustak, *Peter Lougheed*, 75.

81. Minutes of Meeting of Communications Committee Held in Palliser Hotel on August 21, 1965, PAA, PR1997.0111 Lougheed Papers Box 9 122-135 The PC Election Campaign 1965–1971, 4.

82. Alan Hustak, *Peter Lougheed*, 76.

83. Progressive Conservative Party of Alberta, "Press Release," May 15, 1967, University of Alberta Archives, Peter Lougheed fonds 2012-46 Box 2 File 1967-F1.

84. Joe Lougheed, interview by author, January 8, 2020.

85. Eva Reid, "Eavesdrop," *The Albertan*, August 6, 1976, 8. Retrieved from University of Alberta Archives, Peter Lougheed fonds 2012-46 Box 8, File 1976-F1.

86. Trudy Soby, *Be It Ever So Humble* (Calgary: Century Calgary Publications, 1975), 9.

87. Paul Voisey, "Entrepreneurs in Early Calgary," in *Frontier Calgary: Town, City, and Region, 1875–1914*, ed. Anthony W. Rasporich and Henry Cornelius Klassen (Calgary: McClelland and Stewart West, 1975), 240.

88. "Lougheed's Lesson," *Calgary Herald*, May 17, 1994, University of Alberta Archives, Peter Lougheed fonds 2012-46 Box 33 Lougheed 1994-F1.

CHAPTER THREE: MÉTIS ACTIVISM IN ALBERTA

1. Metis Settlements of Alberta, "A Metis homeland in Alberta. A Constitutional first in Canada," msgc.ca/.

2. Alberta Register of Historic Places, "Buffalo Lake Métis Settlement," Hermis Heritage Resources Management Information System, hermis.alberta.ca/ARHP/Details. aspx?DeptID=1&ObjectID=4665-0280.

3. Lawrence Barkwell, "Tail Creek, Alberta Metis Scrip Claims," SCRIBD, scribd.com/document/ 111361558/Tail-Creek-Alberta-Metis-Scrip-Claims.

4. William C. Wonders, "Far Corner of the Strange Empire: Central Alberta on the Eve of Homestead Settlement," *Great Plains Quarterly* (Spring 1983): 91-108, core.ac.uk/download/pdf/188079577.pdf.

5. Lawrence J. Barkwell, "Battle River Metis Settlements," SCRIBD, scribd.com/document/114043443/Battle-River-Metis-Settlements.

6. Ibid.

7. Musee Heritage Museum, "The Mission," museeheritage.ca/heritage-sites/founders-walk/the-mission/

8. Yvon Beaudoin, "Saint-Albert, Alberta, Canada, from 1861," OMIWorld, omiworld.org/lemma/saint-albert-alberta-canada-1861/.

9. Government of Alberta, "Father Lacombe Chapel," fatherlacombechapel.ca/about. Also Alberta Register of Historic Places, "Father Lacombe Church," Hermis Heritage Resources Management Information System, hermis.alberta.ca/ARHP/Details.aspx?DeptID=1&ObjectID=4665-0212.

10. Canada's Historic Places, "Father Lacombe Church," historicplaces.ca/en/rep-reg/place-lieu.aspx?id=5004.

11. Alberta Register of Historic Places, "Baptiste River Métis Settlement Site," Hermis Heritage Resources Management Information System, hermis.alberta.ca/ARHP/Details.aspx?DeptID=1&ObjectID=4665-0290.

12. Chantal A. Roy Denis, "Wolf Lake: The Importance of Métis Connection to Land and Place" (master's thesis, University of Alberta, 2017), era.library.ualberta.ca/items/16ccd632-3412-4e2d-81e2-abdc8b9de045.

13. Trudy Nicks and Kenneth Morgan, "Grande Cache: The Historic Development of an Indigenous Population," in *The New Peoples: Being and Becoming Métis in North America*, ed. Jacqueline Peterson and Jennifer S.H. Brown (Lincoln: University of Nebraska Press, 1985), 163–84. Also Margaret Inoue, "Who Are the Métis: Olive Dickason and the Emergence of a Métis Historiography in the 1970s and 1980s" (master's thesis, University of British Columbia, 2004), open.library.ubc.ca/cIRcle/collections/ubctheses/831/items/1.0091598.

14. Mountain Metis website, mountainmetis.com/.

15. Nathalie Kermoal, "From Saint Paul des Métis to Saint Paul: A Patch of Franco-Albertan History," *Encyclopedia of French Cultural Heritage in North America*, ameriquefrancaise.org/en/article-706/From_Saint_Paul_des_Métis_to_Saint_Paul:_A_Patch_of_Franco-Albertan_History.html. Also Carl Betke and Nathan Baker, "St. Paul," The Canadian Encyclopedia (2009; update October 26, 2020), thecanadianencyclopedia.ca/en/article/st-paul.

16. Oblates (Oblati) is a word used to describe the religious congregation of priests and brothers set aside for special missionary work of the Roman Catholic church. They are essentially missionaries who work in many countries. François Blanchin, "Oblates of Mary Immaculate," Catholic Encyclopedia, vol. 11 (New York: Robert Appleton Co., 1911), https://www.newadvent.org/cathen/11184b.htm.

17. Heather Devine, *The People Who Own Themselves: Aboriginal Ethnogenesis in a Canadian Family, 1660–1900* (Calgary: University of Calgary Press, 2014), 183–84.

18. Alexandra Olshefsky, "Revisionist History: St. Paul des Metis," McGill Human Rights Interns, 2013, blogs. mcgill.ca/humanrightsinterns/2013/06/843.

19. "Laurent Garneau Monument," Edmonton Maps Heritage, edmontonmapsheritage.ca/location/ laurent-garneau-monument/.

20. "The Garneau Tree," University of Alberta Faculty of Native Studies, ualberta.ca/native-studies/research/ rupertsland-centre-for-metis-research/news-and-events/news/the-garneau-tree.html/.

21. "Remembering Laurent Garneau and Métis Heritage," Nation Talk, April 10, 2008, nationtalk.ca/story/ remembering-laurent-garneau-and-metis-heritage.

22. James Brady, "The St. Paul Half-Breed Reserve," Gabriel Dumont Institute Virtual Museum, https://www.metis-museum.ca/resource.php/03835.

23. Caleb Anacker, Tanya Fontaine, Megan Tucker, Pierre Lamoureux, Goddy Nzonji and Roy Missal, *Restoring the History of St. Paul de Métis: Understanding Métis Perspectives* (St. Paul: St. Paul Community Learning Association, 2020). Also Jeff Gaye, "St. Paul des Métis history book aims to heal old divisions," Respect News, January 26, 2021, respectnews.ca/news/st-paul-des-metis-history-book-aims-to-heal-old-divisions/.

24. Quoted in Métis Settlements General Council, *Making History: Our Land. Our Culture. Our Future*, metissettlements.files.wordpress.com/2017/01/msgc_centennial_book.pdf.

25. Lawrence J. Barkwell, "Rooster Town: A Métis Road Allowance Community," Gabriel Dumont Institute Virtual Museum, January 3, 2008, metismuseum.ca/ resource.php/07242.

Notes

26. Maria Campbell, "Foreword: Charting the Way," in *Contours of a People: Metis Family, Mobility, and History*, ed. Brenda Macdougall, Carolyn Podruchny and Nicole St-Onge (Norman: University of Oklahoma Press, 2012), xiii–xiv.

27. Canadian Geographic, "Activism 1950s to 1970s," *Indigenous Peoples Atlas of Canada*, indigenouspeoplesatlasofcanada.ca/article/activism-1950s-to-1970s/.

28. Amanda Robinson and Michelle Filice, "Métis Scrip in Canada," *The Canadian Encyclopedia* (2018; update October 2, 2019), https://www.thecanadianencyclopedia.ca/en/article/metis-scrip-in-canada. In 2013, the Supreme Court of Canada ruled that the federal government failed to provide the Métis with the land grant they were promised in the *Manitoba Act of 1870*.

29. Gerhard Ens, *A Son of the Fur Trade: The Memoirs of Johnny Grant* (Edmonton: University of Alberta Press, 2008).

30. Parks Canada, "Smith, Sir Donald A. (Lord Strathcona) National Historic Person," Directory of Federal Heritage Designations, pc.gc.ca/apps/dfhd/page_nhs_eng.aspx?id=1426.

31. Royal Commission on the Condition of the Halfbreed Population of the Province of Alberta, "To The Honourable The Lieutenant Governor in Council Edmonton," on the Métis Settlements of Alberta website, https://msgc.ca/wp-content/uploads/2019/10/Ewing-Commission-report-1.pdf.

32. Canadian Geographic, "Métis Settlements and Farms," *Indigenous Peoples Atlas of Canada*, https://indigenouspeoplesatlasofcanada.ca/article/metis-settlements-and-farms/.

33. Nicole C. O'Byrne, "No other weapon except organization": The Métis Association of Alberta and the 1938 Metis Population Betterment Act," *Journal of the Canadian Historical Association* 24, no. 2 (2013):

311–52, erudit.org/en/journals/jcha/1900-v1-n1-jchao1408/1025081ar/.

34.   Ibid.

35.   Canadian Geographic, "Métis Settlements and Farms," *Indigenous Peoples Atlas of Canada*, indigenouspeoplesatlasofcanada.ca/article/metis-settlements-and-farms/.

36.   Victoria Callihoo, "Early Life in Lac Ste. Anne and St. Albert in the 1870s," *Alberta Historical Review* 1, no. 3 (1953): 21–26; Victoria Callihoo, "The Iroquois in Alberta," *Alberta Historical Review* 7, no. 2 (1959): 17–18; Victoria Callihoo, "Our Buffalo Hunts," *Alberta Historical Review* 8, no. 1 (1960): 24–25.

37.   Lawrence Barkwell, "Callihoo (Belcourt), Victoria Anne," Gabriel Dumont Institute Virtual Museum, metismuseum.ca/resource.php/13921.

38.   Coral Taylor, *Victoria Callihoo: An Amazing Life* (Edmonton: Eschia Books Inc., 2008).

39.   Doris Jeanne MacKinnon, *The Identities of Marie Rose Delorme Smith: Portrait of a Métis Woman, 1861–1960* (Regina: Canadian Plains Research Center, 2012). In January 2023, Marie Rose was designated as a person of national historic significance by the Historic Sites and Monuments Board of Canada: https://www.newswire.ca/news-releases/government-of-canada-recognizes-the-national-historic-significance-of-marie-rose-delorme-smith-889534799.html.

40.   Nancy Millar, *Remember Me as You Pass By: Stories From Prairie Graveyards* (Glenbow Museum, 1994), 136–37. Also "Pioneer Pilot Crosses the Bar at 72 Years: Captain Shott, Most Picturesque of Northern Sailors, Dies at Athabasca," *Calgary Albertan*, June 2, 1914. Also *Edmonton Sun*, April 3, 2000, interview with historian E. David Gregory. Also Henry Thompson, "Louis Fosseneuve, later known as Captain Shot," in *Lac La Biche Yesterday and Today* (Lac La Biche

Heritage Society, 1975), 23. Also Janey Canuck (Emily Murphy), *Seeds of Pine* (1914), Archives.org. Also Robert Service, "Athabaska Dick," in *Rhymes of a Rolling Stone* (1912), www.gutenberg.org/files/309/309-h/309-h.htm

41. Bruce Cinnamon, The "Grand Lady of the Metis": Dr. Anne Anderson's mission to preserve the Cree language," Edmonton City as Museum Project, November 10, 2020, citymuseumedmonton. ca/2020/11/10/the-grand-lady-of-the-metis-dr-anne-andersons-mission-to-preserve-the-cree-language.

42. Lisa Kozleski, "Passion and Purpose: Thelma Chalifoux Changed, Challenged and 'Set on Fire' in the Canadian Senate," *Wider Horizons* (Fall 2014), lethbridgecollege. ca/wider-horizons/fall-2014/passion-and-purpose-thelma-chalifoux-changed-challenged-and-set-fire.

43. Kevin Ma, "Edmonton Public names school after Thelma Chalifoux," *St. Albert Today*, May 11, 2018, stalberttoday.ca/local-news/ edmonton-public-names-school-thelma-chalifoux-1298649.

44. *An Act Respecting the Metis Population of the Province*, SA 1938(2), c 6, November 22, 1938, https://canlii.ca/t/540xk.

45. Jean Teillet, *The North-West is Our Mother: The Story of Louis Riel's People, the Métis Nation* (Toronto: HarperCollins Canada, 2019).

46. "Lougheed Is Really an Indian," *Castor Advance*, February 24, 1977. Retrieved from University of Alberta Archives, Peter Lougheed fonds 2012-46 Box 10 Lougheed File 1977-F1 Folder 1.

47. Chris Anderson, *"Metis": Race, Recognition, and the Struggle for Indigenous Peoplehood* (Vancouver: UBC Press, 2014), 5.

48. Brenda Macdougall, "Metis means much more than 'mixed blood,'" CBC Radio, April 25, 2019, https://www.cbc.ca/radio/ unreserved/from-scrip-to-road-allowances-canada- s-complicated-history-with-the-métis-1.5100375/ métis-means-much-more-than-mixed-blood-1.5100783.

49. Brenda Macdougall, *One of the Family: Metis Culture in Nineteenth-Century Saskatchewan* (Vancouver: UBC Press, 2010), 242.

50. Devine, *The People Who Own Themselves*, xi.

51. Nicole St-Onge, *Saint-Laurent, Manitoba: Evolving Metis Identities, 1830–1914* (Regina: Canadian Plains Research Center, 2004).

52. Anderson, *"Metis": Race, Recognition, and the Struggle for Indigenous Peoplehood*, 6.

53. "Virtual Exhibition—Hiding in Plain Sight," Library and Archives Canada, bac-lac.gc.ca/eng/discover/ aboriginal-heritage/metis/Pages/metis-nation- collection-lac.aspx.

54. Rhiannon Johnson, "Exploring Identity: Who Are the Métis and What Are Their Rights?" CBC News, April 28, 2019, cbc.ca/news/indigenous/ metis-identity-history-rights-explainer-1.5098585.

55. Heather Conn, "Daniels Case," *The Canadian Encyclopedia* (January 18, 2019), thecanadianencyclo- pedia.ca/en/article/daniels-case.

56. Metis Settlements of Alberta website, msgc.ca.

57. Adam Gaudry, Mary Agnes Welch and David Gallant, "Métis," *The Canadian Encyclopedia* (2009; update January 13, 2023), thecanadianencyclopedia. ca/en/article/metis. Also Government of Canada, "Canada-Métis Nation Accord," pm.gc.ca/en/ canada-metis-nation-accord.

1. Dr. Donald B. Smith made this comment on several occasions in reference to his research into the life of John A. Macdonald. Most recently, Smith has noted that "the story of Sir John A. Macdonald (1815–1891) is both very complex and very large." Donald B. Smith, *Seen But Not Seen: Influential Canadians and the First Nations from the 1840s to Today* (Toronto: University of Toronto Press, 2021), 4.

2. Smith, *Seen But Not Seen*, 38.

3. Harold Innis, *The Fur Trade in Canada* (1930; repr. Toronto: University of Toronto Press, 1999). Innis was the first to formulate the argument that Canada existed primarily because of its geography and its reliance on the export of various staples including cod, lumber and, most importantly, fur.

4. Richard Foot and Andrew McIntosh, "Editorial: The Stanley Flag and the 'Distinctive Canadian Symbol,'" *The Canadian Encyclopedia* (2014; update November 29, 2019), thecanadianencyclopedia.ca/en/article/the-stanley-flag.

5. George F.G. Stanley, *The Birth of Western Canada: A History of the Riel Rebellions* (1936; repr. Toronto: University of Toronto Press, 1961), vii. Quoted in Doris J. MacKinnon, *The Identities of Marie Rose Delorme Smith: Portrait of a Métis Woman, 1861–1960* (Regina: Canadian Plains Research Center, 2012), 40.

6. Aritha Van Herk, *Mavericks: An Incorrigible History of Alberta* (Toronto: Penguin Random House, 2002).

7. David Robertson, "Last Best West," *Encyclopedia of the Great Plains*, plainshumanities.unl.edu/encyclopedia/doc/egp.ii.038.

8. Bradford J. Rennie, ed., *Alberta Premiers of the Twentieth Century* (Regina: Canadian Plains Research Center, 2004), xiii.

9. David C. Jones, *Empire of Dust: Settling and Abandoning the Prairie Dry Belt* (Calgary: University of Calgary Press, 2002), 21. Quoted in Doris Jeanne MacKinnon, *Metis Pioneers: Marie Rose Delorme Smith and Isabella Clark Hardisty Lougheed* (Edmonton: University of Alberta Press, 2018), 146. Also Jean Bruce, "The Last Best West: Advertising for Immigrants to Western Canada, 1870–1930," Canadian Museum of History, historymuseum.ca/cmc/exhibitions/hist/advertis/ads1-01e.html.

10. See, for example, W.L. Morton, "The Canadian Métis," in *Contexts of Canada's Past: Selected Essays of W.L. Morton*, ed. A.B. McKillop (Toronto: Macmillan of Canada, 1980); Innis, *The Fur Trade in Canada*; and Stanley, *The Birth of Western Canada*.

11. Marcel Giraud, *The Métis in the Canadian West*, trans. George Woodcock (1945; repr., Edmonton: University of Alberta Press, 1986).

12. Brenda Macdougall, "The Myth of Metis Cultural Ambivalence," in *Contours of a People: Metis Family, Mobility, and History*, ed. Nicole St-Onge, Carolyn Podruchny and Brenda Macdougall (Norman: University of Oklahoma Press, 2012), 433. Reference to Marcel Giraud, *Les Métis Canadiens*, 329.

13. Morton, "The Canadian Métis," 61.

14. Ibid., 62.

15. Innis, *The Fur Trade in Canada*.

16. Arthur Ray, *Indians in the Fur Trade* (1974; repr., Toronto: University of Toronto Press, 1998). Also Carol M. Judd and Arthur J. Ray, eds., *Old Trails and New Directions: Papers of the Third North American Fur Trade Conference* (Toronto: University of Toronto Press, 1980). This anthology demonstrated the quickening pace of fur trade research, which was now becoming interdisciplinary, with studies within archaeology, economics, ethnohistory, geography, history and

anthropology.

17. John Foster, "The Métis: The People and the Term," Prairie Forum 3, no. 1 (1978): 79–90.

18. Sylvia Van Kirk, *"Many Tender Ties": Women in Fur-Trade Society, 1670–1870* (Winnipeg: Watson & Dwyer Publishing Ltd., 1980).

19. Jennifer S.H. Brown, "Women as Centre and Symbol in the Emergence of Métis Communities," *Canadian Journal of Native Studies* 3, no. 1 (1983): 39–46. Another major study was Brown's *Strangers in Blood: Fur Trade Company Families in Indian Country* (Vancouver: UBC Press, 1980).

20. Jacqueline Peterson, "Many Roads to Red River: Métis Ethnogenesis in the Great Lakes Region, 1680–1815," in *The New Peoples: Being and Becoming Métis in North America*, ed. Jacqueline Peterson and Jennifer S.H. Brown (Winnipeg: University of Manitoba Press, 1985), 37–72. Peterson saw the interrelationships of family and community as personal and social constructs.

21. Lucy Eldersveld Murphy, *A Gathering of Rivers: Indians, Métis and Mining in the Western Great Lakes, 1727–1832* (Lincoln: University of Nebraska Press, 2004).

22. Tanis C. Thorne, *The Many Hands of My Relations: French and Indians on the Lower Missouri* (Columbia: University of Missouri Press, 1996).

23. Susan Sleeper-Smith, *Indian Women and French Men: Rethinking Cultural Encounter in the Western Great Lakes* (Amherst: University of Massachusetts Press, 2001).

24. Susan Sleeper-Smith, "Women, Kin, and Catholicism," *Ethnohistory* 47, no. 2 (2000): 423–52.

25. Ibid.

26. Sarah Carter, *The Importance of Being Monogamous: Marriage and Nation Building in Western Canada to*

1915 (Edmonton: University of Alberta Press, 2008). As many historians have now concluded, the concept of punishing Indigenous women for "marrying out" was a manifestation of the *Indian Act*, instituted in 1876 and aimed at both saving money and forcing Indigenous people to adopt Christian European standards of patriarchal and monogamous marital unions.

27. Sylvia Van Kirk, "Toward a Feminist Perspective in Native History," *Centre for Women's Studies in Education Occasional Papers* no. 14 (1987): 6.

28. For one recent study, see Nathalie Kermoal, *Un passé métis au féminin* (Québec: Les Éditions GID, 2006).

29. Heather Devine, *The People Who Own Themselves: Aboriginal Ethnogenesis in a Canadian Family, 1660–1900* (Calgary: University of Calgary Press, 2004).

30. Brenda Macdougall, *One of the Family: Metis Culture in Nineteenth-Century Northwestern Saskatchewan* (Vancouver: UBC Press, 2009), 242.

213

31. Martha Harroun Foster, *We Know Who We Are: Métis Identity in a Montana Community* (Norman: University of Oklahoma Press, 2006), 205. Harroun Foster studied the group of Red River and Pembina Métis who went to the Judith Basin area of central Montana to found Lewisten in 1879. The United States government negotiated with these people as a segment of Chippewa society.

32. Ibid.

33. Ibid., 207.

34. Ibid., 220.

35. Thorne, *The Many Hands of My Relations*. Thorne studied kinship networks between Creoles and Central Siouan people along the lower Missouri River up to the removal era in the 1870s.

36. Harroun Foster, *We Know Who We Are*, 220.

37. Ibid., 9.

38. Melinda M. Jetté, "Ordinary Lives: Three Generations of a French-Indian Family in Oregon, 1827–1931" (master's thesis, Université Laval, 1996), 127.

39. Devine, *The People Who Own Themselves.*

40. Brenda Macdougall, "*Wahkootowin*: Family and Cultural Identity in Northwestern Saskatchewan Metis Communities," *Canadian Historical Review* 87, no. 3 (2006): 434.

41. Chris Anderson, *"Métis": Race, Recognition, and the Struggle for Indigenous Peoplehood* (Vancouver: UBC Press, 2014), 24. Jean Teillet, a descendant of Louis Riel, also makes this argument in several of her publications.

42. Nicole St-Onge and Carolyn Podruchny, "Scuttling Along a Spider's Web: Mobility and Kinship in Metis Ethnogenesis," in *Contours of a People: Metis Family, Mobility, and History*, ed. Nicole St-Onge, Carolyn Podruchny and Brenda Macdougall (Norman: University of Oklahoma Press, 2012), 80.

43. Peter Bakker, *A Language of Our Own: The Genesis of Michif, the Mixed Cree-French Language of the Canadian Métis* (New York: Oxford University Press, 1997), 53.

44. Adam Gaudry, "Métis Are a People, Not a Historical Process," *The Canadian Encyclopedia* (June 21, 2016), thecanadianencyclopedia.ca/en/article/metis-are-a-people-not-a-historical-process.

45. Denis Gagnon, "The 'Other' Métis," *Canadian Encyclopedia* (June 21, 2016), thecanadianencyclopedia.ca/en/article/the-other-metis.

46. Theda Perdue, introduction to *Sifters: Native American Women's Lives*, ed. Theda Perdue (New York: Oxford University Press, 2001), 5.

47. Sarah Carter and Patricia A. McCormack, eds., *Recollecting: Lives of Aboriginal Women of the*

Canadian Northwest and Borderlands (Edmonton: Athabasca University Press, 2011).

48. Gloria Jane Bell, "Oscillating Identities: Re-presentation of Métis in the Great Lakes Area in the Nineteenth Century," in *Métis in Canada: History, Identity, Law and Politics*, ed. Christopher Adams, Gregg Dahl and Ian Peach (Edmonton: University of Alberta Press, 2013), 8.

49. Christopher Adams, Gregg Dahl and Ian Peach, eds., *Métis in Canada: History, Identity, Law and Politics* (Edmonton: University of Alberta Press, 2013), xv.

50. Gerhard Ens and Joe Sawchuk, New Peoples to New Nations: *Aspects of Metis History and Identity from the Eighteenth to Twenty-First Century* (Toronto: University of Toronto Press, 2016), 4.

51. Sherry Farrell Racette, "Sewing for a Living: The Commodification of Métis Women's Artistic Production," in *Contact Zones: Aboriginal and Settler Women in Canada's Colonial Past*, ed. Katie Pickles and Myra Rutherdale (Vancouver: UBC Press, 2005), 17–46.

52. Brown, "Women as Centre," 41.

53. Racette, "Sewing for a Living," 5.

54. Sleeper-Smith, *Indian Women and French Men*, 4.

55. Adams, Dahl and Peach, *Métis in Canada*, xviii.

56. Laura-Lee Kearns, "(Re)claiming Métis Women Identities: Three Stories and the Storyteller," in *Métis in Canada: History, Identity, Law and Politics*, ed. Christopher Adams, Gregg Dahl and Ian Peach (Edmonton: University of Alberta Press, 2013), 59–92.

57. Ibid., 60.

58. Anderson, *"Métis": Race, Recognition, and the Struggle for Indigenous Peoplehood*.

59. Lawrence Barkwell, "Lougheed, Peter, PC, CC, AOE, QC," Gabriel Dumont Institute Virtual Museum, June 13, 2012, metismuseum.ca/resource.php/13483. Source includes documentation verifying scrip for William Lucas Hardisty (file 1404822) and Frank Allen Hardisty (file 1404822).

60. Adam Gaudry, Mary Agnes Welch and David Gallant, "Metis," *The Canadian Encyclopedia* (2009; update January 13, 2023), thecanadianencyclopedia.ca/en/article/metis.

61. Donna McDonald, *Lord Strathcona: A Biography of Donald Alexander Smith* (Toronto: Dundurn Press, 1996), 448. Reference letter from Minto to Peter Elliot (his brother), November 30, 1901, MG 27 II BI, vol 35, Library and Archives Canada.

62. McDonald, *Lord Strathcona*, 358–62. Isabella Hardisty Smith and her husband, Donald, worked hard at carving a position of importance for themselves. Part of that networking involved making rather large endowments to many causes. For example, in 1883, Isabella and Donald donated $30,000 to the Trafalgar Institute, a boarding school for Protestant girls in Montreal. In 1884, when the board of McGill University still hesitated to admit women as students, the couple donated $50,000 in order to establish an endowment fund for women's education. In 1886, the Smiths provided a further $70,000 so that the third and fourth years of women's degrees could be offered. They continued as benefactors through the establishment of the Royal Victoria College for Women.

63. Ibid., 402.

64. Alan Hustak, *Peter Lougheed* (Toronto: McClelland and Stewart, 1979), 12.

65. Digital Museums Canada, "Conflicting Loyalties: The Hardisty Family Legacy," Community Stories, communitystories.ca/v2/conflicting-loyalties_allegeances-contradictoires/story/identity/#_ftn4.

66. Métis Nation of Ontario, "Otipemisiwak," February 18, 2020, https://www.metisnation.org/news/otipemisiwak/.

67. Gerald Friesen, *The Canadian Prairies: A History* (Toronto: University of Toronto Press, 1987), 23.

68. Parks Canada, "Grant, Cuthbert National Historic Person," Directory of Federal Heritage Designations, pc.gc.ca/apps/dfhd/page_nhs_eng.aspx?id=962.

69. Sheila McManus, *The Line Which Separates: Race, Gender, and the* Making of the Alberta–Montana Borderlands (Lincoln: University of Nebraska Press, 2005), 149. Reference Mary Inderwick to sister-in-law Alice, ca. fall 1884, correspondence 1883–91, M559, GAIA.

70. Jennifer S.H. Brown, "Linguistic Solitudes and Changing Social Categories," in *Old Trails and New Directions: Papers of the Third North American Fur Trade Conference*, ed. Carol M. Judd and Arthur J. Ray (Toronto: University of Toronto Press, 1980), 150–51. By the time Inderwick arrived in 1833, the terms "squaw" and "Half-breed" had become more commonplace and uncomplimentary.

71. McManus, *The Line Which Separates*, 150. Another early settler, Carolyn Abbott Tyler, while denouncing the "Indians" as "savage," provided elaborate descriptions of Indigenous customs and artefacts but did not identify how she came to know those details. By not revealing her sources, perhaps Tyler was inadvertently admitting she had witnessed some of those customs herself but preferred to maintain a physical separation for the benefit of her readers, 153.

72. Sarah Carter, *Capturing Women: The Manipulation of Cultural Imagery in Canada's Prairie West* (Montreal/Kingston: McGill-Queen's University Press, 1997), 159.

73. McManus, *The Line Which Separates*, 143.

74. Ibid., 140.

75. Sheila McManus, "Unsettled Pasts, Unsettling Borders: Women, Wests, Nations," in *One Step Over the Line: Toward a History of Women in North American Wests*, ed. Elizabeth Jameson and Sheila McManus (Edmonton and Athabasca: University of Alberta Press and Athabasca University Press, 2008), 38. Reference Inderwick, diary entry October 29, 1883, M559, GAIA.

76. McManus, *The Line Which Separates*, 141.

77. Ibid., 144.

78. Ibid., 116.

79. Judith Hudson Beattie and Helen M. Buss, eds., *Undelivered Letters to Hudson's Bay Company Men on the Northwest Coast of America, 1830–1857* (Vancouver: UBC Press, 2003), 42.

80. Diane P. Payment, *"The Free People—Otipemisiwak": Batoche, Saskatchewan 1870–1930* (Hull: Supply and Services Canada, 1990), xvii.

81. John Portwood, "Private and Enterprising," *Calgary* (July 1980): 10, in University of Alberta Archives, Peter Lougheed fonds 2012-46 Box 28 Lougheed File 1986-F2.

82. Joe Lougheed, interview by author, January 8, 2020.

83. Gillian Lindgren, "Friend of the Bloods, Lougheed Made Chief," *Calgary Herald*, July 22, 1974. Retrieved from University of Alberta Archives, Peter Lougheed fonds 2012-46 Box 6 File 1974 F1.

84. Kainai Chieftainship, "Crop Eared Wolf," Image and Naming Document Presented to Peter Lougheed, University of Alberta Archives, Peter Lougheed fonds 2012-46 O.S. 6.

85. Lindgren, "Friend of the Bloods, Lougheed Made Chief."

86. Peter Lougheed, Letter to Head Chief Him Shot-Both-Sides, July 24, 1974, University of Alberta Archives,

Peter Lougheed fonds 2012-46 Box 36 Lougheed File 1998-F9.

87. Hugh Dempsey, *Tribal Honors: A History of the Kainai Chieftainship* (Calgary: Kainai Chieftainship, 1997), 19.

88. Dempsey, *Tribal Honors*, 25.

89. Kainai Chieftainship, "The Story of the Kainai Chieftainship and the Blood Indian Tribe of the Blackfoot Confederacy from Standoff, Alberta," January 2, 1984. Retrieved from University of Alberta Archives, Peter Lougheed fonds 2012-46 Box 6 File 1974 F5.

90. Alberta Memorandum, from Harold E. Millican to Honourable Peter Lougheed, July 9, 1974, PAA PR1985.0401/1642 PR22071974 Kanai.

91. Dempsey, *Tribal Honors*, 55–56.

92. Peter Linehan, ed., *St. John's College Cambridge: A History* (Woodbridge: Boyden Press, 2011), 441. Harry Richard Ragg, ordained in 1912, was educated at Hereford Cathedral School and St. John's College in Cambridge. Also Glenbow Museum Archives, Image NA-2746-5.

93. Dempsey, *Tribal Honors*, 71. Taken from letter, Ragg to Gooderham, February 8, 1958, KCP/M6812.

94. Dempsey, *Tribal Honors*, 74; *Lethbridge Herald*, June 28, 1960.

95. Jay Smith, "Peter Lougheed on Leadership," *Athabasca University Magazine*, 710, University of Alberta Archives, Peter Lougheed fonds 2012-46 Box 28 Lougheed File 1986-F1.

96. Dempsey, *Tribal Honors*, 74.

97. Kainai Chieftainship, Minutes of Meeting, Blood Tribal Council Chambers, February 15, 1975, University of Alberta Archives, Peter Lougheed fonds 2012-46 Box 36 Lougheed, File 1998-F9.

98.   Conversation between author and historian Donald B. Smith.

99.   Ric Dolphin, "From Wards of the State to Third Order of Government," in *Alberta in the 20th Century*, ed. Paul Bunner, vol. 12, *Alberta Takes the Lead* (Edmonton: History Book Publications Ltd., 2003), 90.

100. Joe Lougheed, interview by author, January 8, 2020.

101. Ibid. Joe Lougheed asserts that had it not been for Peter Lougheed's championing of Section 35 itself, there is a good chance it would not have been included, resulting in no recognition of Indigenous status for the Metis and no constitutional protection of Indigenous and Treaty Rights for all Indigenous people.

102. Dempsey, *Tribal Honors*, 97.

103. Ibid., 94–97.

104. Ibid.

105. Joe Lougheed, interview by author, January 8, 2020.

106. Peter Lougheed "Chief Thunderbird," to Chief Norman Yellowbird, August 17, 1971, PAA, PR1972.0059/188 PR2207 1967–1969, Box 14, Indians, Metis and Eskimos. On January 1, 2014, the people of Maskwacis recognized their territory by its Cree name for Bear Hill to replace the colonial naming of Hobbema (a Dutch landscape painter). "Hobbema to change name in New Year," CBC News, December 26, 2013, cbc. ca/news/canada/edmonton/hobbema-to-change-name-in-new-year-1.2476653. Also Samson Cree Nation, "Official name change to Maskwacis (Bear Hills) in place of 'Hobbema,'" samsoncree.com/ nov-nipisihkopahk-acimowin/name-change/.

107. Jean Johnston, letter to Peter Lougheed, Premier of Alberta, May 5, 1975, "Unknown File," LHA.

108. Archibald Belaney (1888–1938) was born in England but assumed the name Grey Owl after marrying an

Indigenous woman in Ontario. He became a conservationist and respected author who even gained an audience with the queen as Grey Owl.

109. Sylvester Clark Long (1890–1932), born in North Carolina of Lumbee, Cherokee and Euro–North American ancestry, assumed the name Buffalo Child Long Lance when he came to Canada in 1919 after serving in the war and when Black immigration was discouraged.

110. Onoto Watanna was the pen name of Winnifred Eaton, a woman born in Montreal to Chinese and English parents. Eaton came to Cochrane, Alberta, in 1917 with her husband to ranch. As an author, she chose a pen name intended to portray herself as being of Japanese ethnicity at a time when Chinese were the subject of racism.

111. Coleen Collins, "Re: Premier Lougheed's Native Heritage," October 18, 1984, "Unknown File," LHA.

112. Beckles Willson, *The Life of Lord Strathcona and Mount Royal G.C.M.G., G.C.V.O., 1820–1914* (London: Cassell, 1915), 83. Willson wrote that Isabella's grandfather Richard Sr. married Marguerite Sutherland, a "dark, petite woman of remarkable beauty, undoubtedly derived from her mixed-blood or Indian mother." Willson also references Kipling Records 62. Also Donald B. Smith Collection, Hardisty Family File, Box 1, LHA. Reference Manuscript Group 25G vol. 14 Scrip certificate No. 734, application made in Edmonton in 1885, LAC. Scrip application references the marriage.

113. David G. Wood, *The Lougheed Legacy* (Toronto: Key Porter Books, 1985), 27.

114. John English, *Just Watch Me: The Life of Pierre Elliott Trudeau, 1968–2000* (Toronto: Knopf Canada, 2009), 514.

115. Ibid.

116. Ibid. Also Elizabeth Bailey Price, "The First White Girl Born in Alberta," *Lethbridge Herald*, October 23, 1926.

Even contemporaries seemed to sometimes forget Hardisty's Indigenous ancestry, as evidenced by Price's claim that Richard's daughter was the first white girl born in Alberta.

117. English, *Just Watch Me*, 514. Reference to René Lévesque, *Memoirs* (Toronto: McClelland and Stewart, 1986), 42.

118. BC Métis Federation. "BC Metis Federation Remembers Peter Lougheed," September 14, 2012, bcmetis.com/2012/09/ bc-metis-federation-remembers-peter-lougheed/.

119. Government of Alberta, "News Release," May 31, 1985, PAA, GR1990.0066, Box 11, Item 000228, "Motion: Metis Betterment Legislation."

120. Alberta Hansard, "Government Motions," June 3, 1985, 1291.

121. Ibid.

122. Ibid.

CHAPTER FIVE: THE COMPLEXITIES OF LEADERSHIP

1. Donald B. Smith, "The Original Peoples of Alberta," in *Peoples of Alberta: Portraits of Cultural Diversity*, ed. Howard Palmer and Tamara Palmer (Saskatoon: Western Producer Prairie Books, 1985), 67. Reference Archibald Oswald MacRae, *History of the Province of Alberta*, vol. 2 (Western Canadian History Co., 1912), 50–64. See photo (dated 1906), GAIA NA-3899.2, which includes the young Norman Lougheed and his classmates with the schoolmaster Archibald Oswald MacRae.

2. R. Douglas Francis, "Writing Alberta's History," in *Writing Alberta: Building on a Literary Identity*, ed. George Melnyk and Donna Coates (Calgary: University of Calgary Press, 2017), 201–22, 206.

3. Smith, "The Original Peoples of Alberta," 67. Smith references MacRae, *History of the Province of Alberta*, 430.

4.   "Builders of Canada: Peter Lougheed," interview by Laurier LaPierre in 1999, on CPAC website, https://cpac.ca/episode?id=86a8a7ce-1bbc-4da7-94fc-971c83b01528.

5.   Bernie Shiesser to Premier Peter Lougheed, March 25, 1980, PAA, PR1985.0401/2019 PR2207, 1980, Box 168, Climb of Mt. Lougheed.

6.   *Lougheed: A Man and a Mountain*, University of Alberta Archives, Peter Lougheed fonds 2012-46-T22. This video traces Peter Lougheed's personal effort to conquer the 10,200-foot peak named after his grandfather.

7.   Joe Lougheed, interview by author, January 8, 2020.

8.   Alan Hustak, *Peter Lougheed: A Biography* (Toronto: McClelland and Stewart, 1979), 67.

9.   Peter C. Newman, *Titans: How the New Canadian Establishment Seized Power* (Toronto: Penguin Books, 1999), 452.

10.   Conor Mahoney, Asha Siad and Matthew Hayhurst, "Albertans remember Peter Lougheed (Naheed Nenshi)," *Calgary Journal*, September 14, 2012, calgaryjournal.ca/index.php/news/1004-albertans-remember-peter-lougheed.

11.   Robert Sheppard, "Moose Nose on the Menu?" *Globe and Mail*, August 16, 1983, University of Alberta Archives, Peter Lougheed fonds 2012-46 Box 21 Lougheed.

12.   Fil Fraser, *Alberta's Camelot: Culture and the Arts in the Lougheed Years* (Edmonton: Lone Pine Publishing, 2003), 44.

13.   Tabita Marshall, "IODE (Imperial Order Daughters of the Empire)," *The Canadian Encyclopedia* (March 4, 2021), thecanadianencyclopedia.ca/en/article/imperial-order-daughters-of-the-empire#:~:text=Originally%20known%20as%20the%20Imperial,than%20200%20branches%20across%20Canada.

14. *Morning Albertan*, October 21, 1907, 1.

15. Donald B. Smith, *Calgary's Grand Story, Calgary* (Calgary: University of Calgary Press, 2005), 1.

16. Richard Hardisty Fonds, Accession No. M5908, Series 23-3, 1572, Bella Hardisty to Dear Aunt Eliza, December 10, 1877, GAIA.

17. Smith, *Calgary's Grand Story*, 126. Reference Calgary Herald, October 5, 1912.

18. Ibid. Reference "Bishop McNally," *Calgary Herald*, March 19, 1914.

19. Ibid. Reference *Morning Albertan*, January 3, 1914, 4.

20. *Morning Albertan*, January 5, 1914, 5. By this time, furor over the tango was beginning to subside in other areas. Also *Morning Albertan*, January 17, 1914, 4. As the *Albertan* reported, the "Naughty Tango" received the approval of an audience of "duchesses, countesses, and bishops," who deemed the version they witnessed as "so modest it bored . . . to tears."

21. Calvin Demmon, "The Arts: Enter the Professional," in *Alberta in the 20th Century*, vol. 3, *The Boom and the Bust, 1910–1914* ed. Ted Byfield (Edmonton: United Western Communications Ltd., 1994), 61.

22. Jennifer Bobrovitz Files, notes, 11, note 71, LHA. Reference Marjorie Norris, A Leaven of Ladies (Calgary: Detselig Enterprises, 1995); John T. Saywell, ed., *Canadian Journal of Lady Aberdeen* (Toronto: Champlain Society, 1960). Also *Calgary Tribune*, November 30, 1895; *Calgary Herald*, November 29, 1895.

23. Lee Gibson, "Nicholas Flood Davin," *The Canadian Encyclopedia* (2008; update December 14, 2017), thecanadianencyclopedia.ca/en/article/nicholas-flood-davin. A journalist, lawyer and politician, Davin was known as the "voice of the North-West." Among other notable events, Davin wrote the "Report on Industrial Schools

for Indians and Half-Breeds," which recommended the implementation of these schools after investigating American industrial schools for Indigenous children.

24. Donald B. Smith Collection, Lougheed Box 2, James Lougheed 1890–1922 File, LHA. Reference *Calgary Herald*, November 26, 1898.

25. Ibid. Reference *Alberta Magazine*, December 1981, from Charles D. Denney Papers, GAIA. The article in *Alberta Magazine* referenced the earlier edition of the *Calgary Herald*.

26. "The Honourable Peter Lougheed," Canadian Medical Hall of Fame, cdnmedhall.org/inductees/ honourable-peter-lougheed.

27. Max Foran, *Calgary: An Illustrated History* (Toronto: James Lorimer and the National Museum of Man, 1978), 60. Calgary Tribune, October 21, 1885, and April 3, 1886.

28. Southern Alberta Pioneers and Descendants Fonds, Accession No. M2077 B1.6.5727, GAIA, "The Southern Alberta Women's Pioneer and Old Timer Association Constitution," Article 1. In 1922, when the Women's Pioneer Association of Southern Alberta was formed, its mandate was, as with so many clubs of that era, to be a benevolent association meant to cultivate social intercourse. However, another major component of its mandate was to "rescue from oblivion the memory of its early pioneers and to obtain and preserve narratives of their exploits, perils and adventures; to promote the study of the history of the Province and to diffuse and publish information as to its past and present condition and resources and in all appropriate matters to advance the interests and perpetuate the memory of those whose sagacity, energy and enterprise induced them to settle in the west," 1.

29. Joe Lougheed, interview by author, January 8, 2020.

30. Progressive Conservative Party of Alberta, "Press Release," May 15, 1967, University of Alberta Archives, Peter Lougheed fonds 2012-46 Box 2 File 1967-F1.

225

31. Hustak, *Peter Lougheed*, 7.

32. Ibid., 12.

33. Calgary Legal Guidance Legal Humanitarian of the Year Award Dinner, 1987, University of Alberta Archives, Peter Lougheed fonds 2012-46 Box 29 Lougheed 1987-F1.

34. "Lougheed Is Really an Indian," *Castor Advance*, February 24, 1977. Retrieved from University of Alberta Archives, Peter Lougheed fonds 2012-46 Box 10 Lougheed File 1977-F1 Folder 1.

35. Jean Teillet and Carly Teillet, "Devoid of Principle: The Federal Court Determination that section 91(24) of the Constitution Act, 1867 is a race-based provision," *Indigenous Law Journal* 13, no. 1 (2016): 1–20, ilj.law. utoronto.ca/sites/ilj.law.utoronto.ca/files/media/Teillet. pdf.

36. Ibid., 18.

37. Paul Jackson (*Herald* correspondent)," Lougheed Given Nod," Ottawa newspaper not identified, April 1977. Retrieved from University of Alberta Archives, Peter Lougheed fonds 2012-46 Box 10 Lougheed File 1977-F1 Folder 1.

38. Ibid.

39. Satya Das, "You made us feel welcome—Steinhauer," *Edmonton Journal*, September 19, 1979, EPL Exhibit Research Box, File 5, LHA.

40. "Ralph Steinhauer, lieutenant governor of Alberta," March 22, 1979, CBC Digital Archives, https://www. cbc.ca/player/play/1768961160.

41. "The Lieutenant Governors," Government of Canada website, February 28, 2019, canada.ca/en/canadian-heritage/services/crown-canada/lieutenant-governors. html.

42. Joe Lougheed, interview by author, January 8, 2020.

43. "Muriel Stanley Venne," Alberta Government, The Alberta Order of Excellence, alberta.ca/aoe-muriel-stanley-venne.aspx.

44. "The Honourable Ralph G. Steinhauer," The Governor General of Canada website, gg.ca/en/honours/recipients/146-3447. Also Eric J. Holmgren and Michelle Filice, "Ralph Garvin Steinhauer," *The Canadian Encyclopedia* (2008; update July 20, 2016), thecanadianencyclopedia.ca/en/article/ralph-garvin-steinhauer.

45. "Builders of Canada: Peter Lougheed."

46. Donald B. Smith, "Alberta Cree Victims of Callous Disregard," *Toronto Star*, March 1, 1988, A17. Insertions by author.

47. Ibid.

48. Sylvia Van Kirk, "Tracing the Fortunes of Five Founding Families of Victoria," *BC Studies*, no. 115–16 (Autumn/Winter 1997/98): https://doi.org/10.14288/bcs.voi115/6.1729. Van Kirk studied the women in these founding families, arguing that they served as agents of transition.

49. Hustak, *Peter Lougheed*, 15.

50. D.N. Sprague, *Canada and the Métis, 1869–1885* (Waterloo, ON: Wilfrid Laurier University Press, 2009); Frank Tough, *"As Their Natural Resources Fail": Native Peoples and the Economic History of Northern Manitoba* (Vancouver: UBC Press, 1996); Gerhard J. Ens, *Homeland to Hinterland: The Changing Worlds of the Red River Metis in the Nineteenth Century* (Toronto: University of Toronto Press, 1996); Joe Sawchuk, *The Dynamics of Native Politics: The Alberta Metis Experience* (Saskatoon: Purich Publishing, 1998). These scholars provide thorough analyses of scrip politics.

51. Hustak, *Peter Lougheed*, 16.

52. Donald B. Smith Collection, Lougheed #2 Box 2, Lougheed 1922 File, LHA. Reference *Calgary Herald*, June 26, 1999.

53. Ibid.

54. Ibid.

55. Ibid. Secord Jr. did go on to defend his great-grand-father somewhat, saying, "From what I understand he was one of the few who paid a fair price for scrip." Coincidentally, Richard Secord Jr. discovered his great-grandfather's signature on Treaty 8 documents when he was appearing on behalf of Jim Badger in 1994. Badger was Chief of Sucker Creek Reserve, where the original treaty was signed, and was challenging a hazardous waste plant near Swan Hills. Badger pointed the treaty signatories out to the younger Secord, also noting that one of those signing was Badger's own great-grandfather, Chief Moostoos.

56. Donald B. Smith Collection, Lougheed #2 Box 2, Lougheed 1922 File, LHA. *Calgary Herald*, June 26, 1999.

57. Donald B. Smith Collection, Hardisty Box 1, Hardisty Descendants File, LHA. Reference MacRae, *History of the Province of Alberta*, 890.

negotiated with these people as a segment of Chippewa society, 207.

3. Tanis C. Thorne, *The Many Hands of My Relations: French and Indians on the Lower Missouri* (Columbia: University of Missouri Press, 1996). Thorne studied kinship networks between Creoles and Central Siouan tribes along the lower Missouri River up to the removal era in the 1870s.

4. Harroun Foster, *We Know Who We Are*, 220.

5. Joe Lougheed, interview by author, January 8, 2020. According to Joe, whose ten-year tenure as a board member of Lougheed House National Historic Site continues today, preserving this history and its stories were important to Peter. He notes that we should recall that, as a young boy, Peter watched the house repossessed by the city. To see the home restored as a national historic site was very powerful, and "that its stories could be shared with all as a public site meant even more to him."

6. Joe Lougheed, interview by author, January 8, 2020.

7. Parks Canada, "Beaulieu National Historic Site of Canada," Directory of Federal Heritage Designations, pc.gc.ca/apps/dfhd/page_nhs_eng.aspx?id=11.

8. Caroline Loewen, "Calgary Metis History," Lougheed House, October 22, 2020, lougheedhouse.com/lh_blog/calgarys-metis-history/.

9. John Roe, "New Exhibit at the Lougheed House explores Metis culture and the Lougheed's Metis history," *Calgary Herald*, July 4, 2019, calgaryherald.com/entertainment/local-arts/new-exhibit-at-the-lougheed-house-explores-metis-culture-and-the-lougheeds-metis-history.

10. Peter Lougheed, "Take Proud Aim on History," *Globe and Mail*, July 3, 2001, A11, in EPL Exhibit Research, Box 1 of 3, Lougheed, Peter Clippings, LHA.

Bibliography

PRIMARY SOURCES

THESES AND DISSERTATIONS

Bojechko, Cynthia. "Lougheed's Energetic Bureaucrats: A Study of Senior Civil Servants in Province-Building Departments." Master's thesis, University of Alberta, 1982.

Denis, Chantal A. Roy. "Wolf Lake: The Importance of Métis Connection to Land and Place." Master's thesis, University of Alberta, 2017. era.library.ualberta.ca/items/16ccd632-3412-4e2d-81e2-abdc8b9de045.

Herbert, Rachel. "Ranching Women in Southern Alberta, 1880–1930." Master's thesis, University of Calgary, 2011.

Inoue, Margaret. "Who Are the Métis: Olive Dickason and the Emergence of a Métis Historiography in the 1970s and 1980s." Master's thesis, University of British Columbia, 2004. open.library.ubc.ca/cIRcle/collections/ubctheses/831/items/1.0091598.

Jetté, Melinda M. "Ordinary Lives: Three Generations of a French-Indian Family in Oregon, 1827–1931." Master's thesis, Université Laval, 1996.

MacKinnon, Doris Jeanne. "Métis Pioneers: Isabella Hardisty
Lougheed and Marie Rose Delorme Smith." PhD dissertation, University of Calgary, 2012.

Pollard, Juliet Thelma. "The Making of the Metis in the Pacific
Northwest Fur Trade." PhD dissertation, University of
British Columbia, 1990.

ARCHIVAL COLLECTIONS

ARCHIVES OF MANITOBA

Glenbow Alberta Institute Archives. Charles D. Denney
Fonds; Elizabeth Bailey Price Fonds; George and John
McDougall Fonds; McDougall Family Papers; Richard
Hardisty Fonds; Southern Alberta Pioneers and
Descendants Fonds.

Hamilton Public Library Archives.

Hudson's Bay Company Archives.

Library and Archives Canada.

Lougheed House National Historic Site Archives. Donald
B. Smith Collection; Jennifer Bobrovitz Files; Lougheed
House Fonds; Lougheed House Research Files.

Provincial Archives of Alberta. Peter Lougheed Fonds.

University of Alberta. Peter Lougheed fonds 2012-46.

INTERVIEWS

Bobrovitz, Jennifer, researcher, Lougheed House National
Historic Site. Interviews by author, Calgary, AB.
2007–2009.

"Builders of Canada: Peter Lougheed." Interview by Laurier
LaPierre in 1999. On CPAC website. cpac.ca/en/
programs/builders-of-canada/episodes/50189794.

Learn Alberta. "Peter Lougheed: Education in Alberta (interview response—Question 16), Learn Alberta.ca. Updated
July 31, 2006. learnalberta.ca/content/sspl/html/peter_
lougheed_question16.html.

Lougheed, Joe. Interview by author. January 8, 2020.

MacDonald, L. Ian. "A Conversation with Peter Lougheed."
  Policy Options, June 1, 2012. policyoptions.irpp.org/
  fr/magazines/the-best-premier-of-the-last-40-years/a-
  conversation-with-peter-lougheed/.
Macdougall, Brenda. "Metis means much more
  than 'mixed blood.'" Interview by CBC Radio,
  April 25, 2019. https://www.cbc.ca/radio/
  unreserved/from-scrip-to-road-allowances-canada-
  s-complicated-history-with-the-métis-1.5100375/
  métis-means-much-more-than-mixed-blood-1.5100783.
"Ralph Steinhauer, lieutenant governor of Alberta." March 22,
  1979. CBC Digital Archives. https://www.cbc.ca/player/
  play/1768961160.

SECONDARY SOURCES

BOOKS

Adams, Christopher, Gregg Dahl and Ian Peach, eds. *Métis in
  Canada: History, Identity, Law and Politics.* Edmonton:
  University of Alberta Press, 2013.
Anacker, Caleb, Tanya Fontaine, Megan Tucker, Pierre
  Lamoureux, Goddy Nzonji and Roy Missal. *Restoring
  the History of St. Paul de Métis: Understanding Métis
  Perspectives.* St. Paul: St. Paul Community Learning
  Association, 2020.
Anderson, Chris. *"Métis": Race, Recognition, and the Struggle
  for Indigenous Peoplehood.* Vancouver: UBC Press, 2014.
Bakker, Peter. *A Language of Our Own: The Genesis of Michif,
  the Mixed Cree-French Language of the Canadian Métis.*
  New York: Oxford University Press, 1997.
Beattie, Judith Hudson, and Helen M. Buss, eds. *Undelivered
  Letters to Hudson's Bay Company Men on the Northwest
  Coast of America, 1830–1857.* Vancouver: UBC Press, 2003.
Bell, Gloria Jane. "Oscillating Identities: Re-presentation
  of Métis in the Great Lakes Area in the Nineteenth
  Century." In *Métis in Canada: History, Identity, Law and
  Politics*, edited by Christopher Adams, Gregg Dahl and
  Ian Peach. Edmonton: University of Alberta Press, 2013.

233

Breen, David H., and R.C. Macleod, eds. *William Stewart Herron: Father of the Petroleum Industry in Alberta.* Calgary: Alberta Records Publication Board, 1984.

Brennan, Brian. *Building a Province: 60 Alberta Lives.* Calgary: Fifth House Publishing, 2000.

Brown, Jennifer S.H. *Strangers in Blood: Fur Trade Company Families in Indian Country.* Vancouver: UBC Press, 1980.

Bunner, Paul, ed. *Alberta in the 20th Century.* Vol. 10, *The Sixties Revolution and the Fall of the Social Credit.* Edmonton: United Western Communications Ltd., 2002.

———. *Alberta in the 20th Century.* Vol. 11, *Lougheed and the War With Ottawa, 1971–1984.* Edmonton: United Western Communications Ltd., 2003.

———. *Alberta in the 20th Century.* Vol. 12, *Alberta Takes the Lead, 1984–2000.* Edmonton: History Book Publications Ltd., 2003.

Carter, Sarah. *Capturing Women: The Manipulation of Cultural Imagery in Canada's Prairie West.* Montreal/Kingston: McGill-Queen's University Press, 1997.

———. *The Importance of Being Monogamous: Marriage and Nation Building in Western Canada to 1915.* Edmonton: University of Alberta Press, 2008.

Carter, Sarah, and Patricia A. McCormack, eds. *Recollecting: Lives of Aboriginal Women of the Canadian Northwest and Borderlands.* Edmonton: Athabasca University Press, 2011.

Chartrand, Paul L.A.H., ed. *Who Are Canada's Aboriginal People? Recognition, Definition, and Jurisdiction.* Saskatoon: Purich Publishing, 2002.

Cook-Bobrovitz, Jennifer, and Trudy Cowan. *Lougheed House: More Than a Century of Stories.* Calgary: Lougheed House, 2006.

Coutts, George Ballantine. *The Ranchmen's Club: A Short Historical Sketch, 1891–1952.* Calgary: Calgary Ranchmen's Club, 1953.

Cunniffe, Richard. *Calgary in Sandstone.* Calgary: Historical Society of Alberta, Calgary Branch, 1969.

Daschuk, James. *Clearing the Plains: Disease, Politics of Starvation, and the Loss of Aboriginal Life.* Regina: University of Regina Press, 2013.

234

Dempsey, Hugh. *Tribal Honors: A History of the Kainai Chieftainship*. Calgary: Kainai Chieftainship, 1997.

Devine, Heather. *The People Who Own Themselves: Aboriginal Ethnogenesis in a Canadian Family, 1660–1900*. Calgary: University of Calgary Press, 2014.

English, John. *Just Watch Me: The Life of Pierre Elliott Trudeau, 1968–2000*. Toronto: Knopf Canada, 2009.

Ens, Gerhard J. *Homeland to Hinterland: The Changing Worlds of the Red River Metis in the Nineteenth Century*. Toronto: University of Toronto Press, 1996.

———. *A Son of the Fur Trade: The Memoirs of Johnny Grant*. Edmonton: University of Alberta Press, 2008.

Ens, Gerhard, and Joe Sawchuk. *New Peoples to New Nations: Aspects of Métis History and Identity from the Eighteenth to Twenty-First Centuries*. Toronto: University of Toronto Press, 2016.

Foran, Max. *Calgary: An Illustrated History*. Toronto: James Lorimer and the National Museum of Man, 1978.

Fraser, Fil. *Alberta's Camelot: Culture and the Arts in the Lougheed Years*. Edmonton: Lone Pine Publishing, 2003.

Friesen, Gerald. *The Canadian Prairies: A History*. Toronto: University of Toronto Press, 1987.

Garroutte, Eva Marie. *Real Indians: Identity and the Survival of Native America*. Los Angeles: University of California Press, 2003.

Giraud, Marcel. *The Métis in the Canadian West*. Translated by George Woodcock. 1945; repr., Edmonton: University of Alberta Press, 1986.

Harroun Foster, Martha. *We Know Who We Are: Metis Identity in a Montana Community*. Norman: University of Oklahoma Press, 2006.

Hayes, Alan L. *Holding Forth the Word of Life: Little Trinity Church, 1842–1992*. Toronto: Corporation of Little Trinity Church, 1991.

Hogue, Michel. *Metis and the Medicine Line: Creating a Border and Dividing a People*. Chapel Hill: University of North Carolina Press, 2015.

Hustak, Allan. *Peter Lougheed*. Toronto: McClelland and Stewart, 1979.

Innis, Harold. *The Fur Trade in Canada: An Introduction to Canadian Economic History*. 1930; repr., Toronto: University of Toronto Press, 1999.

Institute of Intergovernmental Relations, Queen's University. *Constitutional Patriation: The Lougheed-Levesque Correspondence*. Kingston: Queen's University, 1999.

Jones, David C. *Empire of Dust: Settling and Abandoning the Prairie Dry Belt*. Calgary: University of Calgary Press, 2002.

Judd, Carol M., and Arthur J. Ray, eds. *Old Trails and New Directions: Papers of the Third North American Fur Trade Conference*. Toronto: University of Toronto Press, 1980.

Karsh, Yousuf. *Karsh Canadians*. Toronto: University of Toronto Press, 1978.

Kermoal, Nathalie. *Un passé métis au féminin*. Québec: Les Éditions GID, 2006.

Law Society of Alberta, *Just Works: Lawyers in Alberta, 1907–2007*. Toronto: Irwin Law Inc., 2007.

Lévesque, René. *Memoirs*. Toronto: McClelland and Stewart, 1986.

Linehan, Peter, ed., *St. John's College Cambridge: A History*. Woodbridge: Boyden Press, 2011.

MacDonald, George Heath. *Edmonton: Fort, House, Factory*. Edmonton: Douglas Print Company, 1959.

Macdougall, Brenda. *One of the Family: Metis Culture in Nineteenth-Century Saskatchewan*. Vancouver: UBC Press, 2010.

MacGregor, James Grierson. *Senator Hardisty's Prairies, 1849–1889*. Saskatoon: Western Producer Prairie Books, 1978.

MacKinnon, Doris J. *The Identities of Marie Rose Delorme Smith: Portrait of a Métis Woman, 1861–1960*. Regina: University of Regina Press/Canadian Plains Research Center, 2012.

———. *Metis Pioneers: Marie Rose Delorme Smith and Isabella Clark Hardisty Lougheed*. Edmonton: University of Alberta Press, 2018.

MacRae, Archibald Oswald. *History of the Province of Alberta*. Vol. 2. Western Canadian History Co., 1912.

McDonald, Donna. *Lord Strathcona: A Biography of Donald Alexander Smith*. Toronto: Dundurn Press, 1996.

McManus, Sheila. *The Line Which Separates: Race, Gender, and the Making of the Alberta–Montana Borderlands.* Lincoln: University of Nebraska Press, 2005.

Melnyk, George and Donna Coates, eds. *Writing Alberta: Building on a Literary Identity.* Calgary: University of Calgary Press, 2017.

Métis Settlements General Council. *Making History: Our Land. Our Culture. Our Future.* metissettlements.files. wordpress.com/2017/01/msgc_centennial_book.pdf.

Millar, Nancy. *Remember Me as You Pass By: Stories From Prairie Graveyards.* Calgary: Glenbow Museum, 1994.

Miller, J.R. *Shingwauk's Vision: A History of Native Residential Schools.* Toronto: University of Toronto Press, 1997.

Morton, W.L. "The Canadian Métis." In *Contexts of Canada's Past: Selected Essays of W.L. Morton,* edited by A.B. McKillop. Toronto: Macmillan of Canada, 1980.

Murphy, Lucy Eldersveld. *A Gathering of Rivers: Indians, Métis and Mining in the Western Great Lakes, 1727–1832.* Lincoln: University of Nebraska Press, 2004.

Newman, Peter C. *Titans: How the New Canadian Establishment Seized Power.* Toronto: Penguin Books, 1999.

Newton, William. *Twenty Years on the Saskatchewan.* London: Elliot Stock, 1897.

Norris, Marjorie. *A Leaven of Ladies.* Calgary: Detselig Enterprises, 1995.

Palmer, Howard, and Tamara Palmer. *Alberta: A New History.* Edmonton: Hurtig Publishers, 1990.

———, eds. *Peoples of Alberta: Portraits of Cultural Diversity.* Saskatoon: Western Producer Prairie Books, 1985.

Payment, Diane P. *"The Free People—Otipemisiwak": Batoche, Saskatchewan 1870–1930.* Hull: Supply and Services Canada, 1990.

Payne, Michael. *The Most Respectable Place in the Territory: Everyday Life in Hudson's Bay Company Service—York Factory, 1788 to 1870.* Ottawa: National Historic Parks and Sites, Canadian Parks Service, Environment Canada, 1989.

Payne, Michael, Donald Wetherell and Catherine Cavanaugh, eds. *Alberta Formed, Alberta Transformed.* Vol. 1. Calgary: University of Calgary Press, 2006.

237

Perry, J. Fraser, ed. *They Gathered at the River*. Calgary: Central United Church, 1975.

Pratt, Larry. *The Tar Sands: Syncrude and the Politics of Oil*. Edmonton: Hurtig Publishers, 1976.

Pratt, Larry, and Garth Stevenson, eds. *Western Separatism: The Myths, Realities and Dangers*. Edmonton: Hurtig Publishers, 1981.

Price, Richard. *The Spirit of the Alberta Indian Treaties*. Edmonton: University of Alberta Press, 1999.

Ray, Arthur. *The Canadian Fur Trade in the Industrial Age*. Toronto: University of Toronto Press, 1990.

———. *Indians in the Fur Trade*. 1974; repr., Toronto: University of Toronto Press, 1998.

Rennie, Bradford J., ed. *Alberta Premiers of the Twentieth Century*. Regina: Canadian Plains Research Center, 2004.

Richards, John, and Larry Pratt. *Prairie Capitalism: Power and Influence in the New West*. Toronto: McClelland and Stewart, 1979.

Sawchuk, Joe. *The Dynamics of Native Politics: The Alberta Metis Experience*. Saskatoon: Purich Publishing, 1998.

Saywell, John T., ed. *Canadian Journal of Lady Aberdeen*. Toronto: Champlain Society, 1960.

Sharpe, Sydney, Roger Gibbins, James H. Marsh and Heather Bala Edwards, eds. *Alberta: A State of Mind*. Toronto: Key Porter Books, 2005.

Simpson, Jeffrey. *Discipline of Power: The Conservative Interlude and the Liberal Restoration*. Toronto: University of Toronto Press, 1980.

Sleeper-Smith, Susan. *Indian Women and French Men: Rethinking Cultural Encounter in the Western Great Lakes*. Amherst: University of Massachusetts Press, 2001.

Smith, Donald B. *Calgary's Grand Story: The Making of a Prairie Metropolis from the Viewpoint of Two Heritage Buildings*. Calgary: University of Calgary Press, 2005.

———. *Chief Buffalo Child Long Lance: The Glorious Impostor*. Red Deer: Red Deer Press, 1999.

———. *Seen But Not Seen: Influential Canadians and the First Nations from the 1840s to Today*. Toronto: University of Toronto Press, 2021.

Soby, Trudy. *Be It Ever So Humble*. Calgary: Century Calgary Publications, 1975.

Sprague, D.N. *Canada and the Métis, 1869–1885*. Waterloo, ON: Wilfrid Laurier University Press, 2009.

Stanley, George F.G. *The Birth of Western Canada: A History of the Riel Rebellions*. 1936; repr. Toronto: University of Toronto Press, 1961.

St-Onge, Nicole. *Saint-Laurent, Manitoba: Evolving Metis Identities, 1850–1914*. Regina: Canadian Plains Research Center, 2004.

St-Onge, Nicole J.M., Carolyn Podruchny and Brenda Macdougall, eds. *Contours of a People: Metis Family, Mobility, and History*. Norman: University of Oklahoma Press, 2012.

Taylor, Coral. *Victoria Callihoo: An Amazing Life*. Edmonton: Eschia Books Inc., 2008.

Teillet, Jean. *The North-West is Our Mother: The Story of Louis Riel's People, the Métis Nation*. Toronto: HarperCollins Canada, 2019.

Thorne, Tanis C. *The Many Hands of My Relations: French and Indians on the Lower Missouri*. Columbia: University of Missouri Press, 1996.

Tough, Frank. *"As Their Natural Resources Fail": Native Peoples and the Economic History of Northern Manitoba*. Vancouver: UBC Press, 1996.

Van Herk, Aritha. *Mavericks: An Incorrigible History of Alberta*. Toronto: Penguin Random House, 2002.

Van Kirk, Sylvia. *"Many Tender Ties": Women in Fur-Trade Society, 1670–1870*. Winnipeg: Watson & Dwyer Publishing Ltd., 1980.

Wasylow, Walter J. *History of Battleford Industrial School for Indians*. Saskatoon: University of Saskatchewan, 1972.

Willson, Beckles. *The Life of Lord Strathcona and Mount Royal G.C.M.G., G.C.V.O., 1820–1914*. London: Cassell, 1915.

Wood, David G. *The Lougheed Legacy*. Toronto: Key Porter Books, 1985.

ARTICLES AND CHAPTERS

Alberta Teachers' Association. "Peter Lougheed's commitment to education recognized by Alberta teachers." *ATA News* 30, no. 17 (1995–96): teachers.ab.ca/News%20Room/ata%20news/Volume%2030/Number%2017/In%20

the%20News/Pages/Peter%20Lougheeds%20commit-
ment%20to%20education%20recognized%20by%20
Alberta%20teachers.aspx.

Arnett, E. James. "The Associates: Railway cohort among
greatest business partnerships." *Canada's History*,
February 23, 2015. canadashistory.ca/explore/
business-industry/the-associates.

Barkwell, Lawrence J. "Battle River Metis Settlements."
SCRIBD. scribd.com/document/114043443/
Battle-River-Metis-Settlements.

———. "Callihoo (Belcourt), Victoria Anne." Gabriel Dumont
Institute Virtual Museum. metismuseum.ca/resource.
php/13921.

———. "Lougheed, Peter, PC, CC, AOE, QC." Gabriel Dumont
Institute Virtual Museum. metismuseum.ca/resource.
php/13483.

———. "Rooster Town: A Métis Road Allowance Community."
Gabriel Dumont Institute Virtual Museum. January 3,
2008. metismuseum.ca/resource.php/07242.

———. "Tail Creek, Alberta Metis Scrip Claims."
SCRIBD. scribd.com/document/111361558/
Tail-Creek-Alberta-Metis-Scrip-Claims.

Bateman, Tom. "The White Paper and Alberta Politics."
Edmonton: Government of Alberta, 1985.

Beaudoin, Yvon. "Saint-Albert, Alberta, Canada,
from 1861." OMIWorld. omiworld.org/lemma/
saint-albert-alberta-canada-1861/.

Bellman, Jennifer L., and Christopher C. Hanks. "Northern
Métis and the Fur Trade." In *Picking Up the Threads:
Métis History in the Mackenzie Basin*, edited by Metis
Heritage Association of the Northwest Territories, 5–29.
Winnipeg: Metis Heritage Association of the Northwest
Territories and Parks Canada–Canadian Heritage, 1998.

Betke, Carl, and Nathan Baker. "St. Paul." *The Canadian
Encyclopedia*. 2009; update October 26, 2020. thecana-
dianencyclopedia.ca/en/article/st-paul.

Blanchin, François. "Oblates of Mary Immaculate." *Catholic
Encyclopedia*, vol. 11. New York: Robert Appleton Co.,
1911. https://www.newadvent.org/cathen/11184b.htm.

Brady, James. "The St. Paul Half-Breed Reserve." Gabriel Dumont Institute Virtual Museum. https://www.metis-museum.ca/resource.php/03835.

Brown, Jennifer S.H. "Linguistic Solitudes and Changing Social Categories." In *Old Trails and New Directions: Papers of the Third North American Fur Trade Conference*, edited by Carol M. Judd and Arthur J. Ray. Toronto: University of Toronto Press, 1980.

———. "Women as Centre and Symbol in the Emergence of Métis Communities." *Canadian Journal of Native Studies* 3, no. 1 (1983): 39–46.

Bruce, Jean. "The Last Best West: Advertising for Immigrants to Western Canada, 1870–1930." Canadian Museum of History. historymuseum.ca/cmc/exhibitions/hist/advertis/ads1-01e.html.

Callihoo, Victoria. "Early Life in Lac Ste. Anne and St. Albert in the 1870s." *Alberta Historical Review* 1, no. 3 (1953): 21–26.

———. "The Iroquois in Alberta." *Alberta Historical Review* 7, no. 2 (1959): 17–18.

———. "Our Buffalo Hunts." *Alberta Historical Review* 8, no. 1 (1960): 24–25.

Campbell, Maria. "Foreword: Charting the Way." In *Contours of a People: Metis Family, Mobility, and History*, edited by Brenda Macdougall, Carolyn Podruchny and Nicole St-Onge, xiii–xiv. Norman: University of Oklahoma Press, 2012.

Careless, J.M.S. "The Emergence of Cabbagetown in Victorian Toronto." In *Gathering Place: Peoples and Neighbourhoods of Toronto, 1834–1945*, edited by Robert F. Harney. Toronto: Multicultural History Society of Ontario, 1985.

———. "Frontierism, Metropolitanism, and Canadian History." *Canadian Historical Review* 35, no. 1 (March 1954): 1–21. doi.org/10.3138/CHR-035-01-01.

Climenhaga, David. "Alberta's NDP Borrowed More than Export-cut Threats From Peter Lougheed for Yesterday's Throne Speech." Alberta Politics. ca. March 9, 2018. albertapolitics.ca/2018/03/albertas-ndp-borrowed-more-than-export-cut-threats-from-peter-lougheed-for-yesterdays-throne-speech/.

Coates, K.S., and W.R. Morrison. "More Than a Matter of Blood: The Federal Government, the Churches and the Mixed Blood Populations of the Yukon and the Mackenzie River Valley, 1890–1950." In *1885 and After: Native Society in Transition*, edited by F. Laurie Barron and James B. Waldram. Regina: Canadian Plains Research Center, 1986.

Conn, Heather. "Daniels Case." *The Canadian Encyclopedia*. January 18, 2019. thecanadianencyclopedia.ca/en/article/daniels-case.

Cook-Bobrovitz, Jennifer, and Trudy Cowan. "Reasoned Speculation: The Challenge of Knowing Isabella Clarke Hardisty Lougheed." In *Remembering Chinook Country: 1905–2005 Centennial Edition*, edited by Chinook Country Historical Society, 23–36. Calgary: Detselig Enterprises, 2005.

Cosh, Colby. "Peter Lougheed was more than just a provincial man." *Maclean's*, September 12, 2012. macleans.ca/news/canada/more-than-just-a-provincial-man/.

de Bruin, Tabitha, and Gerald Robertson. "Eugenics in Canada." Canadian Encyclopedia (2006; update June 7, 2019). thecanadianencyclopedia.ca/en/article/eugenics.

Demmon, Calvin. "The Arts: Enter the Professional." *In Alberta in the 20th Century. Vol. 3, The Boom and the Bust, 1910–1914*, edited by Ted Byfield, 56–71. Edmonton: United Western Communications Ltd., 1994.

Devine, Heather. "Conversations with 'Les gens de la Montagne Tortue'—1952." Presented at *Resistance and Convergence: Francophone and Métis Strategies of Identity in Western Canada*. Centre d'études franco-canadiennes de l'Ouest, Institut Français, University of Regina, Regina, SK, October 20–23, 2005.

Dolphin, Ric. "From Wards of the State to Third Order of Government." In *Alberta in the 20th Century*. Vol. 12, *Alberta Takes the Lead, 1984–2000*, edited by Paul Brunner, 90–113. Edmonton: History Book Publications, 2003.

Ellis, Faron. "A Storied Name from the Past Leads a Modern Populist Uprising." In *Alberta in the 20th Century*. Vol. 12, *Alberta Takes the Lead, 1984–2000*, edited by Paul Brunner, 240–57. Edmonton: History Book Publications Ltd., 2003.

Engelmann, Frederick C. "Reforming Canadian Federalism." In *Western Separatism: The Myths, Realities and Dangers*, edited by Larry Pratt and Garth Stevenson, 229–42. Edmonton: Hurtig Publishing, 1981.

Finlay, Patricia. "Edgar Peter Lougheed." *The Canadian Encyclopedia*. 2012; update June 16, 2022. thecanadianencyclopedia.ca/en/article/edgar-peter-lougheed.

Foot, Richard, and Andrew McIntosh. "Editorial: The Stanley Flag and the 'Distinctive Canadian Symbol.'" *The Canadian Encyclopedia*. 2014; update November 29, 2019. thecanadianencyclopedia.ca/en/article/the-stanley-flag.

Foran, Max. "The Boosters in Boosterism: Some Calgary Examples." *Urban History Review* 8, no. 2 (October 1979): erudit.org/fr/revues/uhr/1979-v8-n2uhr0895/1019378ar.pdf.

Foster, John. "The Métis: The People and the Term." *Prairie Forum* 3, no. 1 (1978): 79–90.

Francis, R. Douglas. "Writing Alberta's History." In *Writing Alberta: Building on a Literary Identity*, edited by George Melnyk and Donna Coates, 201–22. Calgary: University of Alberta Press, 2017.

Friesen, Gerald. "The Prairies as Region: The Contemporary Meaning of an Old Idea." In *The Constitutional Future of the Prairie and Atlantic Regions of Canada*, edited by James N. McCrorie and Martha L. MacDonald. Regina: Canadian Plains Research Center, 1992.

Gagnon, Denis. "The 'Other' Métis." *Canadian Encyclopedia*. June 21, 2016. thecanadianencyclopedia.ca/en/article/the-other-metis.

Gaudry, Adam. "Métis Are a People, Not a Historical Process." *The Canadian Encyclopedia*. June 21, 2016. thecanadianencyclopedia.ca/en/article/metis-are-a-people-not-a-historical-process.

Gaudry, Adam, Mary Agnes Welch and David Gallant. "Métis." *The Canadian Encyclopedia*. 2009; update January 13, 2023. thecanadianencyclopedia.ca/en/article/metis.

Gerson, Jen. "Alberta's 'Blue-eyed Sheikh' Peter Lougheed dead at 84." *National Post*, September 13, 2012. nationalpost.com/news/canada/peter-lougheed-dead-Thursday.

243

Gibson, Lee. "Nicholas Flood Davin." *The Canadian Encyclopedia*. 2008; update December 14, 2017. thecanadianencyclopedia.ca/en/article/nicholas-flood-davin.

Hall, David J., and Donald B. Smith. "Lougheed, Sir James Alexander." In *Dictionary of Canadian Biography*, vol. 15. University of Toronto/Université Laval, 2003–. http://www.biographi.ca/en/bio/lougheed_james_alexander_15E.html.

Hannaford, Nigel. "Art Becomes the Battleground as the Culture Wars Erupt in Alberta." In *Alberta in the 20th Century*. Vol. 12, *Alberta Takes the Lead, 1984–2000*, edited by Paul Brunner, 114–31. Edmonton: History Book Publications Ltd., 2003.

Harper, Tim. "Peter Lougheed Once Stood Tallest Among Premiers." *Toronto Star*, September 11, 2012. thestar.com/news/canada/2012/09/11/tim_harper_peter_lougheed_once_stood_tallest_among_premiers.html.

"Hobbema to change name in New Year." CBC News, December 26, 2013. cbc.ca/news/canada/edmonton/hobbema-to-change-name-in-new-year-1.2476653.

Holmgren, Eric J., and Michelle Filice. "Ralph Garvin Steinhauer." *The Canadian Encyclopedia*. 2008; update July 20, 2016. thecanadianencyclopedia.ca/en/article/ralph-garvin-steinhauer.

Innis, H.A., ed. "Notes and Documents: Rupert's Land in 1825." *Canadian Historical Review* 7, no. 4 (1926): 320.

Johnson, Rhiannon. "Exploring Identity: Who Are the Metis and What Are Their Rights?" CBC News, April 28, 2019. cbc.ca/news/indigenous/metis-identity-history-rights-explainer-1.5098585.

Judd, Carol M. "'Mixt Bands of Many Nations': 1821–70." In *Old Trails and New Directions: Papers of the Third North American Fur Trade Conference*, edited by Carol M. Judd and Arthur J. Ray. Toronto: University of Toronto Press, 1980.

Kearns, Laura-Lee. "(Re)claiming Métis Women Identities: Three Stories and the Storyteller." In *Métis in Canada: History, Identity, Law and Politics*, edited by Christopher Adams, Gregg Dahl and Ian Peach, 59–92. Edmonton: University of Alberta Press, 2013.

Kermoal, Nathalie. "From Saint Paul des Métis to Saint

Paul: A Patch of Franco-Albertan History." In
*Encyclopedia of French Cultural Heritage in North
America*. ameriquefrancaise.org/en/article-706/
From_Saint_Paul_des_Métis_to_Saint_Paul:_A_Patch_
of_Franco-Albertan_History.html.

Larson, Jackie E. "Mountains of tributes pour in for Alberta
premier Peter Lougheed." *Edmonton Sun*, September
14, 2012. afl.org/mountains_of_tributes_pour_in_for_
alberta_premier_peter_lougheed.

Leighton, David. Foreword to *Alberta's Camelot: Culture
and the Arts in the Lougheed Years*, by Fil Fraser, 6–8.
Edmonton: Lone Pine Publishing, 2003.

Lougheed, Peter. "Why a Notwithstanding Clause." Library
and Archives Canada. (Modified February 13, 2017).
bac-lac.gc.ca/eng/discover/politics-government/building-
just-society/Pages/honourable-peter-lougheed.aspx.

Macdougall, Brenda. "The Myth of Metis Cultural
Ambivalence." In *Contours of a People: Metis Family,
Mobility, and History*, edited by Nicole St-Onge, Carolyn
Podruchny and Brenda Macdougall. Norman: University
of Oklahoma Press, 2012.

MacLeod, R.C., and Heather Rollason Driscoll. "Natives,
Newspapers and Crime Rates in the North-West
Territories, 1878–1885." In *From Rupert's Land to
Canada: Essays in Honour of John E. Foster*, edited by
Theodore Binnema, Gerhard Ens and R.C. MacLeod.
Edmonton: University of Alberta Press, 2001.

Marshall, Tabita. "IODE (Imperial Order Daughters of the
Empire)." *The Canadian Encyclopedia*. March 4, 2021.
thecanadianencyclopedia.ca/en/article/imperial-order-
daughters-of-the-empire#:~:text=Originally%20
known%20as%20the%20Imperial,than%20200%20
branches%20across%20Canada.

McCarthy, Martha. "Northern Métis and the Churches." In
*Picking Up the Threads: Métis History in the Mackenzie
Basin*, edited by Metis Heritage Association of the
Northwest Territories, 111–36. Winnipeg: Metis Heritage
Association of the Northwest Territories and Parks Canada–
Canadian Heritage, 1998.

245

McKenna, Marian C. "Sir James Alexander Lougheed: Calgary's First Senator and City Builder." In *City Makers: Calgarians after the Frontier*, edited by Max Foran and Sheilagh S. Jamieson. Calgary: The Historical Society of Alberta, Chinook Country Chapter, 1987.

McManus, Sheila. "Unsettled Pasts, Unsettling Borders: Women, Wests, Nations." In *One Step Over the Line: Toward a History of Women in North American Wests*, edited by Elizabeth Jameson and Sheila McManus. Edmonton and Athabasca: University of Alberta Press and Athabasca University Press, 2008.

Métis Nation of Alberta. "Advancing Métis Rights and Claims in Alberta: Understanding the New Objective and Oath of Membership in the Metis Nation of Alberta's Bylaws." albertametis.com/wp-content/uploads/2013/08/Advancing-M%C3%A9tis-Rights-and-Claims-in-Alberta.pdf.

Newman, Peter C. "A Positive View of Conservatism's Future. *Maclean's*, May 27, 1996. archive.macleans.ca/article/1996/5/27/a-positive-view-of-conservatisms-future.

Nicks, Trudy, and Kenneth Morgan. "Grande Cache: The Historic Development of an Indigenous Population." In *The New Peoples: Being and Becoming Métis in North America*, edited by Jacqueline Peterson and Jennifer S.H. Brown, 163–84. Lincoln: University of Nebraska Press, 1985.

Nikiforuk, Andrew. "Peter Lougheed's Radical Legacy." *The Tyee News*, September 17, 2012. thetyee.ca/Opinion/2012/09/17/Radical-Peter-Lougheed/.

O'Byrne, Nicole C. "No other weapon except organization": The Métis Association of Alberta and the 1938 Metis Population Betterment Act." *Journal of the Canadian Historical Association* 24, no. 2 (2013): 311–52. erudit.org/en/journals/jcha/1900-v1-n1-jcha01408/1025081ar/.

Owram, Doug. "Reluctant Hinterland." In *Western Separatism: The Myths, Realities and Dangers*, edited by Larry Pratt and Garth Stevenson, 45–64. Edmonton: Hurtig Publishing, 1981.

Palmer, Howard. "Ethnic Relations and the Paranoid Style: Nativism, Nationalism and Populism in Alberta, 1945–50." *Canadian Ethnic Studies* 23, no. 3 (1991): 7–31.

Perdue, Theda. Introduction. In *Sifters: Native American Women's Lives*, edited by Theda Perdue. New York: Oxford University Press, 2001.

Peterson, Jacqueline. "Many Roads to Red River: Métis Ethnogenesis in the Great Lakes Region, 1680–1815." In *The New Peoples: Being and Becoming Métis in North America*, edited by Jacqueline Peterson and Jennifer S.H. Brown, 37–72. Winnipeg: University of Manitoba Press, 1985.

Pratt, Larry. "Whose Oil Is It?" In *Western Separatism: The Myths, Realities and Dangers*, edited by Larry Pratt and Garth Stevenson, 155–71. Edmonton: Hurtig Publishing, 1981.

Racette, Sherry Farrell. "Sewing for a Living: The Commodification of Métis Women's Artistic Production." In *Contact Zones: Aboriginal and Settler Women in Canada's Colonial Past*, edited by Katie Pickles and Myra Rutherdale, 17–46. Vancouver: UBC Press, 2005.

Robertson, David. "Last Best West." *Encyclopedia of the Great Plains*. plainshumanities.unl.edu/encyclopedia/doc/egp. ii.038.

Robinson, Amanda, and Michelle Filice. "Métis Scrip in Canada." *The Canadian Encyclopedia*. 2018; update October 2, 2019. https://www.thecanadianencyclopedia. ca/en/article/metis-scrip-in-canada.

Schenck, Theresa. "Border Identities: Métis, Halfbreed, and Mixed-Blood." In *Gathering Places: Aboriginal and Fur Trade Histories*, edited by Carolyn Podruchny and Laura Peers, 233–48. Vancouver: UBC Press, 2010.

Sleeper-Smith, Susan. "Women, Kin, and Catholicism." *Ethnohistory* 47, no. 2 (2000): 423–52.

Smith, Donald B. "Alberta Cree Victims of Callous Disregard." *Toronto Star*, March 1, 1988, p. A17.

——. "Color Conscious: Racial Attitudes in Early 20th Century Calgary." In *Remembering Chinook Country: 1905-2005 Centennial Edition*, edited by Chinook Country Historical Society, 119–32. Calgary: Detselig Enterprises, 2005.

——. "The Original Peoples of Alberta." In *Peoples of Alberta: Portraits of Cultural Diversity*, edited by Howard Palmer and Tamara Palmer. Saskatoon: Western Producer Prairie Books, 1985.

247

Smith, Shirlee Anne. "Hardisty, Richard Charles." In
Dictionary of Canadian Biography, vol. 11. University
of Toronto/Université Laval, 2003–. biographi.ca/en/bio/
hardisty_richard_charles_11E.html.

St-Onge, Nicole, and Carolyn Podruchny. "Scuttling
Along a Spider's Web: Mobility and Kinship in Metis
Ethnogenesis." In *Contours of a People: Metis Family,
Mobility, and History*, edited by Nicole St-Onge, Carolyn
Podruchny and Brenda Macdougall, 59–92. Norman:
University of Oklahoma Press, 2012.

Taras, David. "The Winds of Right-wing Change in Canadian
Journalism." *Canadian Journal of Communication* 21, no. 4
(1990): cjconline.ca/index.php/journal/article/view/962/868.

Teillet, Jean, and Carly Teillet. "Devoid of Principle: The
Federal Court Determination that section 91(24) of
the Constitution Act, 1867 is a race-based provision."
Indigenous Law Journal 13, no. 1 (2016): 1-20. ilj.law.
utoronto.ca/sites/ilj.law.utoronto.ca/files/media/Teillet.pdf.

Thompson, Henry. "Louis Fosseneuve, later known as Captain
Shot." In *Lac La Biche Yesterday and Today*. Lac La Biche
Heritage Society, 1975.

Van Kirk, Sylvia. "Toward a Feminist Perspective in Native
History." *Centre for Women's Studies in Education
Occasional Papers* no. 14 (1987): 6.

———. "Tracing the Fortunes of Five Founding Families
of Victoria." *BC Studies*, no. 115–16 (Autumn/Winter
1997/98): https://doi.org/10.14288/bcs.voi115/6.1729.

Voisey, Paul. "Entrepreneurs in Early Calgary." In *Frontier
Calgary: Town, City, and Region, 1875–1914*, edited by
Anthony W. Rasporich and Henry Cornelius Klassen,
221–41. Calgary: McClelland and Stewart West, 1975.

Vowel, Chelsea. "What a landmark ruling means—and
doesn't—for Metis, non-status Indians." CBC News,
April 16, 2016. https://www.cbc.ca/news/indigenous/
landmark-supreme-court-decision-metis-non-status-
indians-1.3537419.

Ward, Rachel. "Albertan rediscovers theatregoer's fight
against segregation 104 years ago." CBC News,
September 17, 2018. cbc.ca/news/canada/calgary/
charles-daniels-train-porter-racism-lawsuit-1.4826763.

Wonders, William C. "Far Corner of the Strange Empire:
Central Alberta on the Eve of Homestead Settlement."
Great Plains Quarterly (Spring 1983): 91-108. core.ac.uk/
download/pdf/188079577.pdf.
Wright, Janet. "Beaulieu Revitalized." *Heritage Canada*
(January/February 1998): 6–8.

MEDIA

Banff Centre for Arts and Creativity. Jens Lindemann. A
Musical Tribute to an Old Friend, Peter Lougheed.
April 30, 2015. banffcentre.ca/articles/
musical-tribute-old-friend-peter-lougheed.

SELECTED WEBSITES

Alberta Register of Historic Places. "Baptiste River Métis
Settlement Site." hermis.alberta.ca/ARHP/Details.aspx?D
eptID=1&ObjectID=4665-0290.
———. "Buffalo Lake Métis Settlement." hermis.alberta.ca/
ARHP/Details.aspx?DeptID=1&ObjectID=4665-0280.
———. "Father Lacombe Church." hermis.alberta.ca/ARHP/
Details.aspx?DeptID=1&ObjectID=4665-0212.
Canada's Historic Places. "Father Lacombe Church." historic-
places.ca/en/rep-reg/place-lieu.aspx?id=5004.
Canadian *Geographic*. Indigenous Peoples Atlas of Canada.
indigenouspeoplesatlasofcanada.ca.
Métis Nation. metisnation.ca.
Métis Nation of Ontario. https://www.metisnation.org.
Metis Settlements of Alberta. msgc.ca/.
Mountain Metis website, mountainmetis.com/.
Parks Canada, "Beaulieu II, François National Historic
Person." pc.gc.ca/apps/dfhd/page_nhs_eng.aspx?id=1896.
———. "Beaulieu National Historic Site of Canada." pc.gc.ca/
apps/dfhd/page_nhs_eng.aspx?id=11.
———. "Grant, Cuthbert National Historic Person." pc.gc.ca/
apps/dfhd/page_nhs_eng.aspx?id=962.
———. "Smith, Sir Donald A. (Lord Strathcona) National
Historic Person." pc.gc.ca/apps/dfhd/page_nhs_eng.
aspx?id=1426.

249

Index

253

254

255

258

era of inequality, 118, 120
for fur trade elite, 42–43, 45–46,
    56–57, 82, 170
importance of Métis kinship
    networks, 34, 39–43, 51, 57,
    106–108, 114–115, 124, 145,
    169–170
Métis men, 88, 105, 114, 120
Métis survival strategies, 3, 9,
    32–34, 71–72, 78–79, 107,
    124, 133–134, 171
Métis women, 86–89, 105,
    114–115, 120–121, 123, 164
no place for Aboriginal Peoples,
    100–101, 103, 143–144
nouveau riche, 57, 65–66
sense of community, 58
See also fur trade; Hardisty
    family; Hudson's Bay Company;
    Lougheed, Isabella Clark
    Hardisty; Métis people,
    identity; Métis scrip; settlers,
    Euro–North American
Treaty 6, 87
Treaty 8, 165–166
Trudeau, Pierre, 136, 160–161
Turner Valley, 155
Tweed, Thomas, 39
Tyler, Carolyn Abbott, 215n71

United Farmers of Alberta, 101
University of Alberta, 50, 75

Unjust Society, The (Cardinal), 78
Upper Saskatchewan District (of
    HBC), 45

Van Herk, Aritha, 101
Van Horne, William, 39
Van Kirk, Sylvia, 104, 105
Victorian Order of Nurses, 151

wahkootowin, 92
Watanna, Onoto, 134, 219n110
Wesleyan Ladies' College, 14,
    23, 24–25, 27–30, 33–34, 150,
    188n36
West, John, 186n22
Western Canada College, 144
Whitby Ladies' College, 22, 187n25
White Horse Plains, 87
Willamette Valley, 108–109
Winnipeg, MB, 20, 47
Wolf Lake, AB, 85
Wolf Lake Métis Settlement, AB,
    72–73
Women's Pioneer Association,
    53, 223n28. See also Southern
    Alberta Pioneer Association
Wood, David, 136
Wood, Henry Wise, 101

Yellowbird, Chief Norman, 132

DORIS JEANNE MACKINNON was born on a farm in northeastern Alberta and attended school in the historic town of St-Paul-des-Métis. She holds a PhD in Indigenous and post-Confederation Canadian history. An independent researcher, author, and post-secondary instructor, she lives in Central Alberta. Her publications focus on Western Canadian topics that expand readers' understanding of our diverse people and experiences. Her books are written in an engaging style that appeals to a broad cross-section of the population.